Global Shakespeares

Series Editor
Alexa Alice Joubin, Department of English, George Washington University, Washington, DC, USA

The Global Shakespeares series, edited by Alexa Alice Joubin, explores the global afterlife of Shakespearean drama, poetry and motifs in their literary, performative and digital forms of expression in the twentieth and twenty-first centuries. Disseminating big ideas and cutting-edge research in e-book and print formats, this series captures global Shakespeares as they evolve.

More information about this series at
https://link.springer.com/bookseries/15016

Alexa Alice Joubin · Victoria Bladen
Editors

Onscreen Allusions to Shakespeare

International Films, Television, and Theatre

Editors
Alexa Alice Joubin
George Washington University
Washington, DC, USA

Victoria Bladen
University of Queensland
Brisbane, QLD, Australia

ISSN 2947-8901 ISSN 2947-891X (electronic)
Global Shakespeares
ISBN 978-3-030-93785-0 ISBN 978-3-030-93783-6 (eBook)
https://doi.org/10.1007/978-3-030-93783-6

Cover illustration: Victoria Bladen

This Palgrave Macmillan imprint is published by the registered company Springer Nature Switzerland AG
The registered company address is: Gewerbestrasse 11, 6330 Cham, Switzerland

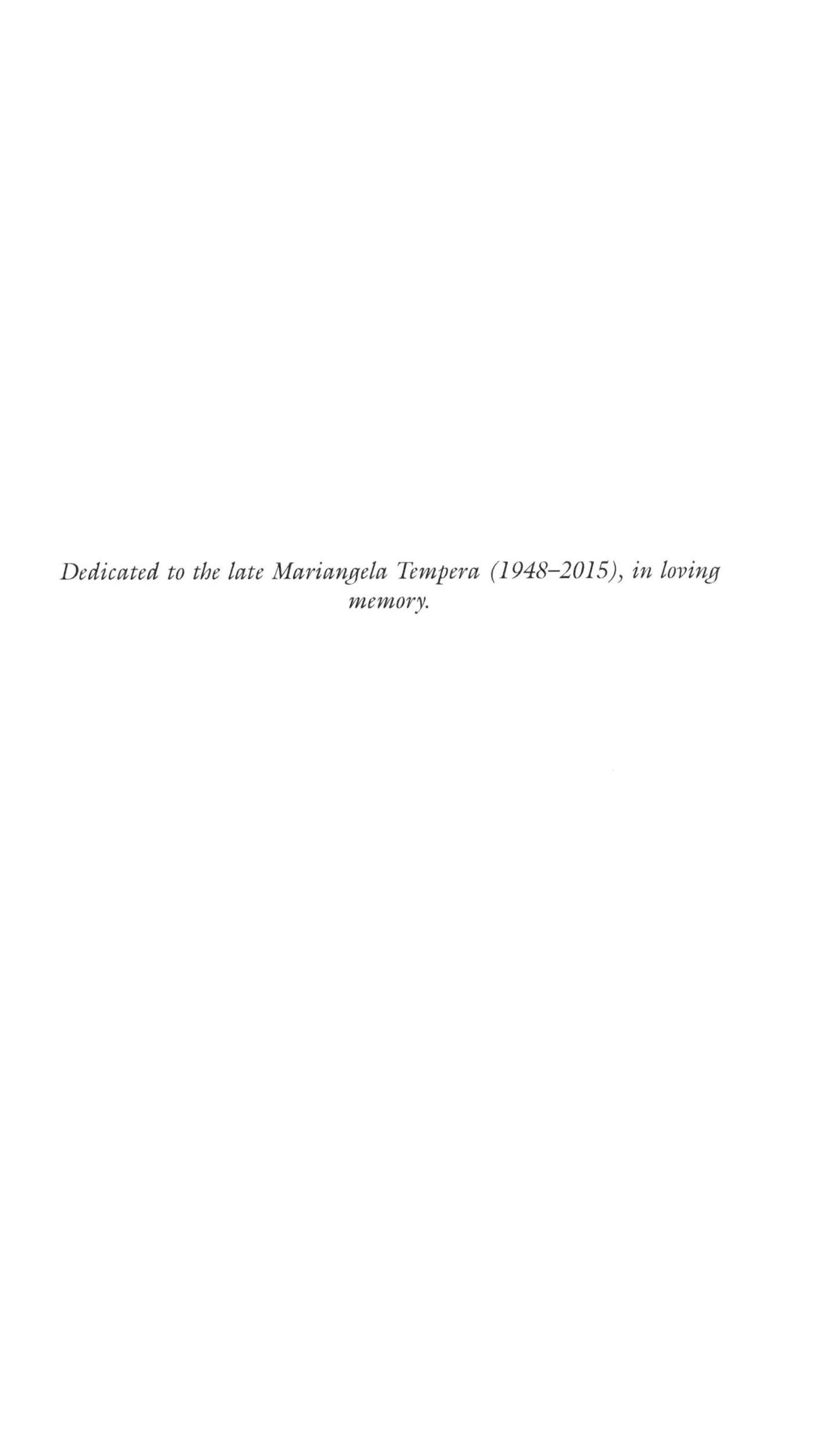

Dedicated to the late Mariangela Tempera (1948–2015), in loving memory.

Acknowledgements

This volume is dedicated to the loving memory of the late Mariangela Tempera (1948–2015), scholar, educator and founder of Centro Shakespeariano Ferrara, Italy, whose pioneering work in the study of Shakespeare adaptations continues to inspire us. To celebrate the twentieth anniversary of the Centro Shakespeariano Ferrara, Professor Tempera organized a conference, "Shakespeare in Tatters: Referencing His Works on Film and Television, in Ferrara," May 10–11, 2013, where the essays in this collection first took shape. We gratefully acknowledge the support of the Centro Shakespeariano Ferrara, Dipartimento di Studi Umanistici at the Università degli Studi di Ferrara, Dipartimento di Lingue e Letterature Straniere of the Università degli Studi di Milano, Comune di Ferrara Assessorato alla Cultura Turismo e Giovani, the Institut de recherches sur la Renaissance, l'âge Classique et les Lumière of the Université Montpellier 3 Paul Valéry in France, the Russian Foundation for the Humanities, the National Research Foundation of South Africa, Facultad de Filosofía y Letras of the Universidad Nacional Autónoma de México and Gandarela Cultural Complex and the Globe Brasil.

Victoria Bladen has graciously provided her striking illustration for use as the cover image of this book.

Washington, DC, USA — Alexa Alice Joubin
Brisbane, Australia — Victoria Bladen

Contents

Notes on Contributors

Victoria Bladen teaches in literary studies and adaptation at the University of Queensland, Australia, and has twice received a Faculty award for teaching excellence. Her publications include: *The Tree of Life and Arboreal Aesthetics in Early Modern Literature* (Routledge, 2021); six Shakespearean text guides in the Insight (Melbourne) series, including *The Merchant of Venice* (2020) and *Much Ado About Nothing* (2019); and five co-edited volumes, including *Shakespeare on Screen: King Lear* (Cambridge University Press, 2019), and *Shakespeare and the Supernatural* (Manchester University Press, 2020). Current projects include the co-edited volume *Shakespeare on Screen: Romeo and Juliet* (Cambridge University Press, forthcoming 2022).

Maurizio Calbi is Professor of English at the University of Palermo in Italy. He has published on Shakespeare, the representations of the body in early modern culture, postcolonial literature and postcolonial rewriting of Shakespeare. His most recent book is *Spectral Shakespeares. Media Adaptations in the Twenty-First Century* (Palgrave, 2013; paperback 2016). He is currently working on Shakespeare in the French *nouvelle vague*, "Prison Shakespeare," and Shakespeare in social media. He is also preparing a monograph on "interstitial Shakespeare," which uses examples of adaptations in different media to address current debates about the notion of "global Shakespeare."

Mariacristina Cavecchi works in the Department of Foreign Languages and Literatures at the State University of Milan, where she teaches History of British Drama and English Literature. Her research interests include twentieth-century and twenty-first-century British drama and theatre. She has also written on contemporary appropriations of Shakespeare's plays for theatre and cinema, Shakespeare in popular culture, and Prison Shakespeare. Her most recent edited volumes include *SceKspir al Bekka. Romeo Montecchi dietro le sbarre dell'Istituto Penale Minorile Beccaria* (2020) and *Will forever young! Shakespeare & Contemporary Culture* (a special number of *Altre Modernità/Other Modernities*, 2017). She served on the executive board of IASEMS.

Aimara da Cunha Resende is the founding President of the Brazilian Shakespeare Studies Centre and a retired Full Professor of English Literature from the Catholic University of Minas Gerais and retired Associate Professor from the Federal University of Minas Gerais. She has published extensively on Shakespeare and his time, both in Brazil and abroad. She translated *Love's Labours Lost* (Selo CESh/Tessitura, 2006) and edited *Foreign Accents: Brazilian Readings of Shakespeare* (University of Delaware Press, 2002). She serves as the General Editor of the Brazilian CESh/Tessitura series on Shakespeare and his contemporaries and Associate Editor of the *Cambridge Guide to the Worlds of Shakespeare* (2016). Professor Resende devised and has been developing for 16 years now, in the rural town of São Francisco de Paula, Minas Gerais, a project for the education of children through Shakespeare's work, "Shakespeare and the Children."

Boris N. Gaydin is Head of the Laboratory of Electronic Research and Educational Projects at the Institute of Fundamental and Applied Studies, Moscow University for the Humanities. He serves as Senior Lecturer in the Department of Romance and Germanic Philology at the St. Tikhon's Orthodox University, Academic Secretary of the Shakespeare Committee at the Russian Academy of Sciences and editor-in-chief of the journal *The Horizons of Humanities Knowledge*. He has co-edited, with Nikolay V. Zakharov, a number of digital humanities projects, including the Information Research Databases "Russian Shakespeare" (rus-shake.ru) and "Shakespeare's Contemporaries" (around-shake.ru), the Electronic Encyclopedia "The World of Shakespeare" (world-shake.ru) and "Digital Tools for Comparative Thesaurus Analysis of Russian Translations of W. Shakespeare's Works" (shakespearecorpus.ru).

Alexa Alice Joubin teaches in the Departments of English, Women's, Gender and Sexuality Studies, Theatre, International Affairs, and East Asian Languages and Literatures at George Washington University in Washington, DC, where she serves as founding Co-director of the Digital Humanities Institute. Her recent books include *Shakespeare and East Asia* (Oxford University Press, 2021), *Race* (co-authored with Martin Orkin, Routledge, 2018), *Local and Global Myths in Shakespearean Performance* (co-edited, Palgrave, 2018) and *Shakespeare and the Ethics of Appropriation* (co-edited, Palgrave, 2014).

Márta Minier is Associate Professor of Theatre and Media Drama at the University of South Wales, UK. Her research interests include Shakespeare (Shakespeare reception in particular), adaptation, translation, dramaturgy, the culture of East-Central Europe, and the biopic and biographical drama. Her publications include the co-edited *Adaptation, Intermediality and the British Celebrity Biopic* (2014, Ashgate) and *Shakespeare and Tourism: Place, Memory, Participation* (2019, E.S.I.) as well as Shakespearean special issues for *New Readings* (2012) and *Multicultural Shakespeare: Translation, Appropriation and Performance* (2017). She is joint editor of the *Journal of Adaptation in Film & Performance*.

Chris Thurman is a Professor of English and Director of the Tsikinya-Chaka Centre at the University of the Witwatersrand (Johannesburg, South Africa). Thurman is the editor of *South African Essays on 'Universal' Shakespeare* (2014), *Sport versus Art: A South African Contest* (2010) and twelve volumes of the journal *Shakespeare in Southern Africa*. His other books are the monograph *Guy Butler: Reassessing a South African Literary Life* (2010) and *Text Bites*, an anthology for high schools (2009); and two collections of arts journalism, *At Large: Reviewing the Arts in South Africa* (2012) and *Still at Large: Dispatches from South Africa's Frontiers of Politics and Art* (2017).

Poonam Trivedi taught at the University of Delhi. She has co-edited books on Indian and Asian Shakespeare: *Asian Interventions in Global Shakespeare: 'All the World's his Stage'* (2020), *Shakespeare and Indian Cinemas: 'Local Habitations'* (2018) and *Shakespeare's Asian Journeys: Critical Encounters, Cultural Geographies, and the Politics of Travel* (2017), *Re-playing Shakespeare in Asia* (2010) and *India's Shakespeare: Translation, Interpretation and Performance* (2005) and has authored a CD 'King Lear *in India*' (2006). She is on the editorial board of the

Shakespeare on Screen series and is a Vice Chair of the Asian Shakespeare Association.

Nathalie Vienne-Guerrin is Professor in Shakespeare studies at the Université Paul-Valéry Montpellier 3 and a member of the Institut de Recherche sur la Renaissance, l'âge Classique et les Lumières (IRCL, UMR 5186 CNRS). She is co-editor-in-chief of the international journal *Cahiers Élisabéthains* and co-director (with Patricia Dorval) of the *Shakespeare on Screen in Francophonia Database*. She has extensively on Shakespeare's evil tongues and Shakespeare on screen and has published *The Unruly Tongue in Early Modern England, Three Treatises* (2012) and *Shakespeare's Insults: A Pragmatic Dictionary* (2016). She is co-editor, with Sarah Hatchuel, of the Shakespeare on Screen series.

Nikolay V. Zakharov is Director of the Shakespeare Center in the Institute of Fundamental and Applied Studies at Moscow University for the Humanities. He is the co-Chairman of the Shakespeare Committee in the Russian Academy of Sciences. He has co-edited, with Boris N. Gaydin, a number of digital humanities projects, including the Information Research Databases "Russian Shakespeare" (rus-shake.ru) and "Shakespeare's Contemporaries" (around-shake.ru), the Electronic Encyclopedia "The World of Shakespeare" (world-shake.ru) and "Digital Tools for Comparative Thesaurus Analysis of Russian Translations of W. Shakespeare's Works" (shakespearecorpus.ru).

List of Figures

CHAPTER 1

Introduction to Onscreen Allusions to Shakespeare

Alexa Alice Joubin and Victoria Bladen

Shakespeare's plays and motifs have been cited and appropriated in fragmentary forms on screen since motion pictures were invented in 1893 when the Kinetoscope was demonstrated in public for the first time. Allusions to Shakespeare, often disconnected from their original contexts, haunt our contemporary culture in a myriad of ways, whether through brief references or sustained intertextual engagements. For example, in a play-within-a-film, a production of *Macbeth* is interrupted in James McTeigue's crime thriller *The Raven* (2012).[1] Lady Macbeth's lines are not fully audible, but her performance in the mad scene provides an additional layer of significance to the film's main plot, which revolves around

A. A. Joubin (✉)
George Washington University, Washington, DC, USA
e-mail: ajoubin@gwu.edu

V. Bladen
University of Queensland, St Lucia, QLD, Australia
e-mail: v.bladen@uq.edu.au

A. A. Joubin and V. Bladen (eds.), *Onscreen Allusions to Shakespeare*, Global Shakespeares, https://doi.org/10.1007/978-3-030-93783-6_1

a serial killer who commits murders following Edgar Allan Poe's description in his stories. In Tom Hooper's biopic *The King's Speech* (2010), Hamlet's "to be or not to be" speech is recited in key scenes, suggesting that reciting Shakespeare might just cure stuttering. Lionel Logue (Geoffrey Rush), a speech therapist for King George VI, also uses Caliban's speech in an educational game with his children. In a film about a stuttering monarch learning to master the radio to speak to his subjects, the "voices in the air" that Caliban longs to hear become ironic, for both the king, who is struggling with a speech disorder and is robbed of a voice, and his therapist, a subject from the Commonwealth who is more eloquent but is dismissed by the royal family.[2] Neither *The Raven* or *The King's Speech* are Shakespeare films, but they evoke a range of themes and values associated with Shakespeare. Some scholars do reclaim such works as Shakespearean. A work does not have to be an adaptation to qualify as "Shakespearean," writes Eric S. Mallin, whose work examines "movies that do not know they are Shakespeare plays."[3]

Shakespeare has a ubiquitous presence in the twentieth and twenty-first centuries. It has been continually deconstructed, quoted in and out of context, hybridized, recycled and appropriated in a wide range of contexts. Fragments of Shakespeare's texts prove highly mobile. A commercial for the 2012 World Shakespeare Festival reused *The Tempest*, with the phrase "enchanted isle full of noises" taken to refer to the British Isles that were gearing up to welcome guests from afar for the London Olympic games. It constituted a re-appropriation of the voice of Caliban, who paradoxically represented both otherness in opposition to Britain's colonial past and also, in this context, a voice *of* Britain speaking in invitation to outsiders, with his "isle full of noises" speech eloquently describing his world to newcomers. During the Olympics ceremony, Kenneth Branagh recited the same speech when dressed as industrialist Isambard Kingdom Brunel and the closing ceremony again echoed the "Isles of Wonder" theme. Timothy Spall's Winston Churchill recited Caliban's lines: "Be not afear'd / The isle is full of noises"—the same passage spoken by Branagh earlier. Each of these films and performances deploys Shakespeare for varying purposes of foreshadowing, social reparation and intertextual echoes.

Shakespeare may not be the main focus of tattered allusions in cinema, television and theatre, yet even passing references to Shakespeare can have the power to shift the meanings and readings of a work. For instance, "Shakespeare" is deployed as a reminder of human civilization in Miguel

Sapochnik's post-apocalyptic *Finch* (2021). In a philosophical scene that probes the question of what it means to be human, Finch Weinberg (Tom Hanks), the sole survivor, takes a humanoid robot he built into a derelict theatre to salvage food. It may seem coincidental in the plot, but clearly dramaturgically intentional, when that theatre turns out to be the venue for "Springfield Shakespeare Festival." The camera lingers frequently on the marquee with the word "Shakespeare" above the entrance. Inside the theatre, the android passes in front of a poster of a production of *Much Ado About Nothing* and spontaneously offers an analysis of that play in his monotonic, synthetic voice. His analysis, casual as it may seem, echoes the theme of post-apocalyptic mistrust: "This is a play by William Shakespeare, a dramatic comedy about love, deception, and other human misunderstanding." As it turns out, this is a pivotal scene where the android becomes sentient. He discovers himself for the first time in a mirror in the lobby. In a later scene, the android, in more fluid speech, tells Finch that he wishes to be named "William Shakespeare." To have a name, for the android, is to be human, and to choose Shakespeare implies that at some level the idea of Shakespeare encapsulates human identity.

Other instances contain direct quotations from Shakespeare for their indexical value to demonstrate a character's intellect. In Destin Daniel Cretton's *Shang-Chi and The Legend of The Ten Rings* (2021), Ben Kingsley's actor-character Trevor Slattery tells Shang-Chi and Katy that he loves Shakespeare, while dressing like Shakespeare and displaying Shakespearean props and memorabilia from his acting career before his capture. Slattery proceeds to recite iconic lines from monologues in *Macbeth* and *King Lear*. Hands on his temples, in agony, Slattery says, in a dramatic tone: "Whence is that knocking? Wake Duncan with thy knocking!" Ever so proud of his performance of Macbeth, he tells Shang-Chi that "they couldn't get enough of it. I've been doing weekly ghosts for lads ever since." Volunteering to give his audience of two further "previews," Slattery launches into the Fool's speech in *King Lear*: "nuncle, nuncle, nuncle …" Beyond these fragmented quotations in a film that has nothing to do with Shakespeare, this meta-theatrical scene carries extra weight because Kingsley began his career at the Royal Shakespeare Company and starred in multiple Shakespearean productions. Onscreen, he is known for his performance of Feste in Trevor Nunn's 1996 film version of *Twelfth Night*.

The study of "Shakespeare in tatters" and in fragmented citations differs from the study of adaptations of full Shakespearean plays. To make sense of the vast network of fragmented citations and appropriations of Shakespeare, we have to understand it as a palimpsest that contains multiple layers of intertexts and meanings. The meanings of these palimpsests are inherently unstable, because they depend on the knowledge and experiences of the observers. Tattered allusions to Shakespeare circumvent the question of "fidelity," because they constitute a wink to, rather than sustained engagement with, Shakespeare. Some citations—in verbal, textual, or visual forms—are a playful gesture, while others aim to deconstruct Shakespeare's canonical status. For instance, Shakespeare is mentioned briefly, only to be dismissed, in Prano Bailey-Bond's horror film *Censor* (2021). Two British censors debate whether to allow an eye gouging scene in a film they are reviewing. One censor cites *King Lear* to support his argument of keeping the scene intact. Enid retorts: "You lost the argument the moment you brought Shakespeare into the room."

What is the effect of such allusions, whether fleeting references or rewritings inspired by a quote? Furthermore, what are the reception dynamics at play here among "knowing audiences" and amateurs? The meanings of tattered allusions emerge from the oscillation between hypotexts (earlier texts that inspire subsequent works) and hypertexts (texts with embedded allusions that one may or may not pursue).[4] Theorists such as Maurizio Calbi and Dougas Lanier have illuminated both the spectral presence and rhizomatic, dispersed nature of Shakespearean appropriations in contemporary culture. Literary citations often take on a spectral quality in that words from previous works haunt the present performance.

The Politics of Quotation Marks

Marjorie Garber reminds us that a well-chosen quotation used to be a gentleman's calling card, a sign of membership in an elite club.[5] Quoting the right authors at the right moment could signal one's sophistication and class. The act of quoting others is simultaneously an act of deferral to an established authority as well as a form of ventriloquism that enables the speaker to channel that authority. Yet quotation can also be an act of resistance or challenge to the hypotext. Quoting or misquoting lines from Shakespeare carries with it the burden of previous uses of those lines, thus creating irony or solidarity as the case may be.

It is striking, but not coincidental, that the viability of quoting Shakespeare has frequently been critiqued and defended on ethical grounds.[6]

Fragmented references to Shakespeare—whether as direct quotations (often out of context) or visual echoes (such as a man holding up a skull)—signal linkage and distance to a cluster of texts. Screen references to Shakespeare are self-aware about their interdependence with other texts. Each new quotation both appears strange and estranges Shakespeare from itself; at the same time, every work creates some new strand within the ever-changing rhizome that comprises "Shakespeare." Artists invoke Shakespeare for all sorts of reasons under many different guises, and our experience of these films is ghosted by our prior investments in select aspects of the play and in previous performances. In her study of Shakespeare's indirect cultural influence on modern culture, Christina Wald characterized such "returns" or allusions to Shakespeare in unexpected contexts as the old work coming back to "haunt us." Wald urges us to avoid obsessive readings to detect "Shakespearean traces" and instead "acknowledge that intertextual relations are created by readers as much as by authors."[7]

As the field of Shakespeare on screen studies has developed, the focus has extended from adaptation as "announced and extensive transposition"[8] to "a more decisive journey away from the informing source."[9] Allusions to Shakespeare, often out of context, are becoming more and more common, and they redefine the boundaries between Shakespearean and "not Shakespeare."[10] This volume continues that work by extending the focus further along the intertextuality continuum to examine the issue of citation where a screen work may only briefly reference Shakespeare, in direct, implied or ambiguous ways. Nuanced and attenuated references to Shakespeare abound in screen culture. Moving away from the notion of singularity, these works carry with them diverse cultural significance.

Chapter Outlines

Mariangela Tempera (1948–2015), a key scholar who was alert to the potency of Shakespearean fragments, tatters and rhizomatic nodes, founded the Centro Shakespeariano Ferrara which collected, over the years, hundreds of films and television programmes that appropriate or allude to Shakespeare. She gathered an international group of scholars together in Ferrara, Italy, in 2013, to explore the phenomena from a range of perspectives. This volume was her vision and was inspired by her initiatives. Mariangela's legacy lives on in her studies of the rich complexities of Shakespearean allusion and citation, no matter how fleeting. All of the contributors and editors to this volume offer their work in dedication and loving memory to her pioneering work.

This collection explores allusions to Shakespeare in lesser-known films, television works and theatres in India, Brazil, Russia, France, Australia, South Africa, East-Central Europe and Italy. The scope of the volume extends beyond the US-UK axis, taking up the challenge for the critical field inspired by Mark Thornton Burnett in his landmark *Shakespeare and World Cinema*.[11] This volume invites consideration of how Shakespeare has been drawn on as a rich source by a range of directors and in a diverse set of cultural contexts. What emerges from this book is a strong sense of the infinite ways in which contemporary directors engage in dialogue with Shakespeare and how Shakespeare, ever our contemporary, is in dialogue with the concerns of contemporary culture.

Maurizio Calbi, in his book, *Spectral Shakespeares: Media Adaptations in the Twenty-First Century*, demonstrated the ways in which Shakespearean allusion and citation haunt and permeate contemporary culture. In his chapter in this volume, "The Boundaries of Citation: Shakespeare in Davide Ferrario's *Tutta colpa di Giuda* (2008), Alfredo Peyretti's *Moana* (2009), and Connie Macatuno's *Rome and Juliet* (2006)," he tests the conceptual boundaries of citation, focusing on three films that include Shakespearean fragments: Davide Ferrario's *Tutta colpa di Giuda* (*Blame it on Judas*), set in an Italian prison with some inmates playing themselves, which references *Hamlet*; Alfredo Peyretti's *Moana*, centred on the life of Italian porn star Moana Pozzi, and incorporating lines from *A Midsummer Night's Dream*; and Connie Macatuno's *Rome and Juliet*, an experimental film that turns Shakespeare's tragic love story into a lesbian romance. Fragments and traces of Shakespeare appear in each of these films in different ways. Yet the fragmented nature of these references, Calbi argues, does not render them less significant. In fact, an audience can hardly respond fully to the logic of these films without understanding these Shakespearean traces. At the same time, the chapter points to the ways that these films give new and unexpected meanings to the Shakespearean material. The chapter shows that the Shakespeare of these films—one that is simultaneously marginal and central—often touches upon, and is involved in, the question of boundaries. This self-reflexive aspect prompts Calbi's more general, theoretical discussion about the boundaries of what constitutes Shakespeare, taking up the theories and discourse of Desmet et. al.'s *Shakespeare/Not Shakespeare* volume. Is there a clear-cut dividing line between what constitutes adaptation and what is not, between an extended engagement with the adapted text and one that is a rewriting, between verbatim, occasional citation and full adaptation, and between the so-called straight adaptation and the vast field of Shakespearean spin-offs? Calbi's chapter suggests that to speak of performative allusions to Shakespeare is to speak of Shakespearean citationality—simultaneously a textual *and* media phenomenon—without any clear beginning or predetermined end, a field within which citation and other forms of Shakespearean afterlife situate themselves as variables that cannot be so easily separated from one another.

Shakespearean citation is often bound up with questions of national identity, as several of the chapters illustrate. Victoria Bladen's chapter "Antipodean Shakespeares: Appropriating Shakespeare in Australian film" illuminates the ways that Shakespearean intertexts appear in a diverse range of Australian films. It examines three films that use various modes of appropriation—a play-within-a-film and the transposition of Shakespearean language in Raymond Longford's *The Sentimental Bloke* (1919), a fleeting citation in Peter Weir's *Picnic at Hanging Rock* (1975), and an extended intertextual engagement in Jerzy Domaradzki's *Lilian's Story* (1996). Bladen argues that Australian screen culture has shaped Shakespeare in its own unique ways, rendering Shakespeare a crucial part and active force in the process of negotiating complex questions of national identity and articulating the postcolonial relationship between Australia and Britain. Shakespeare has also been a key medium for articulating human relationships and experiences of loss, absence and resilience, as these three films demonstrate.

Staying in the southern hemisphere, Chris Thurman's chapter "Othello Surfing: Fragments of Shakespeare in South Africa" considers the ways in which Shakespeare is recruited towards particular narrative and thematic purposes in the Zulu-language South African film *Otelo Burning* (2011) directed by Sara Blecher. Set in the townships outside Durban in the late 1980s, *Otelo Burning* is based on a true story about a group of young men who discover surfing as a means of escape from their material and historical circumstances. Fragments of Shakespeare's *Othello* were layered into the film in order to make it a story of betrayal and greed. While, in one sense, this appropriation subverts the traditional invocation of *Othello* in South Africa (based on parallels between the play and the country's fractious race relations), the film-makers' choice to "use the structure of [Othello's] story to tell ours" is problematic, as Thurman argues. It both reduces the play/text to an archetypal point of reference and reinscribes some of the false assumptions about what "Shakespeare" means in a South African context. The film nonetheless demonstrates that onscreen allusions to Shakespeare can be liberating for the reception of Shakespeare's plays in a South African context.

Turning to India, Poonam Trivedi points out that citations, references, allusions and intertextualities with Shakespeare are found everywhere in Indian culture: in newspapers, magazines, journals, fiction, poetry, theatre, television and increasingly in films. Some of these are unself-conscious citations of words and phrases that have become part of the English language, while others are reverential allusions or appropriative borrowings; still others are pointedly parodic and ironic, or subtle and suggestive of shades of Shakespeare. In her chapter "Shakespeare in bits and bites in Indian Cinema," Trivedi considers whether a taxonomy of this diverse range of referencing is possible, and if so what are the implications of this increasing usage and does the surfacing of Shakespeare in recent films point to a shift in attitude, visualization and vocalization with the bard? She focuses on examples in which there is a tangential, parodic or unacknowledged relation to the source and where each represents differing modes of referencing Shakespeare: *Eklavya: The Royal Guard* (2007), directed by Vinod Vidhu Chopra, *Matru ki Bijlee ka Mandola* (2013), directed by Vishal Bharadwaj, and *Bodyguard* (2011), directed by Siddique. Trivedi's examination traces an evolving cultural trajectory of Shakespeare citations in Hindi cinema.

The iconic balcony scene in *Romeo and Juliet* is arguably one of the most recurrent Shakespearean allusions on screen. Aimara da Cunha Resende's chapter "'Doth grace for grace and love for love allow': Recreations of the Balcony Scenes on Brazilian Screens" explores the various ways the scene has been appropriated in Brazilian film and TV. Her chapter discusses the ways in which it has been appropriated, either as serious borrowing or as comic parody in two films: *Carnaval no Fogo (Carnival in Fire,* 1949) and *Mônica e Cebolinha no Mundo de Romeu e Julieta* (*Mônica and Cebolinha in Romeo's and Juliet's World*, 1979); and in three TV productions, Globo TV's "caso especial" ("special affair") *Romeu e Julieta (Romeo and Juliet,* 1980), two "novelas" (Brazilian serials): *Pedra Sobre Pedra* (*Stone Over Stone*, 1992) and *Fera Ferida* (*Wounded Beast*, 1993), and a series of comic sketches broadcast in 1968 by SBT. The discussion focuses on the appropriative nuances emerging from the cultural constraints characteristic of Brazilian cultural and social identities as well as of the time of their creation, and on the different treatment required by the two filmic formats. Diversity and national identity are here seen as a way to bring to the fore the sense of nationality as it has been developed since the publication of Oswald de Andraded's *"Manifesto Antropófago" (Anthropophagic Manifesto)* in 1928.

What is the effect when Shakespearean allusion is mediated through a double layer of intertextuality, for example where the references occur in a work that is itself an adaptation of another text? Nathalie Vienne-Guerrin's chapter, "*Mon petit doigt m'a dit…*: Referencing Shakespeare or Agatha Christie?" explores the issues at stake in examining a French film version of Agatha Christie's novel *By the Pricking of my thumbs* (1968), entitled *Mon petit doigt m'a dit* (2005), directed by Pascal Thomas. It alludes to Shakespeare's *Macbeth* yet through the filters of Agatha Christie's detective novel and its film adaptation. Vienne-Guerrin considers these palimpsestic layers of reference, and generic multiplicity, asking what meanings can emerge, particularly for a French audience. What remains of Shakespeare in such a work when the allusive fragments are both concealed and revealed by Christie's work and its afterlives? She asks, how do Shakespeare and Christie share the seeds and roots of such a reference?

Mariacristina Cavecchi's chapter "Shakespeare's *Julius Caesar* in Federico Fellini's *Rome*" explores the porous boundary of Shakespeare / not Shakespeare through an examination of Federico Fellini's *Rome* (1972). She argues that the film exemplifies the conundrum by including a very short and bizarre fragment from a play about the Roman leader Julius Caesar. Shakespeare has played a key role in forging Italian national identity and Julius Caesar, herald and founder of the Roman Empire, and has undoubtedly been a key figure in Italian history and culture. References to Shakespeare's *Julius Caesar* are common in Italian film culture but is Fellini's one of them? The Fellinian quotation evidences the way in which such passing references, so marginal to the narrative of the films, are often interpreted by Shakespeareans as offshoots from Shakespeare's plays. Cavecchi considers the evidence for classifying the fragment. Whether or not it derives from Shakespeare, Fellini's brief reference reminds us of Shakespeare's crucial role in the process of negotiating questions of national identity and in articulating the contradictory relationship between Italian culture and its troublesome Fascist history.

Márta Minier's chapter, entitled "Still Our Contemporary in East-Central Europe? Post-socialist Shakespearean Allusions and Frameworks of Reference," focuses on two films, one from East-Central Europe and one with a strong East-Central European connection, that evidence the breadth of East-Central European recourse to Shakespeare. The Polish television film *Żółty szalik* (*Yellow Scarf*) (2000), directed by Janusz Morgenstern, makes only a slight reference to *Hamlet*; however, Minier argues that upon closer inspection, the connection is more than superficial. She illuminates the ways in which the film's themes and characters invoke Hamlet and his existential questioning, lending the protagonist gravitas in dealing with his alcoholism and giving him the potential of being a modern-day tragic hero, while his petty situation and quixotic struggle fuse the tragic overtone with that of comedy. The second film is Ronald Harwood's internationally acclaimed *The Pianist* (2002), based on Władysław Szpilman's memoir, that quotes from The *Merchant of Venice*. It is Wladek's brother Henryk who reads *The Merchant of Venice* as the family are made to wait before they are pushed onto the trains, and Minier explores the resonances of the allusion to Shylock's famous "Hath not a Jew eyes?" speech, in the face of the horrors of the Holocaust.

Boris N. Gaydin and Nikolay V. Zakharov in their chapter "Soviet and Post-Soviet References to *Hamlet* on Film and Television" explore the iconic place of *Hamlet* on the Russian screen. Since Grigori Kozintsev's landmark adaptation of 1964, *Hamlet* has been evoked in Russian film in a variety of ways. They trace how Hamlet is turned into an icon in popular culture and in commercials. Hamlet is presented as the embodiment of a thinker, a nobleman, a lover, a lunatic and an enigma. Their examples constitute a diverse range of genres, including an episode of a children's comedy TV show *Yeralash*, an "Interesting Movie or Poor Yurik" (1977); an episode in a comedy TV series *33 Square Meters* (1999–2000), "Hamlet, Prince of Dacha"; a student pop sketch "Hamlet" in *the Club of the Funny and Inventive* (2002); and Hamlet's soliloquy read by Elizaveta Arzamasova in an episode of the TV series *Daddy's Daughters* (2007). These diverse screen allusions to Hamlet point to the figure's popularity and range of uses to which Shakespearean appropriation has been put in Russian culture.

Finally, Mark Thornton Burnett's afterword concludes the volume with valuable reflections on the chapters outlined here and by exploring the short film *Daqqet ix-Xita* (*Plangent Rain*, 2010), directed by Kenneth Scicluna and set in Valletta, Malta, and its intertextual dialogue with *Hamlet*. Burnett also contributes some personal reflections on Mariangela Tempera.

Conclusion

This volume ultimately asks: what can Shakespeare do to a filmic text? What versions of Shakespeare emerge from these intertexts and how do these fragments transform our readings of films? Our hope is that the chapters presented here will increase awareness of Shakespeare's spectral reach and the potential richness of interpretation, critique and international dialogue when we take these intertextual mosaics into account.

Notes

1. *Raven*, directed by James McTeigue (Intrepid Pictures, 2012), is a serial-killer crime thriller set in the nineteenth century.
2. Alexa Alice Joubin, "Screening Social Justice: Performing Reparative Shakespeare Against Vocal Disability," *Adaptation*, vol. 14, no. 2 (August 2021): 187–205.
3. Eric S. Mallin, *Reading Shakespeare in the Movies: Non-Adaptations and Their Meanings* (New York: Palgrave Macmillan, 2019), 1.
4. Linda Hutcheon, *A Theory of Adaptation*, 2nd ed. (New York: Routledge, 2013), 121.
5. Marjorie Garber, *Quotation Marks* (New York: Routledge, 2003).
6. Alexa Alice Joubin and Elizabeth Rivlin, eds., *Shakespeare and the Ethics of Appropriation* (New York: Palgrave Macmillan, 2014).
7. Christina Wald, *Shakespeare's Serial Returns in Complex TV* (London: Palgrave Macmillan, 2020), 1 and 8.
8. Hutcheon, 7.
9. Julie Sanders, *Adaptation and Appropriation* (New York: Routledge, 2006), 26.
10. Christy Desmet, Natalie Loper and Jim Casey, eds., *Shakespeare/Not Shakespeare* (New York: Palgrave Macmillan, 2017).
11. Burnett, Mark Thornton, *Shakespeare and World Cinema* (Cambridge: Cambridge University Press, 2013), 2.

Works Cited

Burnett, Mark Thornton. *Shakespeare and World Cinema*. Cambridge: Cambridge University Press, 2013.

Calbi, Maurizio. *Spectral Shakespeares: Media Adaptations in the Twenty-First Century*. London: Palgrave Macmillan, 2013.

Desmet, Christy, Natalie Loper and Jim Casey, ed. *Shakespeare/Not Shakespeare*. New York: Palgrave Macmillan, 2017.

Garber, Marjorie. *Quotation Marks*. New York: Routledge, 2003.
Hutcheon, Linda. *A Theory of Adaptation*. 2nd ed. New York: Routledge, 2013.
Joubin, Alexa Alice. "Screening Social Justice: Performing Reparative Shakespeare against Vocal Disability." *Adaptation*, vol. 14, no. 2 (August 2021): 187–205.
Joubin, Alexa Alice and Elizabeth Rivlin, eds. *Shakespeare and the Ethics of Appropriation*. New York: Palgrave Macmillan, 2014.
Lanier, Douglas. "Shakespearean Rhizomatics: Adaptation, Ethics, Value." In *Shakespeare and the Ethics of Appropriation*, eds. Alexa Alice Joubin and Elizabeth Rivlin. New York: Palgrave Macmillan, 2014.
Mallin, Eric S. *Reading Shakespeare in the Movies: Non-Adaptations and Their Meanings*. New York: Palgrave Macmillan, 2019.
Sanders, Julie. *Adaptation and Appropriation*. London and New York: Routledge, 2006.
Wald, Christina. *Shakespeare's Serial Returns in Complex TV*. London: Palgrave Macmillan, 2020.

CHAPTER 2

The Boundaries of Citation: Shakespeare in Davide Ferrario's *Tutta colpa di Giuda* (2008), Alfredo Peyretti's *Moana* (2009), and Connie Macatuno's *Rome and Juliet* (2006)

Maurizio Calbi

To write about Shakespearean citations in twenty-first century media is to enter what Douglas Lanier calls the perilous "netherworld of 'Shakespeareana,'" "the realm of bastard, deformed, or wayward children of the Bard" ("Introduction" 132), a world whose boundaries are indeterminate and unstable. This is a world, if one adopts the theoretical framework of "post-fidelity Shakespeare" (of which Lanier is one of the most acute proponents), that cannot be clearly separated from the domain of "straight" Shakespearean adaptation. In a way, this "netherworld"

M. Calbi (✉)
Università degli Studi di Palermo, Palermo, Italy
e-mail: maurizio.calbi@unipa.it

A. A. Joubin and V. Bladen (eds.), *Onscreen Allusions to Shakespeare*, Global Shakespeares, https://doi.org/10.1007/978-3-030-93783-6_2

continually "overflows the measure" (*Ant.* 1.1.2),[1] and it is perhaps not by chance that theories of adaptation often attempt to define the "measure," the criteria whereby an adaptation can be said to be an adaptation "proper," as distinct from other engagements with the "source." For instance, Linda Hutcheon's influential *A Theory of Adaptation* defines adaptation as "an *acknowledged* transposition of a *recognizable* other work," or "an *extended* intertextual engagement with the adapted work" (8, my emphases), thus appealing to an unexamined notion of critical consensus or invoking a highly problematic quantitative criterion. The emphasis on what is "acknowledged" or "recognizable" reintroduces a sense of hierarchy of taste, or at least an unquestioned concept of an ideal viewer / reader, that a "post-fidelity" perspective attempts to undermine.[2] In short, who is it that acknowledges and / or recognizes? And if "allusions to and brief echoes of other works" do not qualify as adaptations in the sense of "extended engagements" (9), where would one situate, for instance, "engagements" with *Hamlet* such as Kurosawa's *The Bad Sleep Well* (1960) or Kaurismaki's *Hamlet Goes Business* (1987)? And since these films, if one adopts Hutcheon's approach, are *less* "extended engagements" with *Hamlet* than, say, Branagh's "uncut" version of *Hamlet* (1996), a film that goes as far as to visually supplement what is absent or only hinted at in Shakespeare's text, are they also *less* "creative *and* ... interpretive act[s] of appropriation" (8) than Branagh's?[3] In other words, where, when, and how do allusions, echoes, citations *properly* end? Where, when, and how does an adaptation *properly* begin? Moreover, what about the "entity" one extensively engages with (or not): the "adapted work" itself? The problem of boundaries—between what is "acknowledged" as adaptation and what is not, between an "extended engagement" with the adapted text and one that is less so—re-presents itself when one considers the relationship between the work and "its" adaptation, which Margaret Kidnie rephrases and highlights as the "problem" of adaptation. Referring to Hutcheon and other adaptation theorists, she questions the assumption that "there exists a relatively stable distinction between work and adaptation" (4). To Kidnie, the (Shakespearean) work is not "an a priori category" (7); it does not function as "an objective yardstick against which to measure the supposed accuracy of editions and stagings"; it "continually takes shape as a *consequence* of production" (7). ("Production" here includes textual editions, theatrical stagings as well as renditions of plays in other media such as TV). Yet, although she consistently argues that "one *cannot* absolutely separate [the work from its adaptation]" (30, Kidnie's emphasis), she also insists that "in such an indeterminate situation one constructs a provisional definition of the 'truth' of the work through ongoing debate" (31). One may wonder whether Kidnie's radical questioning of the (ontological) status of the work—what she calls "a process without an origin" (7)—is entirely compatible with her matter-of-fact position, her simultaneous emphasis on "the pragmatic truth of the dramatic work of art" as "continually produced among communities of users through assertion and dissension" (31); one may also wonder about the preponderant role she attributes to interpretive communities, and the effectiveness of such role in providing "checks and limits on the work's evolving shape" (7), in making a "genuine" instance of the work emerge, or rather re-emerge, in a contingent manner, as what is *not* adaptation, and especially if one considers the vast proliferation of versions of the work (textual editions, theatrical performances, filmic, TV, and web remediations) in early twenty-first-century media culture.[4]

Therefore, to write about Shakespearean citation in twenty-first century media culture is to raise a number of theoretical questions about boundaries, about the dividing line between work and adaptation, "straight" adaptations and not-quite-so-straight adaptations, spin-offs and citations, meaningful citations and "accidental" citations, and so on.[5] I want to argue that these are not just general theoretical questions; they are also specifically connected with the so-called Shakespeare-on-film boom of the 1990s, a phenomenon that has radically reshaped the place and "nature" of "Shakespeare"—what is meant by "Shakespeare"—in contemporary media culture. This is a phenomenon, according to Douglas Lanier, that has produced various "recalibrations" of the Bard; in particular, by bringing an updated "Shakespeare" (especially in terms of setting and time period) into closer proximity with late twentieth-century visual culture and the "concerns and screen styles of youth culture" (107), it has "loosen[ed] the equivalence between Shakespeare and text" ("Mutations" 106). Lanier goes as far as to argue that the overall effect of these "recalibrations" has been the emergence of a "Shakespeare" that is "definitively post-textual" (106). One may disagree with individual aspects of Lanier's cultural diagnosis, but it would be hard to deny that the "Shakespeare" of our contemporary mediascape is more visual and less textual (at least in the common-sense meaning of the word "textual"), almost exclusively experienced on screen, highly self-reflexive and often ironic, irremediably "global" (also by virtue of the predominance of visual aspects), and moving across multiple media platforms. In short, it is an increasingly heterogeneous and fragmentary textual and mediatized *presence*. In fact, I want to suggest that at the beginning of the new millennium "Shakespeare" is a spectral "entity," what Jacques Derrida calls the "Thing 'Shakespeare'" (*Specters* 22), simultaneously material and evanescent. Like the Ghost in *Hamlet*, it is "here," "here," and then suddenly "gone" (1.1.123). It is an "entity" that "inhabits without residing" (*Specters* 18), that inhabits without *properly* inhabiting. It is because of its fragmentary and spectral status that this "Shakespeare" approximates what one usually understands as citation.[6] In this sense, one may want to speak of a field of (Shakespearean) *citationality*—both a textual *and* media matter—without any clear beginning or predetermined end, a field within which citation and other forms of Shakespearean afterlife situate themselves as variables that cannot be so easily separated from one another. Moreover, "post-textual" may indicate not only the reduced presence of Shakespearean textual material, but also the uncanny, mutual invagination of "part" (i.e. what one commonly calls "citation") and "whole" (i.e. a more extended engagement with the "original").

To stress the indeterminacy of boundaries—for instance, the lack of a clear-cut distinction between citation and "full-blown" adaptation, a Shakespeare "in tatters" and a Shakespeare in "royal robes"—is *not* to give up on the desire to engage with Shakespearean citations and thus to "contribute to the wider, evolving sense of Shakespeare's reach, relevance, importance, or sheer recognition value" in contemporary media culture (Lanier, "Introduction" 132–33). This undoubtedly remains a fetishistic desire, structured from within by the well-known psychoanalytic formula for fetishism: "I know very well … but nonetheless," a compulsive desire for the (Shakespearean) archive—what Derrida may call "archive fever" (cf. *Archive*, esp. 91). It is in order *not* to give up on this desire, but also in order *not* to lose sight of the theoretical problematics of boundaries as concerns and the effects of "Shakespeare" in the current mediascape, that this essay focuses on twenty-first-century media products that are themselves concerned with boundaries, each in its own idiosyncratic way, and often as a result of the Shakespearean citations they incorporate: Davide Ferrario's *Tutta colpa di Giuda* (2008) (*Blame it on Judas*), an Italian film set in a prison in Turin; Alfredo Peyretti's *Moana* (2009), an Italian film about porn star Moana Pozzi; and Connie Macatuno's *Rome and Juliet* (2006), a Filipino lesbian romance. They reference, respectively, *Hamlet*, *A Midsummer Night's Dream*, and *Romeo and Juliet*.

***

Davide Ferrario's *Tutta colpa di Giuda* (*Blame it on Judas*) is an Italian film set in *Le Vallette*, a jail in the Northern Italian city of Turin. Challenging the boundaries of the genre "prison film," it is a postmodern, tongue-in-cheek combination of *cinéma verité* and musical. (It defines itself, in the opening titles, as "a comedy with music," but plays with the conventions of *cinéma verité* by introducing interviews with the convicts conducted with a mini-DV camera). It casts a mix of professional actors (Kasia Smutniak, Gianluca Gobbi, Fabio Troiano) and non-professional actors (i.e. twenty convicts as well as a few security guards playing themselves), and also includes professional musicians making their debut as film actors (i.e. Cristiano Godano, lead singer of the Italian band Marlene Kuntz, and Cecco Signa, who is a "fictional" inmate playing the mouth-organ). In the film, Irena Markovich (Kasia Smutniak), an avant-garde theatre director from Belgrade, is employed to work with a group of convicts. (She is, in a way, a simulacrum of the film director himself, since Davide Ferrario has often been involved with experimental projects in prisons since 1999). Don Iridio (Gianluca Gobbi), a socially progressive priest who coordinates educational activities inside the prison, and an admirer of Pier Paolo Pasolini, suggests that they put on a Passion play for Easter. Irena is a little reluctant at first but then accepts; she buys a copy of the Gospels, and conscientiously starts reading it, also in order to explore what Don Iridio wants her to focus on—the "human" aspect of Jesus. But the trouble with the Passion play is that none of the convicts wants to play the role of the informer, the *infame*; none of them wants to be Judas. And, of course, without Judas, the theological—and teleological—aspects of the Passion of Christ as a drama of suffering and redemption are irremediably undermined. As Irena lucidly summarizes it: "Without Judas, there is no betrayal... without betrayal, there is no trial... without trial, there is no sentence... without sentence, there is no expiation... without expiation or sacrifice... there is no salvation or redemption." However, she does not give up on the project; in the course of the rehearsals, it is the meaning of "passion" that dramatically shifts, from "passion" as suffering to "passion" as joy, love, and zest for life, and this is also as a result of her critical rereading of the figure of Jesus in the Gospels, much to Don Iridio's amazement and irritation. She thus decides to stage a play that responds to this second sense of "passion," a musical that vaguely recalls

Jesus Christ Superstar, and in which Jesus, played by a lifer, is only too human.

A fragment of Shakespeare's *Hamlet*—the "What a piece of work is a man" speech—appears in the early stages of the film, when Irena is still very much undecided about what to do with the convicts, but clearly sees herself as an avant-garde theatre director. This speech emerges in the form of a video clip she plays during a workshop with the inmates. It is thus already mediatized, a video recording within the film. Moreover, it articulates itself as a "piece of work" at the crossroad of different media, a contamination of boundaries: we see Cristiano (Irena's boyfriend) speaking the lines while members of the dance company G.A.P. (Federica and Michela Pozzo, Renato Cravero, Paolo Data Blin, Clelia Riva) perform these lines with their bodies. The whole performance is punctuated by a melancholic, reiterative musical score by Marlene Kuntz (Fig. 2.1).

Cristiano Godano's style of delivery makes Hamlet into a character that is affected by an irreducible hauteur. Moreover, his Hamlet is not just a character but also some kind of stage director: with his gestures, he prompts the movements of the bodies of the dancers, which simultaneously stresses the "infinite" capability of these bodies in terms of "form and moving" *and* the senselessness of any such "faculty." In the midst of the speech, the camera briefly shifts to a prison cell, and we see one of the

Fig. 2.1 Hamlet performance

convicts lying in bed and smoking a cigarette: What a piece of work is *this* man? How noble in reason? Yet, as the clip comes to an end, this ironic juxtaposition is itself irremediably re-marked and transformed. As we shift back to the workshop room, we find one of the convicts carrying on with Hamlet's speech, reading the lines from a script up to "this quintessence of dust." As soon as he ends the speech, he expostulates: "Do I really have to read this?" The other convicts' reaction to the speech is incontrollable laughter, and they are all equally disparaging: "What does it mean?... Dust and bones... we didn't understand a thing." It is only when one of the convicts asks Irena if she has written the speech herself that the object of scorn acquires a name: "It's William Shakespeare!"

For these convicts, there is an unbridgeable chasm between "high" and "low" culture. Shakespeare's words are incomprehensible. They smack of "high" culture even before they are identified as Shakespeare's. (One of the convicts attributes the words to Dante, not because he recognizes them as such, but because they sound like an expression of "high" culture). They function as a mechanism of inclusion / exclusion, implicitly construing the inmates as cultural outsiders: "He offends our ignorance." In a sense, Hamlet's hauteur doubles as the hauteur of "Shakespeare," the iconic sign of the cultural values of the higher classes. Sneering at these words—"What a jerk!"—is thus a form of iconoclasm one often finds in the products of popular culture analysed by Douglas Lanier as "Shakespop." To refer to Lanier's approach, the convicts' reaction can be seen as a form of resistance towards "the network of practices, connotations and hierarchies of taste that dominant cultural institutions attach to Shakespeare's name" (*Shakespeare* 106), or other significant "high" cultural icons. In this specific context, it is also a trenchant criticism of the intellectualism of experimental theatre, of an avant-garde treatment of Shakespeare that does not resonate with the experience of being in jail. As the scene progresses, Irena laughs *with* them *at* Shakespeare, which marks not only the creation of a stronger bond with the convicts turned actors, but also an alteration of her life in both artistic and personal terms: she moves away from avant-garde theatre *and* splits up with her boyfriend Cristiano, who stands for this type of theatre. It is not by chance that in a subsequent scene we are offered Cristiano's reflections on Judas. He finds it odd that none of the convicts wants to play the informer: "It's such a magnificent role." (After he says this, we see him quietly sitting in a corner of the room holding a skull). If the Passion play Irena is originally forced to consider ignores "passion" as forceful affirmation of life, avant-garde "Shakespeare," on the other hand, is too "dis-passionate," cool, and detached.

The irreverent attitude towards the Bard in *Tutta colpa di Giuda* also suggests that the "Shakespeare" included in prison films is not necessarily the "therapeutic Shakespeare" that emerges from a largely US-based tradition of "prison Shakespeare," a tradition whose most emblematic example is perhaps Hank Rogerson's *Shakespeare Behind Bars* (2006), based on Curt Tofteland's work with inmates at Kentucky's Luther Luckett prison.[7] It is not necessarily, that is, a "Shakespeare" as catalyst of spiritual growth, reformation, and redemption, as is predominantly the case with this tradition. The therapeutic model of drama is very much part of Davide Ferrario's film, although not explicitly in connection with Shakespeare. For Don Iridio, theatre is "holy" and "salvific." And, of course, the form of educational theatre he suggests as the most appropriate for convicts—the Passion play—is, or should be, "salvific": it is a play based on sacrifice but leading to redemption. However, as mentioned earlier, none of the convicts wants to play Judas. Moreover, this refusal soon becomes an unwillingness to play *any* role in *any* drama based on rituals—trial, sentence, expiation, and salvation—that disquietingly recall the equally dramatic rituals of the judiciary apparatus. The latter are rituals that require that the convict see himself as an *essentially* disciplined subject (in a Foucaultian sense), subject to the (internalized) "truth" about himself, achieved through some form of suffering qua "passion." When Irene points out the deleterious consequences of a missing Judas for the whole dynamics of the Passion play (speaking as herself but also ventriloquizing Don Iridio's voice), one of the convicts trenchantly replies: "Trial... sentence... expiation... if you speak of these things in here [i.e., in a prison] you're starting off on the wrong foot." Thus, Davide Ferrario's film repeatedly draws attention to the therapeutic model of drama, but only to re-mark and displace it. During the dress rehearsal of a radically transformed Passion play, Jesus descends from the Cross to join the dance, giving up on the idea of sacrifice and performing the same dance steps as the other actors / convicts, and with the same kind of elation, while singing: "The cross... I'll forget about it. And my life I'll begin to live. Come and play with me... Come and dance with me." This is a Jesus who is diametrically opposed to the Jesus who emerges from Irene's rereading of the Gospels. Irene illustrates her findings to Don Iridio as follows: "Allow me... If I was to describe him as a theatrical character, I would define him as an obsessed man... obsessed with saving the world... self-indulgent... He mistreats everybody, including the apostles... He never smiles." The "sacrilegious" Jesus Christ she expounds is of course uncannily similar to her longhaired boyfriend *Crist*iano, who is obsessed with his avant-garde theatrical "mission," is self-indulgent, plays the *prima donna* with his "disciples," and never smiles.

There is no staging as such of the new Passion play: after the dress rehearsal, which obviously disappoints Don Iridio, and after the production runs into yet more problems—the convicts discover that Irene is having an affair with the prison warden, and thus refuse to be directed by somebody who, Judas-like, has betrayed their trust—we learn that the Italian government has proclaimed an amnesty, and that all the convicts will soon be released. The film ends with a scene in which they are all lining up on the threshold of the jail, as if about to leave. But immediately afterwards, we see them looking at themselves on a screen, commenting on their pose, and we realize that the amnesty is itself only a "fiction," "a dream of passion." With this self-reflexive, postmodern *coup de théâtre*, we are back into the film's "fictional" world, along with the convicts, with little hope of escaping it. ("Back inside," one of the guards repeats). The final scene refers back to very beginning of the film, when we witness the first interview with one of the convicts. In retrospect, the words of this convict take on an almost prophetic quality: "Jail? It is like a play. We all pretend... us, the guards, the judges, and then at some point it ends and we start all over again." In short, the play starts before the (actual) play starts. *Tutta colpa di Giuda* is a light "comedy with music" in many respects. Yet, the quasi-Shakespearean motif of *theatrum mundi* enunciated here also bears sinister connotations. It points to the senseless reiteration of the rituals of the disciplinary system. There is no "liberal" idea of improvement of the penal system emerging from the film but only "passion" / joy as that which somehow guards against the most deleterious effects of reiteration, and partially alters the purpose of playing. There is no intimation of reformation of the self or re-discovery of the truth about one's self through "Shakespeare" or other types of drama. It is highly ironic that it is up to the ironically named director of the prison, Libero (i.e. Freedom), to provide an allegorization of the prison system that is superbly alert to the question of boundaries: "Jail is a rip-off... it helps those outside to draw the line, to brush all the garbage under the carpet... And nobody worries about the real problem... the carpet." Libero tells Irene that he was named after his grandfather, an anarchist. And, indeed, the film often foregrounds articulations of what may be called an anarchic and utopian "po-ethics" of boundaries. I want to conclude this section with one such articulation, taken from the lyrics of the song that bears the same title as the film. With much less cynicism than in Libero's speech, these words re-mark the problematics of boundaries and extend the sense of permeability in surprising and unexpected ways: "Listen to my utopia: no more bars, no more jails, let the good mix with the bad, let the wolf go to the lamb, maybe they'll discover that they are brothers." Thus, in this utopian world, poetics—and the poetics of music—overlaps with ethics, and "mix" becomes the rule.

* * *

"Without the cross … we'll do it without the cross," Irene announces when she decides to replace the Passion play with a "neo-hippie" musical. Appearing only to disappear in Ferrario's film, the cross is a lingering, spectral presence in another contemporary Italian movie that references Shakespeare, Alfredo Peyretti's *Moana* (2009), a film about the life of Italian porn star Moana Pozzi and the "netherworld" of porn. Shakespeare emerges when a very young Moana auditions for a role in a film, after moving from the South of Italy to Rome. Since the film appears to be a kind of love story, she decides to recite (in Italian) a shortened version of Hermia's stoical response to the "madness" of Athenian law, a decision the casting director defines, not without irony, "challenging." The lines she delivers roughly correspond to the following: "If then true lovers have been ever crossed, / It stands as an edict in destiny. / Then let us teach our trial patience, because it is a customary cross" (1.1.150–53).[8] Wearing a short pink dress, gesticulating excessively, and adopting a seductive pose that somehow jars with the content of Hermia's lines, Moana (Violante Placido) may be said to reduce "Shakespeare" to "tatters, to very rags" (Fig. 2.2). But whatever the shortcomings of her performance, the film clearly associates "Shakespeare" with the realm of high art. In terms of Moana's personal trajectory, "Shakespeare" symptomatizes her strong desire to become an artist, which she announces when she is still a teenager, after dancing the *pizzica* (the Salento version of the *tarantella* dance) and being severely chastised by her mother because of the exceeding sensuality of her movements.

Shakespeare reappears after Moana makes love to Adrian, a film producer from California who has somehow overheard her audition and used the word "Shakespeare" as a pick-up line. She reiterates Hermia's

Fig. 2.2 Moana's audition

lines while in bed with him and then asks: "Do you like Shakespeare?" Adrian replies: "No, I don't. I like theatre, but you don't make any money with theatre." The philistinism of money-oriented Americans is here opposed to "Shakespeare" as a cultural icon that finds its most appropriate expression in a medium that escapes mere economic imperatives. Unlike *Tutta colpa di Giuda*, Shakespearean theatre is an authentic, genuine medium that not only rivals the medium of film but is also set against the world of porn cinema: it is Adrian who first introduces Moana to this world, and thus becomes an emblem of the dark side of the Californian "industry." Her affair with Adrian is the first of a long series of relationships that function as "trials": not only does she find him in bed with another porn actress; she also discovers that he has breached his promise that her first porn film would only be released abroad, which wreaks havoc on her relationship with her family in the South of Italy. We also have a duke, although in this biopic "Duke" (*il duca*) is only the nickname of a drug dealer with aristocratic descent acting as a lover who has effectively "stol'n the impression of her fantasy" (1.1.32) as well as a surrogate father: he keeps her away from the world of porn and repeatedly prevents her from sniffing cocaine. Moreover, he shelters her with his own body as he is shot dead by two hit men on a motorbike, which is presumably to settle a drug score. In fact, the film opens with Moana in the shower washing away his blood after the murder, and then we see her, still naked, rummaging through her wardrobe desperately looking for what turns out to be the only precious object she can hang on to in order to survive: a cross attached to the beads of a rosary. This sequence is juxtaposed with the aftermath of the episode of the *pizzica* mentioned earlier: a flashback shows us a traumatized Moana clutching the beads of the same rosary, with the cross very much in the foreground. The "customary cross" of Shakespeare's play thus becomes the repeated appearance of a literal "cross," a fetishized object supporting Moana's identity. More generally, Hermia's lines take on an almost spectral quality. They are fragments that mark in advance the vicissitudes of her life, functioning as uncanny premonition, a "warning" for the future.[9]

In Shakespeare's play the strict, patriarchal law of Athens decrees that Hermia is "either to die the death, or to abjure for ever the society of men" (65–66). Unlike Hermia, Moana *does* "die the death"—she is diagnosed with liver cancer at the age of thirty-three, in the middle of her career as an internationally renowned porn star. But she also lives as a votaress *manqué*, the uncanny, reverse mirror image of a "barren sister," a woman "in a shady cloister mewed" (71–72). In fact, as the film progresses, the porn industry increasingly takes on the features of a suffocating, claustrophobic "cloister." After precipitously signing a binding contract with an unscrupulous producer, we see her relentlessly shooting films in a decidedly unglamorous barn in a derelict and deserted area of town, away from "the society of men." Outside this shabby barn, we only ever see go-carts monotonously going round and round, with no sign of human presence, as if to punctuate the senselessness—perhaps the "austerity" (90)—of her routine as a porn star. After her true love is itself "crossed"—her relationship with a simple fisherman and scuba diver who had never heard of her glamorous career as a porn star—she begins to resemble more and more a "rose" that "grows, lives and dies in single blessedness" (78). There is no comedic denouement here as is the case with Hermia and her lover in *Midsummer Night's Dream*, except perhaps Moana's eager expectation of an interview on prime-time TV. This interview should allow her to represent herself not simply—and exclusively—as a porn actress. But perhaps the TV box is itself yet another example of a space of confinement, yet another "cloister."

* * *

Referencing *Midsummer Night's Dream* in Peyretti's Moana is thus only apparently marginal. It keys into significant aspects of the film. This biopic includes "Shakespeare" to draw the boundaries between high culture and cinema, theatre and porn cinema. Yet, the world of porn turns out to be uncannily proximate to a festive comedy gone awry, with the shift from one realm to the other being facilitated by the rigid patriarchal structure that governs them both.

The law of the Father is also one of the main concerns of *Rome and Juliet* (2006), Connie Macatuno's first feature film after much experience as a theatre director. Presumably, the title of the film references *Romeo and Juliet* mainly because of Shakespeare's global cultural prestige. Shakespeare's play is implicitly considered to be the love story *par excellence* and is indeed a story extremely popular in the Philippines in various forms and media formats (cf. Ick). The film translates this story into the quasi-obsessive search for "the one and only." One of its most innovative aspects is that "the one and only" does not necessarily coincide with a heterosexual "object," and that the theme of lesbian love is treated with a rare delicacy of touch. In this film, set in Manila, Juliet Flores (Andrea del Rosario) is engaged to be married to Marc (Rafael Rosell), a rich, ambitious young politician with an overambitious mother. The families of the two lovers are not "alike in dignity": contrary to Marc, who is also about to run for Mayor, Juliet is a kindergarten teacher who comes from a very poor background. Class difference is often emphasized, and language is one of its most significant markers. Upper class, educated people such as the members of Mark's household switch with ease from Tagalog / Filipino to English and back, but this never happens in Juliet's household. The Romeo figure, however, is not Marc but a character with a doubly Shakespearean name, Rome Miranda (Mylene Dizon), a successful, liberated, "Westernized" young businesswoman who starts seeing Juliet precisely because of her business: she is well-renowned for her floral arrangements, and Juliet, after meeting her by chance, asks her to be her wedding planner. Difference of status also informs the relationship between the two women, but sameness of gender appears to be an element that allows for its successful renegotiation.

The film does not end tragically, although this is nearly the case: Juliet is run over by car, and in a coma for several weeks, while Marc and Rome alternate at her hospital bed. This unexplained accident is perhaps the only "unconscious" symptom of homophobia at a structural level, a homophobia the film simultaneously contests. Moreover, if there is feud between families, this is as a result of the scandal, when Marc discovers the relationship between Rome and Juliet and calls off the wedding. One of its most vociferous forms is the dialogue between Mark and Juliet's mother, a confrontation during which questions of class intermix with issues of sexuality: from the perspective of Mark's mother, "deviant" sexuality feeds upon poor upbringing. The "vial" also makes its appearance. It takes the form of an overdose of pills taken by Rome's sister. Its function in the plot is to bring Rome and Juliet closer together and to drive Juliet and Mark apart: as Juliet and Mark are out for dinner on Valentine's Day, Juliet pays little attention to him, and she is much more concerned about replying to Rome's text messages with updates about her sister's health. The film also includes a character who resembles Shakespeare's Nurse, Juliet's co-worker: she repeatedly acts as Juliet's confidante and realizes that Juliet is falling for Rome before Juliet realizes this herself. Later on, we learn that she is herself involved in a lesbian relationship, which is yet another sign of how the film circulates the "naturalness" of female homoeroticism.

In Shakespeare's *Romeo and Juliet*, Juliet's love at first sight is mostly an escape from the patriarchal and gender constraints of the Capulets' household; in the film, Juliet's relationship with Rome allows her to move away from the gentle but obsessive forms of control Mark repeatedly employs to discipline her body. For instance, he insists that she wears her hair tied up. Moreover, the very first time we see them together in a car, he checks whether her blouse is properly buttoned up (and fastens the seat belt for her). The inventiveness of Juliet's language in Shakespeare's play here becomes Juliet's love for poetry: she keeps a diary with her poetry (and, of course, she hides it from Marc). In fact, the film opens with Juliet reciting poetry in voice-over and writing her diary on her way to work. Poetry is also what strengthens the relationship between the two women: one day Rome picks Juliet up from work without telling her where they are going and drives her to a lesbian poetry club; Juliet recites one of her poems to great acclaim, which boosts her confidence and re-marks the intimate connection between art and various forms of deconstruction of patriarchal boundaries.

Unlike *Tutta colpa di Giuda* and *Moana*, the title of Macatuno's film raises expectations about the presence of Shakespeare in the film. If one associates "Shakespeare" with a textual corpus with definite boundaries, these expectations are likely to be largely frustrated. "Shakespeare" remains a shadowy presence. Yet, it sometimes makes itself felt in an idiosyncratic way, as when the film, for instance, engages with the analysis of the name. In the film, this analysis is just as significant as in the balcony scene of the "original"; it acts as a trigger for the transformation of a heterosexual love story into a lesbian romance. When Juliet and Rome meet for the first time, the former confesses to the latter: "I thought Rome was a guy's name... I am a huge fan by the way--of your floral arrangements. I can't believe it–but there you are. So... much... a woman." After talking to each other for a while, sharing food from a street stall, and exchanging phone numbers, Julie comments: "Nice ring to it... our names, I mean" (Fig. 2.3).[10]

There is no "grudge" here—quite the opposite in fact—but the name "Rome" is still a kind of "enemy" to Juliet from the point of view of hetero-normativity, in that it "attaches" itself to a "bearer" of the same gender, to somebody who, in spite of the way the name sounds,

Fig. 2.3 Rome and Juliet

is "so... much... a woman." And, much in the same way as *Romeo and Juliet*, "enmity" *is* irresistible attraction—while exchanging numbers, each surreptitiously glances at each other, and these fleeting looks clearly speak of desire. Moreover, if there is a "nice ring" to these names, it is also because they are always-already mediatized: on the one hand, they literally become indistinguishable from the *ring* tones of their mobile devices; on the other, and more metaphorically, they inscribe themselves, in a tongue-in-cheek and self-reflexive way, in an endless series of names that respond to, and echo, those of the "star-crossed lovers" in *Romeo and Juliet*.

A further revision of words from the balcony scene occurs later on when Rome (ironically) says: "Finally, she speak" (cf. *Rom.* 2.1.68) to address a Juliet who has just broken her silence after frantically preparing breakfast without saying a word. It is early in the morning, like in Shakespeare's play, but the context is entirely different—Juliet is mad at Rome because she thinks that Rome has spent the night with a former boyfriend. This is a minor citation, but within a crucial scene that activates a process whereby a close friendship turns into an explicit sexual liaison. (They nearly kiss in this scene after the argument). It is a scene that shows the intimate connection of pain and desire, a desire that is at this stage so much on the surface and yet hardly acknowledged, or perhaps unacknowledged *because* so much in the open. An allusion to *Romeo and Juliet* may also be glimpsed when the film references that most metaphoric of flowers—the rose. Giving a kind of crash-course on floral arrangements to a captivated audience, Rome speaks of the rose as follows: "The rose is my ultimate favorite flower. Did you know that the Greek goddess of beauty, Aphrodite, named the rose after her son, Eros?" (She is probably thinking of the myth of Adonis, a young man killed by a wild boar sent by Ares, and of the red rose that sprang from his blood). Rome implicitly reminds us that "rose" is an anagram of "Eros." This is part of the logic of the film. Desire has much to do with letters that shift; it is always-already inscribed in the names that the two characters bear: how can Juliet *not* be attracted to Rome? How can a Juliet *Flores* who loves roses *not* desire and admire a floral designer who is called Rome Miranda? "That which we call a rose / By any other word would smell as sweet" (85–86): perhaps Connie Macatuno's film by any other title would work as well, or not work at all. Still, it is a brave film that introduces signs of alterity within what it implicitly identifies as a Western heterosexual myth.

The three films that I have discussed here reference Shakespeare in different and often idiosyncratic ways. In each one of them, "Shakespeare" emerges as a fragmentary, spectral presence, as a "foreign body" within the "body proper" of the film that induces reconsideration of boundaries: between high and low culture (*Tutta colpa di Giuda*), between high art in the form of theatre and (porn) cinema (*Moana*), and between heterosexual normativity and the "naturalness" of homoerotic desire (*Rome and Juliet*). Each film cites and re-contextualizes Shakespeare in its own peculiar way, and thus (literally and metaphorically) puts "Shakespeare" in quotation marks—in scare quotes—as it cites it.[11] Each one of them bears witness to the infinite variety of forms of survival of the "Thing 'Shakespeare'" in contemporary media culture.

Notes

1. All citations of Shakespeare's works are from Welles and Taylor.
2. Of course, Hutcheon's own approach fundamentally contributes to such a "post-fidelity" perspective. See esp. 6–7.
3. "A creative *and* an interpretive act of appropriation / salvaging" is part of Hutcheon's three-pronged definition of adaptation (8).
4. Kidnie's approach is perhaps more pertinent as concerns the field of production of textual and theatrical instances of the work. For further discussion of Kidnie's approach, see Cartelli; see also Calbi, *Spectral* 16–18.
5. For an understanding of the practice of citation, including Shakespearean citation, that raises questions about commonly held notions about this problematic field, see Garber.
6. See Burt on how "Shakespeare's mediatization and consequent fragmentation extends much more broadly than the quotation of famous lines from the plays" ("Introduction" 3). Zoltán Márkus also notes that there is a lack of definite boundaries between citations as "acts of appropriation" and "other cultural practices of textual reiteration such as adaptation, editing, performing, and translation" (n.p.).
7. On "therapeutic Shakespeare," and the difference between European and US tradition of prison Shakespeare, see Wray. On the US tradition of "prison Shakespeare," see Scott-Douglass. On another Italian example of prison Shakespeare, Paolo and Vittorio Taviani's *Cesare deve morire*, and how it situates itself within these traditions, see Calbi, "States."
8. "Se dunque al mondo tutti i grandi amori sono stati in eterno contrastati, vuol dire che è decreto del destino e questa prova cui siamo sottoposti anche noi due ci sia d'ammonimento."

9. Interestingly, in Moana's interpretation of Hermia's lines, "patience" becomes "warning" ("*ammonimento*"). The lines contain the word "warning," and are themselves, as a whole, a kind of uncanny "warning."
10. Rome and Juliet share a passion for food, and food punctuates the development of their relationship. After cooking *adobo de Juliet* for Rome, Juliet says: "You won't forget my name after this."
11. In a theoretically related context, Zoltán Márkus argues that "the quotation marks in 'Shakespeare' indicate an act of extraction, while they also function as markers of alienation–as scare quotes: they simultaneously highlight and mask the word they contain" (n.p.). Arguably, they mark the visible / invisible, "hauntological" status of "Shakespeare" in contemporary media culture (cf. Derrida, *Specters* 50–51; see Calbi, *Spectral* 1–20). On "scare quote" as that which "estranges [the] appearance of the natural," and is thus distinct from "authoritative quotation," see Harries 3 and *passim*.

Works Cited

Burt, Richard, ed. *Shakespeares After Shakespeare: An Encyclopedia of the Bard in Mass Media and Popular Culture*. Vol. 1. Westport and London: Greenwood P, 2007.

Burt, Richard. "Introduction: Shakespeare, More or Less? From Shakespearecccentricity to Shakespearecentricity and Back." Burt, *Shakespeares* 1–9.

Calbi, Maurizio. *Spectral Shakespeares: Media Adaptations in the Twenty-First Century*. New York and London: Palgrave Macmillan, 2013.

Calbi, Maurizio. "'In States Unborn and Accents Yet Unknown': Spectral Shakespeare in Paolo and Vittorio Taviani's *Cesare deve morire* (*Caesar Must Die*)." *Shakespeare Bulletin*, vol. 32, no. 2 (2014): 235–53.

Cartelli, Thomas. Rev. of *Shakespeare and the Problem of Adaptation*, by Margaret Jane Kidnie. Semenza, 218–24.

Derrida, Jacques. *Specters of Marx: The State of the Debt, the Work of Mourning and the New International*. Trans. Peggy Kamuf. London and New York: Routledge, 1994.

Derrida, Jacques. *Archive Fever*. Trans. Eric Prenowitz. Chicago and London: U of Chicago P, 1995.

Tutta colpa di Giuda. Dir. Ferrario, Davide. Warner Bros and Rossofuoco. 2008. Film.

Garber, Marjorie. "" " (Quotation Marks)." *Critical Inquiry*, vol. 25, no. 4 (1999): 653–79.

Hutcheon, Linda and Siobhan O'Flynn. *A Theory of Adaptation*. 2nd ed. London and New York: Routledge, 2013.

Ick, Judy Celine. "The Undiscovered Country: Shakespeare in Philippine Literatures." *Kritika Kultura*, vols. 21/22 (2013/2014): 185–209.
Kidnie, Margaret J. *Shakespeare and the Problem of Adaptation*. London and New York: Routledge 2009.
Lanier, Douglas. "Introduction. On the Virtues of Illegitimacy: Free Shakespeare on Film." Burt, *Shakespeares*, 132–37.
Lanier, Douglas. *Shakespeare and Modern Popular Culture*. Oxford: Oxford UP, 2002.
Lanier, Douglas. "Recent Shakespeare Adaptation and the Mutations of Cultural Capital." Semenza 104–13.
Harries, Martin. *Scare Quotes from Shakespeare: Marx, Keynes, and the Language of Reenchantment*. Stanford, CA, Stanford UP, 2000.
Rome and Juliet. Dir. Connie Macatuno. Regal Capital & Regal Entertainment. 2006. Film.
Márkus, Zoltán. "Shakespeare in Quotation Marks." Ed. Bruce Smith and Katherine Rowe, *Cambridge World Shakespeare Encyclopedia* (forthcoming).
Moana. Dir. Alfredo Peyretti. Sky Cinema and Polivideo. 2009. Film.
Scott-Douglass, Amy. *Shakespeare Inside: The Bard Behind Bars*. London: Continuum, 2007.
Semenza, Greg, ed. *After Shakespeare on Film*. Spec. issue of *Shakespeare Studies*, vol. 38 (2010): 1–285.
Shakespeare, William. *William Shakespeare: The Complete Works*. Ed. Stanley Wells and Gary Taylor. 2nd ed. Oxford: Clarendon Press, 2005.
Wray, Ramona. "The Morals of *Macbeth* and Peace as Process: Adapting Shakespeare in Northern Ireland's Maximum Security Prison." *Shakespeare Quarterly*, vol. 62, no. 3 (2011): 340–63.

CHAPTER 3

Antipodean Shakespeares: Appropriating Shakespeare in Australian Film

Victoria Bladen

Shakespearean intertexts appear in a diverse range of Australian films, and this chapter maps a selection of these, tracing their potential meanings in three films that use various modes of appropriation: a play-within-a-film and the transposition of Shakespearean language in Raymond Longford's *The Sentimental Bloke* (1919), a fleeting citation in Peter Weir's *Picnic at Hanging Rock* (1975) and an extended intertextual engagement in Jerzy Domaradzki's *Lilian's Story* (1996), all adaptations of literary texts.[1] Adaptations further complicate the intertextual relationship with Shakespeare, the films entering into dialogue with the earlier literary hypotexts as well as with the Shakespearean intertexts. Australia has strong historical, constitutional and cultural links with Britain, through its history as a former British colony and its status as a constitutional monarchy, despite widespread support for republicanism. This extended relationship with British culture is a relevant context for all of the focus films. Shakespeare

V. Bladen (✉)
The University of Queensland, Brisbane, QLD, Australia
e-mail: v.bladen@uq.edu.au

A. A. Joubin and V. Bladen (eds.), *Onscreen Allusions to Shakespeare*, Global Shakespeares, https://doi.org/10.1007/978-3-030-93783-6_3

as a key British cultural product has inevitably featured in the history of Australian culture in a diversity of ways.[2] Clearly, however, this has not been a process of mere passive reception of British culture.[3] Australian screen culture, this chapter argues, has shaped Shakespeare in its own unique ways, rendering Shakespeare a crucial part and active force in the process of negotiating complex questions of national identity and articulating the postcolonial relationship between Australia and Britain.[4] Shakespeare has also been a key medium for articulating human relationships and experiences of loss, absence and resilience, as these three films demonstrate.

The Sentimental Bloke (1919)

An appropriate starting point is the silent film *The Sentimental Bloke* (1919),[5] which uses *Romeo and Juliet* as a play-within-a-film and appropriates the play in various other ways. Interestingly, *Romeo and Juliet* was also drawn on for the cover image of a print version of *The Sentimental Bloke* in 1919; the iconic balcony tableau is depicted by artist Hal Gye with the lovers as winged cupids.[6] Regarded as a landmark of early Australian cinema, the film was produced, scripted and directed by pioneering film maker Raymond Longford, with Lottie Lyell (who played Doreen), a co-scriptwriter. Arthur Tauchert played the figure of Bill "the Bloke", a working-class man inspired to reform his gambling, fighting and drinking life when he falls in love with Doreen, who works at a pickle factory.[7]

Early in the film, when the Bloke is jailed for illegal gambling, he laments:

> The World has got me snouted jist a treat.
> Crool forchins dirty left as smote me's soul
> An' all them joys o' life I 'eld so sweet
> Is up the pole.

The intertitles emphasise the colloquial language of the Bloke, following the verse of C.J. Dennis's *The Songs of a Sentimental Bloke* (1915),[8] written mostly in iambic pentameter (Fig. 3.1), thus mirroring Shakespeare by using the common early modern verse metre. The Bloke's reference to "crool forchin" recalls Romeo's railings at Fortune, such as "O, I am fortune's fool" (3.1.127).[9]

Fig. 3.1 Example of intertitles in *The Sentimental Bloke* (1919)

Throughout the film's narrative, there is a sense of naïve romanticism that parallels Romeo's, conveyed primarily through the Bloke's point of view, and he is attributed with a poetic sensibility:

> Another day gone by, another night
> Creepin' along to douse Day's golden light.

Paradoxically, the narrative in verse attributed to the Bloke, with its implication of linguistic skill, is at odds with the character of the Bloke himself. When the Bloke finally gets a formal introduction to Doreen, language at first fails him:

> I sez 'Good day'
> An' blime I 'ad nothin' more ter say!

Nevertheless, he manages to organise a date and the relationship takes off. The Bloke's dumbfounded wonder at his beloved is conveyed through a sense of the inadequacy of his language to articulate his emotions:

> The way she torks!
> 'Er lips! 'Er eyes! 'Er hair! Oh, gimme air!

Waiting is excruciating for him and, in a typically Shakespearean way, love initiates his need to turn to poetry:

> Now, as the poit sez, the days drag by
> On ledding feet. I wish't they'd do a guy.

As love blossoms, the Bloke starts to shun his mates, just like Romeo. The Bloke expresses the idea that love catches up with everyone eventually:

> An, square an' all, no matter 'ow yeh start
> The commin end of most of us is – Tart.

Fittingly, on one of the couple's dates, the Bloke takes Doreen to a performance of *Romeo and Juliet* (Fig. 3.2):

> The drarmer's writ be Shakespeare, years ago
> About a barmy goat called Romeo.

The narrative of the play is mediated through the perceptions of the Bloke, creating humour as we experience the Bloke's initiation into Shakespeare:

> 'Lady, be yonder moon I swear!' sez 'e.
> An' then 'e climbs up on the balkiney
> An' there they smooge a treat wiv pretty words
> Like two love-birds.
> I nudge Doreen. She whispers 'Ain't it grand!'
> 'Er eyes is shinin'; and I squeeze 'er 'and.

There is an implicit comparison created between the Shakespearean lovers on stage and the couple viewing them.

Fig. 3.2 The Bloke and Doreen at a performance of *Romeo and Juliet*

The Bloke finds direct analogues between himself and Romeo, translating Shakespeare and continuing to speak mostly in iambic pentameter verse:

> Fair Juli-et, she gives 'er boy the tip.
> Sez she: 'Don't sling that crowd o'mine no lip;
> An' if yeh run agin a Capulet,
> Just do a get',
> 'E swears 'e's done wiv lash; 'e'll chuck it clean.
> (Same as I done when I first met Doreen).

The Bloke finds Romeo's situation highly relevant to his own; he and Romeo are two blokes in love—he feels their commonality. The Bloke also finds Romeo's promise to avoid street fighting just like his own promise to Doreen. There is a tone of moral censure at Romeo's failure to stick to his promise:

Instid of slopin' soon
As 'e was wed, orf on 'is 'oneymoon,
'Im an' 'is cobber, called Mick Curio,
They 'ave to go
An' mix it wiv that push o' Capulets.
They look fer trouble; an' it's wot they gets.

Through the Bloke's translation of Shakespeare's language, the Italianate name "Mercutio" becomes the very Australian "Mick Curio".

The Bloke takes a strong interest in the plot and can relate to the street fighting. Karenlee Thompson has historicised the Bloke in the context of the Australian figure of the "larrikin", a figure perceived as likeable, yet also associated with violence.[10] The Bloke reports that:

Mick Curio, 'e gits it in the neck,
'Ar rats!' 'e sez, an' passes in 'is check.

The Bloke can empathise with Romeo's response to Mercutio's death:

Quite natchril, Romeo gits wet as 'ell.
'It's me or you!' 'e 'owls, 'an wiv a yell,
Plunks Tyball through the gizzard wiv 'is sword.

There is a point of recognition, of affinity, when he experiences the street fight. The Bloke's reaction is exuberant: "'Ow I ongcored!" In fact, the Bloke forgets he is in a theatre and, to Doreen's distress, he becomes like a bystander in a street fight, blurring the lines between the intra-diegetic and extra-diegetic worlds: "'Put in the boot!' I sez. 'Put in the boot!'" The fourth wall is dissolved for him and he slips back into his natural habit of enjoying street fights. The Bloke is admonished by Doreen and another audience member. The effect of the *mise-en-abyme* is, paradoxically, both to emphasise the Bloke's position as an outsider to the protocols of theatre going and yet to show the relevance of the play to the Bloke. *Romeo and Juliet*, with its street brawling and love plot, presents a world the Bloke can relate to.

The Bloke and Doreen are visibly moved by the tragic ending:

'Dear love,' she sez, 'I cannot live alone!'
An' wiv a moan,

> She grabs his pocket knife, an' ends 'er cares...
> 'Peanuts or lollies!' sez a boy upstairs.

The Bloke translates the Shakespearean dagger as a pocket knife and the intense emotional moment of the ending is deflated, as the curtain falls, with the vendor's call for peanuts or lollies.

In *The Sentimental Bloke*, the play-within-a-film invokes the strong theatrical presence of Shakespeare in Australian culture in the early twentieth century. As David Boyd observes, it relies "for its comic effectiveness on an assumed familiarity" with Shakespeare.[11] Boyd explores the episodes of spectatorship in the film and how they reflect historical changes in terms of social regulation of theatrical and cinematic spectatorship. Drawing from the work of Lawrence W. Levine on the shifts, from the latter part of the nineteenth century, in shared public culture from heterogeneous to more confined homogenising of theatre audiences and from the work of Richard Sennett on the social psychology of capitalism, Boyd points to the way that restraint of emotional responses to performance became a way of marking class and that the Bloke's response to the play signifies him as working class.[12]

The gentle satire of the Bloke's alienation from the theatre is also significant beyond issues of class difference. It embodies an early example from the long history of Australian cultural interest in parodying its own perceived lack of cultural sophistication, its "cultural cringe". The play-within-the-film here reflects something of the Australian cultural relationship with Shakespeare; it is both a postcolonial outsider yet instinctively drawn to a myriad of elements within Shakespeare that it can relate to, reappropriate and transpose into its own idiom; it makes Shakespeare its own.

The early twentieth-century Australian slang (now as opaque to contemporary Australians as Shakespeare's language is for many) is intended to deliberately contrast with the "high" language of Shakespeare.[13] Yet ironically the Bloke's voice, conveyed in iambic pentameter, the metre of Shakespeare, claims his own poetic vision. He confidently appropriates Shakespeare and conveys joy in finding their connections. Here, the slang of a postcolonial culture retells Shakespeare, appropriating, yet transforming its sound, diction and syntax. Shakespeare is thus alien and yet utterly relatable.

Picnic at Hanging Rock (1975)

The 1970s is considered a high point of Australian cinema, when several films, especially those of Peter Weir, gained international recognition. *Picnic at Hanging Rock* (1975), based on the novel by Joan Lindsay (1967), tells the story of a group of school girls who go on a picnic to Mt Macedon in rural Victoria in 1901.[14] Three of the girls and one of the teachers go missing at the mysterious Hanging Rock, and only one is subsequently found. The film, with its haunting soundtrack and evocative cinematography, explores the beauty, strangeness and hostility of the Australian landscape.[15] The girls, in their late Victorian clothing, stage a confrontation between European culture and the alien Australian landscape. Indigenous Aboriginal culture is noticeably absent in this space, historically a sacred site; the local inhabitants were erased by violence and introduced disease during the colonial period.[16]

In the novel, there is no reference to Shakespeare. However, Weir has one of the girls at the picnic recite part of Shakespeare's sonnet number 18, "Shall I compare thee to a summer's day" (Fig. 3.3). The sonnet, expressing the speaker's love for the young man, is self-reflective; it asks whether, in the process of writing poetry, the speaker should compare

Fig. 3.3 Reading Shakespeare's sonnet 18 in *Picnic at Hanging Rock* (1975)

the beloved to a summer's day or whether the analogy, however beautiful, is in fact inadequate because of the natural flaws of reality, such as rough winds and the temporary nature of summer. Ultimately, it is poetry that will preserve and grant immortality to the beauty of the beloved. In *Picnic*, the figure who primarily embodies that of the beloved is Miranda (Anne Lambert), one of the girls who disappear at the rock. She is the central focus of the theme of lost beauty and love. The reciting of poetry in the natural landscape is also a pastoral act, recalling the classical origins of the genre.[17] The filmic episode of reading the sonnet is also metafictional and metafilmic; reading a poem about the immortality of beauty through poetry, in contrast to loss and change in the world, reflects back on the process of creating art itself and the potential immortality of the art object.

The fragment of the sonnet expresses loss; the speaker conveys the shortness of "summer's lease", the fragility and temporal nature of human beauty, the seasons and life. Weir's choice of Shakespeare's sonnet was an apt one. The melancholy tone of the sonnet is appropriate as some of the girls are about to climb the rock and will not return. Thus, the intertextual allusion functions as a foreshadowing of loss and fits the mood of the picnic. Of course, the extent to which the Shakespearean citation holds meaning for a viewer will depend on their knowledge of the intertext. As Julie Sanders has observed of appropriation and adaptation generally, they are:

> dependent on the literary canon for the provision of a shared body of storylines, themes, characters, and ideas upon which their creative variations can be made. The spectator or reader must be able to participate in the play of similarity and difference perceived between the original, source, or inspiration to appreciate fully the reshaping or rewriting undertaken by the adaptive text.[18]

Although the entire sonnet is not read, viewers with knowledge of the sonnet bring that knowledge to their reading of the film. The sonnet articulates the confrontation between decay, loss and pain in the material world, on the one hand, and art as a potential preserver of beauty and source of consolation on the other.

Another confrontation is implied here, between European culture, of which the Shakespearean sonnet is part (Botticelli's art, which is referred to in both novel and film, is another sign of this), and the sublime power and horror of a landscape that has purportedly been colonised yet not understood or controlled. *Picnic* articulates the horror of this inability. The ancient age of the landscape is an unfathomable void into which the youth and beauty of the girls disappear. The sonnet fragment resonates with the mood and tenor of *Picnic*, evidencing the potential power of a Shakespearean fragment to have a relevance far greater than its fleeting intertextual moment.

Lilian's Story (1996)

Yet another mode of appropriating Shakespeare is evident in Jerzy Domaradzki's *Lilian's Story* (1996), based on the 1985 Kate Grenville novel, which relates the story of a woman, Lilian Singer (Ruth Cracknell), who is abused by her father Albion Singer (Barry Otto) and locked up in an asylum, at his instigation, for several decades.[19] She is ultimately released and has to adjust to a new life, on the streets of Sydney. It charts her journey of coming to terms with what has happened to her, a process that ultimately encompasses forgiveness and, despite everything, a willingness to embrace the potential in life. Throughout everything, Shakespeare is Lilian's touchstone. She has a phenomenal memory and recites passages from across his body of work, according to their relevance to her life. As Gerry Turcotte observes, Lilian "has taken the bard's words and stripped them of their codes and referents and has replaced them with her own systems of codification".[20] Similarly, Alice Healy highlights how Lilian "defiantly rewrites–or re-stages– personal history through her streetside recitations of Shakespeare and subversions of a middle-class lady's behaviour".[21] In the novel, the references to Shakespeare are fairly subtle but the film adaptation magnifies the significance of Shakespeare and is rich with quotations.

The film opens with Lilian behind barriers at the asylum and she quotes from the end of *Richard II* (5.5.42–61), ending with "This music mads me. Let it sound no more" (5.5.61). The speech of the deposed king is relevant on multiple levels. It speaks of wasted time ("I wasted time, and now doth time waste me" (5.5.49)), applicable to Lilian's life since she has wasted the best years of her life in the asylum, her youth and early womanhood stolen from her by her abusive and dysfunctional father. The reference to madness is continued when she distributes flowers, thus also invoking Ophelia in her madness. When she commands "Let it sound no more" (*Richard II* 5.5.61), the background music to the film ceases, suggesting the character's power to break through the barrier between the intra- and extra-diegetic worlds.

In the busy dining room where the patients eat, the orderly castigates some of the patients; Lil enters and pulls antics behind his back. She challenges authority, a pattern of behaviour that manifests across her life, despite all that happens to her. It is the day Lil is to be released, and before she goes, her fellow inpatients ask for some Shakespeare. Shakespeare is communal. After suggestions of *Hamlet* and *Julius Caesar* are rejected, they settle on the weird sisters from *Macbeth*: "When shall we three meet again?" (1.1.1). The volume rises; Shakespeare binds them:

> Fair is foul, and foul is fair,
> Hover through the fog and filthy air" (1.1.10–11).

Macbeth articulates the power of outsiders and of female community. The orderly intervenes however, anxious at this communal chanting and keen for Lil to go. He castigates: "come on Lil, no one's ever sad to leave the loony bin".

This intense engagement with Shakespeare at the beginning of the film establishes the centrality of Shakespeare in Lilian's life, which is told in a series of flashbacks, often invoked by particular events. For example, a violent altercation Lilian witnesses between a prostitute and her pimp triggers a flashback of Lilian's father beating her. The flashbacks are presented in sepia tones with Toni Collette playing young Lilian.

As an old woman now, Lilian spends most of her time in public spaces reciting Shakespeare to whomever will listen. She becomes friends with the street prostitutes and quotes from *Venus and Adonis* to Zara (Essie Davis):

> Love is a spirit all compact of fire
> Not gross to sink, but light, and will aspire. (l. 149–50)

Lil is entranced by Zara and her client. Through Lil's eyes, they are as enchanting as any of Shakespeare's lovers. Shakespeare's poetry transforms Lil's view on the world; the ordinary life of the street becomes beautiful, romantic and poetic.

During a night in a bus shelter, she has a flashback of herself as a young woman. The scene shows her with a young man who embraces her as she reads Shakespeare aloud. We find out subsequently that this is Frank

Fig. 3.4 Young Lilian with Frank Stroud reading Shakespeare in *Lilian's Story* (1996)

Stroud (John Flaus), the love of her life. The couple are underneath an upturned boat with the sea in the background (Fig. 3.4), and she quotes Miranda from *The Tempest* to articulate her sense of wonder at being loved:

> I do not know
> One of my sex; no woman's face remember
> Save from my glass mine own; nor have I seen
> More that I may call men than you, good friend,
> And my dear father. (3.1.48–52)

Although it is a joyful moment, the mention of "father" is a chilling reminder and creates a sinister undercurrent. This forewarning of tragedy is reiterated when, as her beau embraces her, they switch to *Romeo and Juliet*. Lilian quotes:

> Romeo, doff thy name,
> And for that name- which is no part of thee-

> Take all myself. (2.1.89–91)

Frank quotes back with Romeo's reply:

> I Take Thee at Thy Word:
> Call me but love and I'll be new baptized.
> Henceforth I never will be Romeo. (2.1.91–93)

Young Lilian and Frank unite verbally and emotionally through the medium of Shakespeare, yet we are warned, by the very play they quote from, that this happiness cannot last. Lilian's father will separate them and incarcerate Lilian.

Back in the present time, a taxi driver (Morgan Smallbone), with whom Lilian gets a ride, quotes from *The Merchant of Venice*: "The man that hath no music in himself...let no such man be trusted" (5.1.82, 87). Lilian responds with a quotation from *Romeo and Juliet*:

> What man art thou that, thus bescreened in night,
> So stumblest on my counsel?" (2.1.94–95)

He responds with Romeo's lines:

> By a name
> I know not how to tell thee who I am. (2.1.95–96)

Lilian realises the taxi driver is Frank, her childhood sweetheart. She continues with Juliet's speech:

> My ears have yet not drunk a hundred words
> Of thy tongue's uttering, yet I know the sound. (2.1.100–101)

Then she says "Frank?", to which he replies: "What's in a name?" (2.1.85), and she continues with Romeo's lines:

> That which we call a rose
> By any other name would smell as sweet. (2.1.86)

The couple have been reunited after 40 years and once more Shakespeare provides their common language.

Ecstatic at their reunion, they spend time together in a park, under a tree; Frank is now an alcoholic who lives on the streets. Once again, however, this happiness is short-lived. Frank passes out and, while he is asleep, police come and complain about the taxi being illegally parked. Lil gets into an altercation with them and, in her anger, she quotes Trinculo from *The Tempest*: "Thou liest, most ignorant monster!" (3.2.23). The relevance of this quotation is that Trinculo's next line is: "I am in case to jostle a constable" (3.2.23–24), which Lil is about to do. Then as she assaults the police officer, she quotes from *Henry 5* "Once more unto the breach" (3.1.1). Shakespeare is part of her assault, her continual challenge to authority.

Lil is arrested so when Frank wakes, like Juliet in the tomb, he finds no one; she is gone and the lovers are separated again. Lilian appears in court and when her father turns up at the back of the room, the courtroom becomes a site where Lil confronts and accuses her father. Her father calls out that he will not pay the fine and says they should lock her up. Lil retorts back to him "and you are a violent and degenerate man". When the judge fines Lil, her father stands, calling out "you are a disgrace to your sex". From his oppressive, patriarchal perspective, she fails to conform to femininity because she speaks out and challenges authority. Lilian then has a flashback of having to bend over, her father continually beating her on the buttocks. In the court, she bends over in her father's direction and pulls up her skirt, repeating the routine brutally ingrained in her and thus linking the punishment of the court with the abuse she has suffered at the hands of her father. It is both an indictment of and yet simultaneously a challenge to her father.

Lil is sent to jail where, in flashback, we are shown the tragic destruction of her happiness, a scene in which Shakespeare is central. Lil and Frank are confronted by her father, who overturns the boat. Lil clutches her volume of Shakespeare protectively to her chest. Frank tells her father that he wants to marry Lilian but Albion replies "no one can marry her" because "she is unstable". He completes the destruction by slandering Lil, telling Frank that she is promiscuous: "By jove boy she is rutting every night like a cat on heat". The potent lie reflects Albion Singer's warped view of his daughter, embodying his incestuous desire and his equation of nonconformity with mental illness. Lil yells at Frank to go; her chances at happiness are ruined. She then resorts to Cordelia's speech in *King Lear* as a means of articulating her rejection of the dysfunctional relationship

Albion Singer seeks to impose on his daughter. Like Cordelia, Lil rejects his attempt to impose more than is due to a father. She quotes:

> Good my lord,
> You have begot me, bred me. (1.1.94–95)

Significantly she omits "loved me" from the line but continues with "I / Return those duties back as are right fit" (1.1.95–96). Her father, enraged, throws the Shakespeare volume into the sea. As Kate Livett observes, in her analysis of the novel, Albion is enraged by Lilian's "attempts to acquire an all-encompassing 'Shakespearean' education on her own terms".[22]

Shakespeare functions in both novel and film as a refuge for the oppressed, a voice of truth; he is the weapon Lilian wields against her father, the abuse of authority and the oppressive forces that seem continually against her. As Ruth Barcan emphasises, Lilian uses Shakespeare as an "instrument of rebellion against patriarchy and convention"; likewise, Healy discerns Lilian's recitations as "creative strategies of resistance".[23] It is this potency of Shakespeare in Lilian's hands that Albion responds to by impotently throwing the volume into the sea.

Lil is eventually released from jail, searches continually for Frank and eventually finds him. They live together in his hovel at the water's edge, joined for a while by Jewel (Susie Lindeman), Lil's friend from the asylum.[24] Lil is granted a period of happiness with Frank until his death, upon which she recites from sonnet 116, which articulates the endurance of love:

> Love's not Time's fool, though rosy lips and cheeks
> Within his bending sickle's compass come;
> Love alters not with his brief hours and weeks,
> But bears it out even to the edge of doom.
> If this be error and upon me proved,
> I never writ, nor no man ever loved. (ll. 9–14)[25]

From then on, she busks on the streets for money by reciting Shakespeare.

In a powerful scene that encapsulates Lil's lifelong challenge to authorities that have oppressed her, she quotes Isabella from *Measure for Measure*:

> The sense of death is most in apprehension,
> And the poor beetle that we tread upon
> In corporal sufferance finds a pang as great
> As when a giant dies. (3.1.76–79)

Through Shakespeare, she expresses her solidarity with the oppressed and the ignored, society's periphery, and she roars it in challenge (Fig. 3.5). There is then a terrible flashback of Lilian screaming in anguish, and a shot of her lying naked on the beach, having slit her wrists in a suicide attempt after being raped by her father.

Back in the present time, after the death of Lilian's father, she and her brother John (also played by Barry Otto) return to the childhood home. They re-enter the study, and Lil recalls her discovery that the book their father was writing, entitled "The Book of Facts", is entirely blank, a tome standing in opposition to the volume of Shakespeare Albion threw

Fig. 3.5 Lilian quoting Shakespeare on the street in *Lilian's Story* (1996)

into the sea. The father's empty book, signifying his impoverished character, contrasts starkly with the rich source that Shakespeare represents for Lilian.

As several critics have observed, that Lil's father's name is Albion, the ancient word for Great Britain, evokes the larger postcolonial dimension to the father-daughter relationship, suggesting that Grenville sought to suggest the destructive potential of empire.[26] Lilian, as Healy describes, "thus becomes allegorical of Australia's adolescence in her transgressive recitation of English 'scripts'".[27] However, Shakespeare adds complexity to this paradigm. For Lilian, there are two fathers, one biological and one literary. The former is destructive and controlling and tellingly his book is blank; his legacy is a void. However, the other parent, Shakespeare, is nurturing; the abundance of quotations in the film points to the way Shakespeare is a rich source of life and meaning for Lilian. The implication is that postcolonial relationships can embody creative dimensions alongside the destructive.

After visiting her father's grave, Lilian recites Portia's speech on mercy from *The Merchant of Venice* (4.1.179–97). Despite all that has happened to her, she draws on Shakespeare to learn to forgive and it is this that sets her free. The last scene is of her going in a taxi out into desert country with an indigenous taxi driver (Bob Maza), which hints at the potential of reconciliation and healing after violence, at the level of the postcolonial allegory. Her philosophical reflections include the statement that "everything matters and it's necessary to make up our lives". For Lilian, Shakespeare has been a key medium through which she has interpreted and remade her life and sense of the world. There is a great sense of optimism to this final scene; Lilian has refused to be kept down by the oppression of the past and is open to the next stage in life. The change from old Lilian to young Lilian in the back of the taxi suggests that her life is still before her and the increasing long shot of a magnifying sky reiterates this potential for optimism.

Postcolonial Shakespearean appropriations inevitably reflect on the wider implications of a "younger" culture entering into dialogue with an "older" one. They speak back to the supposed "centre" from the so-called "margins", bringing new perspectives. As Julie Sanders reminds us, Shakespeare himself was an adaptor and appropriator of other material and "would perhaps have expected to be adapted by future writers and future ages".[28] His "cultural value lies in his availability" and, as Jean

Marsden has observed, "each new generation attempts to redefine Shakespeare's genius in contemporary terms, projecting its desires and anxieties onto his work".[29] Shakespearean references may be fleeting or sustained; either way, they are crucial to filmic meanings. The films briefly explored in this chapter engage with Shakespeare in a diversity of ways, evidencing that intertextual references to Shakespeare are of central importance to our deeper understanding of Australian screen culture.

Notes

1. Another key example of an Australian film appropriating Shakespeare is Fred Schepisi's *The Eye of the Storm* (2011), based on the 1973 novel of Patrick White, which engages with *King Lear*. For a detailed examination of this, see Victoria Bladen, "Looking for Lear in *The Eye of the Storm*," in *Shakespeare on Screen:* King Lear, edited by Victoria Bladen, Sarah Hatchuel and Nathalie Vienne-Guerrin (Cambridge: Cambridge University Press, 2019), 185–201.
2. For explorations of Australian engagements with Shakespeare in theatre, see: Kate Flaherty, *Ours as We Play It: Australia Plays Shakespeare* (Crawley, W.A.: UWA Publishing, 2011) and John Golder and Richard Madelaine, *O Brave New World: Two Centuries of Shakespeare on the Australian Stage* (Sydney: Currency Press, 2001).
3. On the issues at stake in appropriating Shakespeare generally, see: Alexa Alice Joubin and Elizabeth Rivlin, eds. *Shakespeare and the Ethics of Appropriation* (New York: Palgrave Macmillan, 2014); Christy Desmet and Robert Sawyer, eds. *Shakespeare and Appropriation* (London: Routledge, 1999); Jean I. Marsden, ed. *The Appropriation of Shakespeare* (Hemel Hempstead: Harvester Wheatsheaf, 1991); and Julie Sanders, *Adaptation and Appropriation* (The New Critical Idiom. London and New York: Routledge, 2006), Chapter 3. For the ways in which postcolonial drama is a force of resistance to the legacy of imperialism, see Helen Gilbert and Joanne Tompkins, *Post-Colonial Drama: Theory, Practice, Politics* (London: Routledge, 1996).
4. For explorations of the history of Australian film generally, see Felicity Collins, Jane Landman, and Susan Bye, *A Companion to Australian Cinema* (Hoboken, NJ: Wiley-Blackwell, 2019) and Tom O' Regan, *Australian National Cinema* (London: Routledge, 1996). For a useful database of Australian film and access to Australian films that reference Shakespeare, see the Australian *National Film and Sound Archive* http://www.nfsa.gov.au/.
5. *The Sentimental Bloke*, directed by Raymond Longford (1919; Australia: Madman Entertainment Pty Ltd.), DVD.

6. Melissa Bellanta, "A Masculine Romance: *The Sentimental Bloke* and Australian Culture in the War and Early Interwar Years," *Journal of Popular Romance Studies* 4, no. 2 (2014): 6, accessed July 19, 2021, www.jprstudies.org/2014/10/a-masculine-romance-the-sentimental-bloke-and-australian-culture-in-the-war-and-early-interwar-yearsby-melissa-bellanta/.
7. Bellanta contexualises the narrative within the genre of the masculine romance; as she points out, *The Sentimental Bloke* was a multi-media phenomenon, encompassing a successful stage adaptation and radio plays, and with subsequent adaptations on screen and stage throughout the twentieth century: Bellanta, "A Masculine Romance", 3.
8. For a modern edition, see C.J. Dennis, *The Songs of a Sentimental Bloke* (Text Publishing, Melb. Aust.: 2012).
9. Also, "sour misfortune's book" (5.3.82). Furthermore, the police raid on the 2-up game has parallels with the Prince's order to keep the public peace in *Romeo and Juliet*. All quotations from Shakespeare are taken from the Norton edition: William Shakespeare, *The Norton Shakespeare*, eds. Stephen Greenblatt, Walter Cohen, Suzanne Gossett, Jean E. Howard, Katherine Eisaman Maus and Gordon McMullan, 3rd ed. (New York: Norton, 2016).
10. The "larrikin" concept gained social legitimacy in Australian culture after World War I, contributing to the popularity of the film, released in 1919; see generally Melissa Bellanta, *Larrikins: A History* (Brisbane: University of Queensland Press, 2012). Karenlee Thompson, "The Australian Larrikin: C.J. Dennis's [Un]Sentimental Bloke," *Antipodes* 21, no. 2 (2007): 180.
11. Boyd, David, "The Public and Private Lives of a Sentimental Bloke," *Cinema Journal* 37, no. 4 (1998), 4.
12. Boyd, "Public and Private Lives", 4–5. Lawrence W. Levine, *Highbrow/Lowbrow: The Emergence of Cultural Hierarchy in America* (Cambridge, Mass.: Harvard University Press, 1988). Richard Sennett, *The Fall of Public Man: On the Social Psychology of Capitalism* (New York: Vintage, 1974).
13. The restored DVD edition includes a full glossary of the colloquial terms used throughout the film.
14. *Picnic at Hanging Rock*, directed by Peter Weir (Australia: The Australian Film Commission; McElroy & McElroy, 1975), DVD. The screenplay is by Cliff Green. Joan Lindsay, *Picnic at Hanging Rock* (Harmondsworth: Penguin, 1970 [1967]). A subsequent adaptation, a TV mini-series, was released in 2018: *Picnic at Hanging Rock*, directed by Larysa Kondracki, Michael Rymer and Amanda Brotchie, written by Joan Lindsay, Beatrix Christian and Alice Addison, featuring Natalie Dormer and Lily Sullivan,

Amazon Studios, FremantleMedia Australia and Screen Australia, 2018, Blu-Ray.

15. For valuable analyses of the screen adaptation, see Jytte Homqvist, "Contrasting cultural landscapes and spaces in Peter Weir's film *Picnic at Hanging Rock* (1975), based on Joan Lindsay's 1967 novel with the same title," *Coolabah* no. 11 (2013): 25–35; and Saviour Catania, "The Hanging Rock Piper: Weir, Lindsay, and the Spectral Fluidity of Nothing," *Literature/Film Quarterly* 40, no. 2 (2012): 84–95.
16. Despite the absence of indigenous presence, the novel is indebted in some respects to Aboriginal cultural ideology in that there is a suggestion that the girls disappear into a sort of timeless space akin to the Dreaming of Aboriginal mythology. This idea, however, is primarily present in the last chapter of the novel, which was omitted in the first publication, in order to enhance the mystery, and was only published subsequently, after Lindsay's death. Weir's film does not deal with the odd last chapter by Lindsay; he focuses on the power of the unexplained mystery that the original publication created.
17. For an exploration of the pastoral elements of the film, see Victoria Bladen, "The Rock and the Void: Pastoral and Loss in Joan Lindsay's *Picnic at Hanging Rock* and Peter Weir's Film Adaptation," *Colloquy: text theory critique* no. 23 (2012): 0–26, accessed May 12, 2020, https://www.monash.edu/__data/assets/pdf_file/0003/1764300/bladen.pdf.
18. Sanders, *Adaptation and Appropriation*, 45.
19. *Lilian's Story*, directed by Jerzy Domaradzki (Australia: Movieco Australia, 1996), DVD. The screenplay is by Steve Wright. Kate Grenville, *Lilian's Story* (Allen & Unwin: St. Leonard's, NSW, 1997 rev. ed. [1985]).
20. Gerry Turcotte, "'The Ultimate Oppression': Discourse Politics in Kate Grenville's Fiction," *World Literature Written in English* 29, no. 1 (Spring, 1989): 77.
21. Alice Healy, "'Impossible Speech' and the Burden of Translation: *Lilian's Story* from Page to Screen," *Journal of the Association for the Study of Australian Literature* 5 (2006): 162.
22. Kate Livett, "Homeless and Foreign: the Heroines of *Lilian's Story* and *Dreamhouse*", in *Lighting Dark Places: Essays on Kate Grenville* ed. Sue Kossew (Rodopi: Netherlands, 2010), 124.
23. Ruth Barcan, "'Mobility Is the Key': Bodies, Boundaries and Movement in Kate Grenville's *Lilian's Story*," *Ariel: A Review of International English Literature* 29, no. 2 (1998): 44. Healy, "Impossible Speech", 168.
24. When Jewel has a baby, Lil delivers it, afterwards reciting Ariel's song from *The Tempest*: "Where the bee sucks, there suck I" (5.1.88–96).
25. As Frank dies, Lil quotes Juliet: "and, when he [I] shall die,/Take him and cut him out in little stars" (3.2.21–22).

26. For postcolonial readings on the novel, see, for example, Laura Deane, "Cannibalism and Colonialism: *Lilian's Story* and (White) Women's Belonging," *Journal of the Association for the Study of Australian Literature* 14, no. 3 (2014): 1–13; and Bill Ashcroft, "Madness and power: *Lilian's Story* and the decolonised body," in *Lighting Dark Places: Essays on Kate Grenville*, ed. Sue Kossew (Netherlands: Rodopi, 2010), 55–72.
27. Healy, "Impossible Speech", 163.
28. Sanders, *Adaptation and Appropriation*, 47–48.
29. Marsden, *Appropriation of Shakespeare*, 1.

Works Cited

Ashcroft, Bill. "Madness and power: *Lilian's Story* and the decolonised body." In *Lighting Dark Places: Essays on Kate Grenville*, edited by Sue Kossew, 55–72. Netherlands: Rodopi, 2010.

Barcan, Ruth. "'Mobility Is the Key': Bodies, Boundaries and Movement in Kate Grenville's *Lilian's Story*." *Ariel: A Review of International English Literature*, vol. 29, no. 2 (1998): 31–55.

Bellanta, Melissa. "A Masculine Romance: *The Sentimental Bloke* and Australian Culture in the War and Early Interwar Years." *Journal of Popular Romance Studies*, vol. 4, no. 2 (2014): 0–20. Accessed May 12, 2020. www.jprstudies.org/2014/10/a-masculine-romance-the-sentimental-bloke-and-australian-culture-in-the-war-and-early-interwar-yearsby-melissa-bellanta/.

Bellanta, Melissa. *Larrikins: A History*. Brisbane: University of Queensland Press, 2012.

Bladen, Victoria. "Looking for Lear in *The Eye of the Storm*." In *Shakespeare on Screen:* King Lear, edited by Victoria Bladen, Sarah Hatchuel and Nathalie Vienne-Guerrin, 185–201. Cambridge: Cambridge University Press, 2019.

Bladen, Victoria. "The Rock and the Void: Pastoral and Loss in Joan Lindsay's *Picnic at Hanging Rock* and Peter Weir's Film Adaptation." *Colloquy: Text Theory Critique*, vol. 23 (2012): 0–26. Accessed May 12, 2020. https://www.monash.edu/__data/assets/pdf_file/0003/1764300/bladen.pdf.

Boyd, David. "The Public and Private Lives of a Sentimental Bloke." *Cinema Journal*, vol. 37, no. 4 (1998): 3–18.

Catania, Saviour. "The Hanging Rock Piper: Weir, Lindsay, and the Spectral Fluidity of Nothing." *Literature/Film Quarterly*, vol. 40, no. 2 (2012): 84–95.

Collins, Felicity, Jane Landman and Susan Bye. *A Companion to Australian Cinema*. Hoboken, NJ: Wiley-Blackwell, 2019.

Deane, Laura. "Cannibalism and Colonialism: *Lilian's Story* and (White) Women's Belonging," *Journal of the Association for the Study of Australian Literature*, vol. 14, no. 3 (2014): 1–13.

Dennis, C.J. *The Songs of a Sentimental Bloke*. Melb., Aust.: Text Publishing, 2012.

Desmet, Christy and Robert Sawyer, eds. *Shakespeare and Appropriation*. London: Routledge, 1999.

Domaradzki, Jerzy, dir. *Lilian's Story*. Australia: Movieco Australia. DVD, 1996.

Flaherty, Kate. *Ours as We Play It: Australia Plays Shakespeare*. Crawley, W.A.: UWA Publishing, 2011.

Gilbert, Helen and Joanne Tompkins. *Post-Colonial Drama: Theory, Practice, Politics*. London: Routledge, 1996.

Golder, John and Richard Madelaine. *O Brave New World: Two Centuries of Shakespeare on the Australian Stage*. Sydney: Currency Press, 2001.

Grenville, Kate. *Lilian's Story*. St. Leonard's, NSW: Allen & Unwin, 1997 rev. ed. [1985].

Healy, Alice. "'Impossible Speech' and the Burden of Translation: *Lilian's Story* from Page to Screen." *Journal of the Association for the Study of Australian Literature*, vol. 5 (2006): 162–77.

Homqvist, Jytte. "Contrasting cultural landscapes and spaces in Peter Weir's film *Picnic at Hanging Rock* (1975), based on Joan Lindsay's 1967 Novel with the Same Title." *Coolabah*, vol. 11 (2013): 25–35.

Huang, Alexa and Elizabeth Rivlin, eds. *Shakespeare and the Ethics of Appropriation*. New York: Palgrave Macmillan, 2014.

Levine, Lawrence W. *Highbrow/Lowbrow: The Emergence of Cultural Hierarchy in America*. Cambridge, Mass.: Harvard University Press, 1988.

Lindsay, Joan. *Picnic at Hanging Rock*. Harmondsworth: Penguin, 1970 [1967].

Lindsay, Joan, Beatrix Christian and Alice Addison, writers. *Picnic at Hanging Rock*. Directed by Larysa Kondracki, Michael Rymer and Amanda Brotchie, featuring Natalie Dormer and Lily Sullivan. Aired 2018. Amazon Studios, FremantleMedia Australia and Screen Australia. Blu-Ray.

Livett, Kate. "Homeless and Foreign: the Heroines of *Lilian's Story* and *Dreamhouse*." In *Lighting Dark Places: Essays on Kate Grenville*, edited by Sue Kossew, 119–134. Netherlands: Rodopi, 2010.

Longford, Raymond, dir. *The Sentimental Bloke*. Australia, Madman Entertainment Pty Ltd. DVD, 1919.

Marsden, Jean I., ed. *The Appropriation of Shakespeare*. Hemel Hempstead: Harvester Wheatsheaf, 1991.

National Film and Sound Archive. http://www.nfsa.gov.au/.

O' Regan, Tom. *Australian National Cinema*. London: Routledge, 1996.

Sanders, Julie. *Adaptation and Appropriation*. London and New York: Routledge, 2006.

Schepisi, Fred. dir. *The Eye of the Storm*. Australia: Paper Bark Films Pty. Ltd. DVD, 2011.

Sennett, Richard. *The Fall of Public Man: On the Social Psychology of Capitalism.* New York: Vintage, 1974.

Shakespeare, William. *The Norton Shakespeare.* 3rd ed. edited by Stephen Greenblatt, Walter Cohen, Suzanne Gossett, Jean E. Howard, Katherine Eisaman Maus and Gordon McMullan. New York: Norton, 2016.

Thompson, Karenlee. "The Australian Larrikin: C.J. Dennis's [Un]Sentimental Bloke." *Antipodes*, 21, no. 2 (2007): 177–83.

Turcotte, Gerry, "'The Ultimate Oppression': Discourse Politics in Kate Grenville's Fiction." *World Literature Written in English*, 29, no. 1 (Spring 1989): 64–85.

Weir, Peter, dir. *Picnic at Hanging Rock.* Australia: The Australian Film Commission; McElroy & McElroy. DVD, 1975.

CHAPTER 4

Othello Surfing: Fragments of Shakespeare in South Africa

Chris Thurman

In a South African context, the subject of Shakespeare on film and television typically has more to do with reception than it does with production. Yes, there was the 2008 *Shakespeare in Mzansi* series, in which Shakespeare's plays (or rather, the themes, certain plot features and some of the characters associated with a handful of well-known works) were translated and adapted, primarily for a teenage audience.[1] And yes, before that there was Eubulus Timothy's largely forgotten *Othello: A South African Tale* (2005; here it may be noted that one has to go back to 1988 for the other South African screen *Othello*, a filmed version of Janet Suzman's stage production at the Market Theatre the previous year). Of course, South Africa has the common Shakespearean crop of weak puns and misquotations in advertisements, and there are occasional pop cultural references—although these are usually limited to invoking

C. Thurman (✉)
The Tsikinya-Chaka Centre (School of Literature, Language and Media), University of the the Witwatersrand, Johannesburg, South Africa
e-mail: christopher.thurman@wits.ac.za

A. A. Joubin and V. Bladen (eds.), *Onscreen Allusions to Shakespeare*, Global Shakespeares, https://doi.org/10.1007/978-3-030-93783-6_4

Shakespeare-as-metonym for Englishness, for education, or for a long-distant European history, and they rarely have satirical intent or evince any critical distance from the clichés of Bardolatry. Then there are the politicians who quote him: much has been written about South African presidents citing Shakespeare in their speeches.[2] If we discount adverts and televised State of the Nation addresses, however, there has been relatively little "local" Shakespearean content broadcast, projected or streamed to South African screens over the last two or three decades.[3] In 2020 and 2021, the combination of growing internet access for potential audiences, diversification of online platforms and of course the Covid-19 pandemic resulted in a boost in Shakespearean content available on screen. This included film(ed) versions of stage productions, from Third World Bunfight's adaptation of Verdi's *Macbeth* (made available as part of the National Arts Festival's virtual program) to the Abrahamse & Meyer *Hamlet*; extracts from a concept treatment for a production of *Twelfth Night* directed and designed by Greg Homann, and a live-online-reading of a planned stage production of Hamlet directed by Neil Coppen; monologues submitted to Shakespeare ZA's #lockdownshakespeare campaign or filmed for the Market Theatre's "Chilling with the Bard" season and Johannesburg Awakening Minds' "JAM at the Windybrow" series; and the Centre for the Less Good Idea's Shakespearean experiments *Umsebenzi ka Bra Shakes* and *Spactral*.

Collectively, these latter enterprises may indeed be best understood as variations on the main theme of the present volume, and of the 2013 "Shakespeare in Tatters" conference out of which it grew—they are allusive, fragmentary or derivative Shakespearean film phenomena rather than Shakespeare films per se. More broadly, however, the paucity of Shakespeare-on-screen that I have described results in an inversion of the dynamic presented by the original conference's call for papers, because along with "references to Shakespeare's works" in South African TV and film productions one may equally discern "references to South Africa" in the reception of Shakespeare-on-screen: fragments or "tatters" of the nation, as it were, being invoked in response to versions of the plays that have been filmed and produced in other countries.[4] Ralph Fiennes' *Coriolanus* (2011) makes for an interesting case study in this regard. Consider a review of the film by Richard Poplak (writing for leading South African online publication *The Daily Maverick*) that notes:

> The film's politics are dead-on – the landscape calls to mind Iraq, Serbia, Syria and, um, South Africa ... We [in South Africa] are, of course, not quite at the level of Ralph Fiennes' depiction of Shakespearean Rome. But there is something about Coriolanus's contempt for the great unwashed that resonates as particularly South African.[5]

From Jan Smuts to Thabo Mbeki (and, following him, the pseudo-populism of Jacob Zuma—and arguably even the subsequent government under Cyril Ramaphosa), South African history evinces strong parallels with *Coriolanus*.[6] As a result, of course, there is a risk that readings of the play in South Africa become purely allegorical; for example, *Coriolanus* "explains" Thabo Mbeki and becomes a key for interpreting his presidency.[7] Critics have discerned and problematized this use of Shakespeare-as-allegory for national history and politics in a number of prominent South African stage productions: from Suzman's *Othello* (1987) to Gregory Doran's *Titus Andronicus* (1995) and Janice Honeyman's *"African" Tempest* (2009).[8]

Yet the impulse remains. If *Coriolanus* was Mbeki's play, which plays might be applied to other South African politicians? During Zuma's rise to power, *Julius Caesar* came to mind; here was a leader who seemed to reflect the will of the people (which was sometimes even manifested in threatening "mobs") even though this was at odds with the established law and constitution of the state. Similar debates about demagoguery arise in *2 H VI*—at certain points the parallels between Jack Cade and Julius Malema have appeared remarkable. David Schalkwyk has even connected Zuma to corruptible Prince Hal in *1 H IV*.[9] But it is *Julius Caesar* into which the South African (or, more generally, "African") situation is again and again made to fit. Yael Farber's *SeZaR* (2001) is a good example, and even the Royal Shakespeare Company's 2012 production of the play can be seen to continue this trajectory: Doran's idea of an 'all-black' *Julius Caesar*, in which black British actors performed with "African" accents, was justified by quoting John Kani's assertion that "*Julius Caesar* is Shakespeare's African play."[10] And, of course, there is Nelson Mandela's signature in the now-famous Robben Island "Bible" (a copy of the *Collected Works* that was signed by various political prisoners on the island) alongside Caesar's speech in Act 2 Scene 2, "Cowards die many times before their deaths./ The valiant never taste of death but once..." It makes perfect sense that this should be Mandela's favorite passage; he had voiced a similar sentiment from the dock when he was on trial for treason. But neither the narrative of *Julius Caesar* nor the hunger for power of its title character are suited to Mandela's political career. Instead, the Mandela who had long since retired from public life, who spent his later years in and out of hospital, clinging to life, seemed to recall the Shakespearean figure of the dying king or emperor, whose passing may signal renewed political machinations in an already-unstable state.

If we turn again to Fiennes' *Coriolanus*, we see that it is not merely South African narcissism that drives this recognition of "particularly South African" aspects to some of Shakespeare's plays. Here is Philip French in the (British) *Observer*:

> [*Coriolanus*] reaches out in many different directions, and in ways that Shakespeare could never have foreseen ... the great South African actor John Kani, major exponent of Athol Fugard's plays and for decades a victim of apartheid, is cast as General Cominius. This strong, wise leader, ready to fight but always an advocate of peaceful solutions, inevitably reminds us of Nelson Mandela.[11]

These are inaccurate and simplistic characterizations of Kani, Cominius in the play, Cominius in Fiennes' film and Mandela. Yet French is not alone. Other critics have referred to Kani's Cominius as "a benevolent figure" who "recalls images of Kofi Annan and Nelson Mandela."[12] Thus, we have not only Mandela as the most recognizable South African statesman, but Annan as the most recognizable African statesman.

I emphasize these slippages between global perceptions about South Africa, South African self-perception and a certain version of "Shakespeare"—the symbol or the historical signifier, rather than the playwright himself or the plays themselves—because such slippages help to introduce my concerns about the way in which "Shakespeare" functions in another 2011 film (this time an unequivocally South African one): *Otelo Burning*.

***

Otelo Burning is an isiZulu-language film that won numerous awards at international film festivals and was generally a critical (albeit not box office) success. Here is director-producer Sara Blecher's summary of the story with a brief account of the film's provenance:

> It's a coming-of-age story. It's about three friends who discover surfing as a way out of the township. So it's a way out of their shit lives. And then, just when they start making it in the surfing world, they turn on each other. It's a story about greed and betrayal and jealousy ... About seven years ago I met one of the lifeguards on the Durban beachfront and he started telling me a story about how all the [black] lifeguards ... came from one township. They weren't from Umlazi, they weren't from Inanda, they weren't from Kwa Mashu, they were from Lamontville – because it was the only township that had a swimming pool that wasn't destroyed by apartheid and wasn't destroyed by gangsters. One person had a vision and saw that the pool could get people jobs and he fought ... to keep that pool open. So the best [black] swimmers in Durban all learnt to swim in that pool.[13]

To understand the significance of learning to swim in a municipal pool, one must recall the long history of excluding black South Africans from "Whites Only" public amenities (including swimming pools and beaches) that was a daily feature of apartheid racial segregation. One must also consider the stigma attached to black people swimming—a combination of white racism and a putatively superstitious fear of water on the part of some black communities.[14] This emerges early in the film when we learn that Ntwe, the younger brother of the title character, has been banned from swimming by his father until he turns 13 because of a dream in which Ntwe drowns; throughout the film, there are references to the mythological underwater snake that "sings like a girl" and, siren-like, lures swimmers to their deaths.[15] In a film set during the dying days of apartheid, the black surfer is thus a doubly anomalous, potentially liberated and liberating figure.

Otelo and his best friend, nicknamed "New Year" (who narrates the story), gain access to this taboo form of freedom via Mandla, another teenager they meet at the pool. Mandla teaches them to surf and, after a veteran surfer—a white man, Kurt, who speaks isiZulu—takes the trio under his wing, they are soon ready to compete. Gradually, Otelo becomes more skilled than Mandla; this source of tension between them is compounded by friction over the affections of Dezi, New Year's sister. Private and public conflicts merge in the "black-on-black" violence that beset KwaZulu-Natal in the final years of apartheid.[16] New Year's brother, Blade, is one of the "comrades"—banned African National Congress (ANC) or United Democratic Front (UDF)-aligned freedom fighters who are campaigning both against the apartheid state and against the Inkatha Freedom Party (IFP).[17] The black townships are ablaze.

In a climate of mistrust, those who are seen as "informers" to either the government or the IFP are rooted out and subjected to a gruesome death by necklacing: bound by a rubber tire, doused in petrol and set alight. Mandla, who has become involved in the comrades' gun-smuggling, falsely accuses young Ntwe of being an informer (and receives payment for doing so). Ntwe is necklaced shortly before his thirteenth birthday, on the day that Otelo beats Mandla in a major surfing competition for the first time—a perverse fulfillment of his father's prophetic dream. Otelo is expelled by his father and left to grieve on his own. He resorts to alcohol abuse. One drunken night, Mandla rapes Dezi; Otelo catches a glimpse of them together and stumbles away, disappearing for weeks. Dezi eventually finds him at Dead Man's Point, where he has been sleeping rough and surfing the dangerous waves. She tells him about the rape. Otelo subsequently discovers that Mandla was responsible for Ntwe's death. He steals a gun from Blade, hunts Mandla down at a surfing competition and shoots him dead before grabbing his surfboard and swimming out to surf one last time. The end of the film is ambiguous but it seems that, rather than returning to shore to be arrested, Otelo surrenders to the waves and drowns. Either way, the culmination of this domestic, personal tragedy is juxtaposed against a triumphant national narrative—it is February 11, 1990, the day of Nelson Mandela's release from prison.

Where, readers may well ask, is Shakespeare's *Othello* in all this? If we look hard enough, we can find points of (inconsistent) correspondence with the play. Mandla must be "honest" Iago, pretending friendship and loyalty while he plots against Otelo/Othello. Before shooting Mandla, Otelo asks, "Why? Was it the money? Or is it because I am a better surfer than you?"—reinforcing the notion that Mandla's actions are spurred by both jealousy and an almost amoral survival instinct. Iago's deception of Othello may be based partly on jealousy of Othello's position and of his relationship with Desdemona, and partly on Iago's desire to climb military and social hierarchies, but this cannot account for it entirely (even if we factor in the rumor that Iago's wife Emilia has been seduced by Othello). Any reading of *Othello* must, inevitably, address Iago's racism.

Otelo, in turn, shares little with his Shakespearean near-namesake. Certainly, there is a sustained discourse in the film around Dezi's chastity or promiscuity. Repulsed by the behavior of her mother, a "shebeen queen" (a female owner of an informal or illegal tavern) and a possible prostitute, Dezi insists on maintaining sexual innocence in her relationship with Otelo. She will not have sex with him until they have escaped the poverty and depravity of their surroundings—that is, in her imagination, until they can afford to stay in a hotel and order room service. In his drunkenness and grief after the death of Ntwe, Otelo cruelly accuses her of being "just like your mother." When Otelo sees Mandla raping her, and mistakenly thinks she is being unfaithful to him, he is clearly in the position of Othello (if we temporarily conflate Iago and Cassio). But when Dezi finds Otelo and tells him what really happened, he immediately believes her. He enacts no violence against her. Moreover, the neurosis and apparent insecurity about his racial identity that drives Othello to turn against Desdemona shares little with Otelo's self-image. If anything, it is Mandla who exhibits racial self-hatred—when he is "put in his place" by his mother's white employers.[18] What of New Year? He is hardly a peripheral figure; he is one of the central protagonists and the observer-narrator of the story. There is no character in Shakespeare's *Othello* with whom we can equate him.

Othello kills Desdemona, not Iago; Otelo kills Mandla, not Dezi. The characters don't match; the plot doesn't match. At best, then, we can identify thematic overlaps between *Othello* and *Otelo Burning*: jealousy and deception in a social context fraught with racial prejudice. But the ways in which these extremely broad "themes" manifest in the two works are entirely different. *Otelo Burning* does not, in fact, need *Othello*—it is an autonomous narrative, based on concrete South African realities and the history of particular communities in KwaZulu-Natal. The names "Otelo" and "Dezi" are potentially distracting signifiers, encouraging the viewer to seek Shakespearean parallels where they may not exist.

Why, then, did the film-makers insert *Othello* into, or impose *Othello* onto, their film? This wasn't Blecher's original intention. In the interview quoted earlier, she explains that, after their meetings and workshops with the community in Lamontville,

> ... we got the first draft of a script out and we went to the NFVF [National Film and Video Foundation, major funder of film projects in South Africa] and they said the script has a lot of nice textures and it's great but it's all over the place, there's no story. So we hired a writer who came on board, James Whyle, and he started from scratch taking all the material that had come out of the workshop. And then we made a decision, essentially, to tell the story of Othello ... [So the film is] based on a true story but it's

> very fictionalized. We layered Othello's story into it so it becomes a story of betrayal and greed. We wanted to make a story about what's going on in South Africa now, but how do you do that? With a historic story ... Basically we just used the structure of [*Othello*] to tell ... a story about a guy who is really good at surfing and he's really making it and his best friend betrays him. So our lead female character's name is Dezi. Our lead character's name is Otelo. It's like a township version of *Othello*. They say there are seven stories in the world and we needed a structure to put our story around so that's what we did. It worked out kind of nice.[19]

There are some telling details in this anecdote. What it seems to describe is a process in which a South African state-funded foundation would not support a South African film production until it conformed to an archetypal, recognizable, "universal" narrative. While Blecher has since clarified that this is not an entirely accurate summary of her interaction with the NFVF,[20] it remains evident that Shakespeare helped to authorize the South African narrative—he provided a form of cultural authority, a stamp of approval, confirming that the film-makers would reproduce one of the "seven stories in the world," which would in turn guarantee audience buy-in.

There are various ways in which we might interpret Blecher's aim to use an "historic story" to comment obliquely on present-day South Africa. Does it mean that by telling a story set during the final years of apartheid she has produced an historic(al) film—a period piece, albeit one in which the history is fairly recent? Or does it mean, more specifically, that the watershed years of 1989–1990 were "historic," as in history-making and epoch-defining? Both these possibilities are accommodated by David Johnson's appraisal of *Otelo Burning*, which presents the film's refusal to provide a form of Aristotelean catharsis (although such catharsis could have emerged from a slightly different rendering of its narrative) in terms of Augusto Boal's resistance to "the conservative social function of tragedy."[21] For Johnson, the "cautious optimism" of the film's conclusion—New Year committing himself to helping other black boys and young men learn to swim and surf—is deliberately unconvincing:

> The most striking dissonance in the film is between national and individual narratives, as the national joy accompanying Mandela's release is juxtaposed with the individual pain of Mandla's murder and Otelo's demise. Such juxtaposition argues against any glib synthesis celebrating individual

> and national redemption in February 1990, and argues instead for a critical understanding of the uneven transition to post-apartheid democracy ... by foregrounding the historicity of 1988–1990, *Otelo Burning* raises uncomfortable questions about the post-apartheid present of 2011: Has the masculine violence depicted in the film been transcended or has it assumed new forms? Is it really plausible to imagine that the guns – deployed in either the ANC-Inkatha conflict or in post-apartheid gang violence – can be traded for surfboards? Have the gender inequalities assumed in the world of the film been challenged? Has access to middle-class leisure forms (like surfing and swimming) been de-racialised? Has the idealism represented in New Year's swimming club for Lamontville's youth survived?[22]

Blecher's reference to using "a historic story" to make a film about "what's going on in South Africa now" also, however, suggests that Shakespeare's *Othello* is itself historic(al). This introduces new problems. *Othello* is certainly not historically accurate—the playwright's primary concern was dramatic effect, not historiography. Cinthio, Shakespeare's main source, was also not writing history, although he may have been inspired by accounts of actual events. Leo Africanus and Gasparo Contarini, other suggested sources, may have claimed veracity but also took creative liberties. Shakespeare's *Othello* can only be considered historic(al) insofar as it has a four-hundred-year history of performance, appropriation, popular reception and scholarly criticism. There is something in this of the circular logic behind the myth of "universal" Shakespeare: Shakespeare's work transcends time and space because his work has transcended time and space. Such mythologizing eschews investigation into the material circumstances under which Shakespeare spread across the globe.

Shakespeare's history in South Africa is complex. He has been a tool of the oppressor: made complicit in English cultural and linguistic imperialism, employed by the apartheid state as an icon of "white"/"Western" civilization, and far too often the refuge of white English-speaking South Africans enacting a combination of liberalist superiority and colonial cringe. He has also been an icon of the struggle for freedom: hero of Sol Plaatje and of generations of mission school-educated black leaders, brother-spirit to the *Drum* writers of the 1950s and 1960s, inspiration to protest theater-makers, comfort to prison inmates.[23] What he has never been, however, is self-evidently historic(al)—that is to say, unproblematically entrenched in a national inheritance or in past and present cultural identities. South African Shakespeare scholars have spent a great deal of energy trying to show that we should not shy away from Shakespeare's sometimes-vexed, sometimes-awkward history in the country, because to do so is in effect to accept a conservative, anglophile, neo-colonial version of "The Bard" that undermines the radical potential of the plays.[24] We should, then, resist easy recourse to some notion that Shakespeare *is* history—an assumption of familiarity with a static Shakespeare (a canon of plays that contain fixed "themes") recognized from educational curricula, rather than an engagement with the plays as dynamic works of art. We should also caution against the idea that "layering Othello" onto/into a South African story somehow validates that story.

***

The concerns sketched above might be described as emanating from "the theoretical preoccupations of postcolonial Shakespeare criticism;" if so, what can be made of Johnson's assertion that "*Otelo Burning* exceeds the theoretical preoccupations of postcolonial Shakespeare criticism, as the defining features of the film center not upon *Othello*, but upon the contradictions in post-apartheid South Africa"?[25] In what follows, I want to consider how this productive "exceeding" functions.

After first watching and enjoying *Otelo Burning*—then growing increasingly uncomfortable with what appeared to be the authoritative but shadowy presence of Shakespeare, Othello and *Othello* in the film—I came to realize that my response was something of an over-reaction. In subsequent interviews with Blecher and Whyle, it emerged that Shakespeare's role at various stages in the creative process was more of a cameo appearance than a spectral haunting. Blecher explains:

> In the beginning we just had too many stories. We realized we needed a through-line, and *Othello* could do that, and we pulled out some scenes from the play to use. But the only really significant thing that *Othello* does in the film is that it sets up the story as a tragedy from the outset. We know that Otelo will die. It is his fate. For the rest ... In some places the Othello story served us, in other places it didn't serve us. We experimented with reproducing the murder of Desdemona, but couldn't make it work.[26]

Distinguishing the eventual script from the early material gathered by Blecher within the Lamontville community as well as from the "layering" of *Othello* into *Otelo Burning* (and here it should be noted that the co-written script, after being translated from English into isiZulu, was continually revised by the cast during filming), Whyle quotes renowned South African theater practitioner Barney Simon: "You have to close the door on the original inspiration."[27] Shakespeare remains behind one of a number of closed doors through which *Otelo Burning* passed. This kind of uninhibited but ultimately muted borrowing from Shakespeare—part allusion, part pastiche, part tribute, part pragmatism—is a potentially liberating approach, both for South African creative artists and for Shakespeare in a South African context. On the one hand, there is Whyle's assertion (as an experienced performer and director of Shakespeare): "I've never been afraid to edit Will; I just see him as a fellow-writer."[28] On the other hand, *Otelo Burning* does ultimately achieve a thought-provoking renovation of *Othello*—and of Shakespeare—in South Africa.

In a country whose history has been overwhelmingly determined by race and racism, *Othello* is inevitably touted as a politically "relevant" play. The most important production staged in South Africa, referred to above, starred John Kani and Joanna Weinberg under the direction of Janet Suzman. It was 1987, a year before the commencement of the events recounted in *Otelo Burning*, and South Africa was still in the perverse grip of apartheid legislation. The laws directly targeting the miscegenation that makes the Venetians in Shakespeare's play so uncomfortable, the Prohibition of Mixed Marriages Act and the Immorality Act, had effectively been repealed in 1985—but interracial relationships remained explicitly taboo and could still lead to prosecution. Staging *Othello* was a way of protesting against institutionalized, state-driven racism (although Robert Gordon and other critics have questioned the racial stigmatization in the execution of the production even as they have acknowledged the well-meaning political activism that informed its conception).[29]

Othello has been a mainstay of post-apartheid high school and university syllabi, ostensibly as evidence that Shakespeare addresses South African racial anxieties. New generations of theater practitioners and audiences—as well as students and teachers—have, however, sought alternative ways of making the play "relevant" and "current," attempting to remove the constraints that come with what Pamela Mason describes as "the straight-jacket of being a one-issue play."[30] When a reduced-cast production of *Othello* ran at the POPArt theater in Johannesburg in 2013 (one of many renditions of the play pitched at school audiences), the marketing material steered away from race and focused on another social issue:

> ... with the recent tragedy of the killing of Reeva Steenkamp and so many other violent acts against women the play seems like the right choice, speaking as a warning to men to beware of jealousy and not to act rashly. When director, Denel Honeyball, heard the news about Reeva Steenkamp's murder, she could not help draw parallels: an admired hero who had overcome the odds to be respected, but perhaps with some deep-seated insecurity about his own adequacy; a beautiful heroine who was rumored to have been unfaithful and suffered an untimely death on a day of romance just as Desdemona dies on her wedding sheets.[31]

The reference here is to Paralympic and Olympic athlete Oscar Pistorius, the "Blade Runner," whose story of sporting achievement and triumph over adversity collapsed when he shot and killed his girlfriend, the model Reeva Steenkamp, on Valentine's Day 2013. This Oscar-Othello parallel was in fact remarked upon by British journalist John Carlin the day after the shooting.[32] The comparison may be extended further if one considers an unfortunate advertisement for Nike that depicted Pistorius "exploding" from the starting blocks with the caption, "I am the bullet in the chamber"—a thoughtless valorization of gun violence that, predictably, backfired on the sportswear manufacturer. Reinforcing the ancient association of militarism and athletics, this campaign also seemed to foreshadow the similarities between Oscar the gun-toting sportsman and Othello the renowned soldier.

In 2016, reflecting on his experience of performing in the Market Theatre *Othello* in 1987 and reaching for a more contemporary resonance, John Kani returned to this connection:

> When the Supreme Court of Appeal convicted our national hero Oscar Pistorius of murder, the judge remarked that this case is a human tragedy of Shakespearean proportions. Was he thinking of Othello when he said that? The amputee and hero who falls in love with a model, a beautiful Afrikaans girl, and then he kills her. Theirs is a tragedy of love and passion, and of rejection, of the fear of not being loved, of not being accepted. To think that he shot her in the toilet, and that when he walked there, he walked on his stumps. Othello and Desdemona, a tragedy with its roots in disadvantage and being different, and the way in which being different

> and disadvantaged can make you capable of terrible violence. It could be disability. It could be race.[33]

There are two problems here. One is the equivalence drawn between racism and ablism, which seems not to attend to the complex structural considerations pertaining to either but instead refers broadly to the psychological impact of "disadvantage and being different." The second is the implication that, as a consequence, it is Othello's psychology rather than Desdemona's fate that interests us most.

What is significant about the description framing the 2013 POPArt production, therefore, is the focus on Reeva-Desdemona as a representative of the hundreds of thousands of South African women who are subjected to domestic abuse and gender-based violence (often resulting in femicide). In the same year, *Desdemona*, a "dance deconstruction" of *Othello* performed by students at the University of Johannesburg in the months following Steenkamp's death, sought to "reimagine" the narrative from Desdemona's perspective. For choreographer Owen Lazar, the challenge was to "rearticulate Shakespeare's original story to comment on [the] topical issue of violence against women in a way that … will engage and speak to young people."[34]

It may be tempting to locate such movements away from race and toward gender as the focal point in *Othello* within the wider phenomenon of what Douglas Lanier, discussing global film versions of the play in 2010, called "post-racial Othello:" "The emergent trend in adapting *Othello* to the screen has been to shift away from race towards some other form of identity politics – sexuality, class, cosmopolitanism, ethnicity, religious difference."[35] For Lanier, "post-racialization is a [form of] resistance to Anglo-American ownership of Shakespeare" insofar as "a racialized conception of *Othello* has come to look increasingly, perhaps even narrowly, like an Anglo-American preoccupation." What this actually means is a "post black/white" *Othello*, for each of Lanier's cinematic examples demands of the viewer at least some awareness of race dynamics—we cannot but acknowledge that race is bound up in class, ethnicity, religion, gender and other aspects of "identity politics."[36] The very phrasing of the concept, however, has been revealed as short-sighted over the course of the decade since Lanier's coinage. In the same way that the United States was never "post-racial" in the way that many wanted to believe it was during the presidency of Barack Obama (as the election of Donald Trump made all too clear), *Othello* simply cannot be construed in this way. Moreover, any distinction between an Anglo-American preoccupation with race in *Othello* and a "post-racial" (implicitly non-Western) interpretation of the play is undermined by the example of a country like South Africa, where racial categories are a national obsession and *Othello* cannot ever honestly escape "a racialized conception."

Perhaps a more helpful perspective is offered by Victoria Bladen in her 2015 essay on *Othello* on screen, which emphasizes the intersection of race and gender in the play and in film adaptations—or, rather than evincing intersection, "*Othello* is a site where race and gender discourses collide" and thus "Iago's crime is effective because of his ability to draw from the power of cultural metanarratives of [both] race and gender."[37] The treatment of Dezi and her mother in *Otelo Burning* (both their treatment by the male characters in the world of the film and, one could say, their treatment by the film-makers) may be viewed in this light. Such an emphasis complements the ways in which Blecher and Whyle have adopted, adapted and "fragmented" *Othello*.

***

Finally, then, we are left with the question: Why *Othello*? Ayanna Thompson has identified this as one of Shakespeare's three "toxic plays," which "resist rehabilitation and appropriation."[38] Thompson argues that, because the part of Othello was written for a white actor performing in blackface, and the structure of the play invites the audience to sympathize with Iago (and the white actor playing him) as he virtuosically goads "the Moor," *Othello* remains "regressive" and reinscribing of "deep racism" even when a black actor takes on the title role.[39] No matter how much theater-makers might aim to "recuperate" the play or make it "progressive," *Othello* cannot be rejuvenated or redeemed. Perhaps in *Otelo Burning*, we have an alternative: precisely because its plot and characterization deviate from *Othello* so substantially, it offers a "version'" of Shakespeare's play that is not irredeemably tainted by that play's racist premises and conclusions. Yet, the film is very much about race: its premise is dependent on the circumstances of late apartheid society, and indeed one may fairly claim that race is a part of any South African story, or any story told in South Africa.

Otelo Burning could thus be seen as a provocative intervention both in South African and in global Shakespeare studies. But, of course, in developing the story, Blecher and Whyle were not concerned about the state of

South African or global Shakespeare studies. They wanted to make, and sell, a movie. *Othello* is simply a convenient narrative and thematic point of reference. Arguably, it serves a similar purpose to another film that the title *Otelo Burning* brings to mind: Alan Parker's *Mississippi Burning* (1988). Blecher affirms that this was not a deliberate or conscious reference.[40] Still, for many viewers it is likely to function as an invocation, a kind of cinematic shorthand for a story about a "society on fire"—whether through apartheid-fueled township necklacing or Ku Klux Klan crosses and lynching—and the individuals who burn in that fire. In *Otelo Burning*, as in *Mississippi Burning*, the personal merges with the political, while also being at odds with it, resisting it for better and for worse. Viewers may not make the connection between *Otelo Burning* and either *Othello* or *Mississippi Burning*. If they do, the comparison may enrich their experience of the film but it may also leave them confused, seeking intertextual consistency where none exists. Either way, as James Whyle notes, "The necklacing, the township violence, the characters' disillusionment and grief ... that kind of shit completely overpowers Shakespeare."[41]

Shakespeare, then, is very much in the back seat. *Otelo Burning* is driven by South African realities, past and present. For Blecher, the film is ultimately about "what happens when you get freedom. What happens to a country?"[42] Despite Mandela's release and the formal dismantling of apartheid, South Africans have continued to see tragedies like that of Otelo unfold daily. The challenge facing post-apartheid South Africa may be to establish a "normal" society—whatever that may mean—but, Blecher suggests, there is still no remedy for "normal human emotions" or for the consequences of "greed and jealousy and betrayal." And as we see in this case, when historic(al) or "universal" Shakespeare is fragmented, reconstituted and put to use by South African film-makers this can, in turn, be unexpectedly liberating for Shakespeare's plays.

Notes

1. "Mzansi" means "South" in a number of Nguni languages and is used colloquially to refer to South Africa. *Shakespeare in Mzansi* was produced for the South African Broadcasting Corporation (SABC). For discussion of the series, see Seeff, *South Africa's Shakespeare*, 181–226; Roux, "Shakespeare and Tragedy;" and Mushakavanhu, "Shakespeare in Mzansi."

2. See, for example, Hofmeyr, "Reading Debating/Debating Reading"; Gevisser, *Thabo Mbeki*; and Distiller, *Shakespeare and the Coconuts*.
3. Television was banned from South Africa until 1976. The country's citizens thus had just under two decades of television-viewing prior to the first democratic elections in 1994 and have had just over two decades of "post-apartheid TV" since then.
4. Quoted from the original Call for Papers, "Shakespeare in Tatters: Referencing his works on film and television," University of Ferrara, Italy, 10–11 May 2013.
5. Richard Poplak, "Shakespeare in hate: Ralph Fiennes' bloody adaptation of *Coriolanus* seems made for South Africans", *Daily Maverick*, 4 June 2012, n.p. Online: http://www.dailymaverick.co.za/article/2012-06-04-shakespeare-in-hate-ralph-fiennes-bloody-adaptation-of-coriolanus-seems-made-for-south-africans/.
6. See Gevisser, *Thabo Mbeki*; Pearce, "Review: *Coriolanus;*" and Johnson, "*Coriolanus* in South Africa."
7. See Roux, "Shakespeare and Tragedy." Pieter-Dirk Uys' *MacBeki—A farce to be reckoned with*, by contrast, imagines Mbeki as a kind of comic villain in the Scottish Play.
8. See Holmes, "'A World Elsewhere'"; Thurman, "Sher and Doran's *Titus Andronicus;*" Pearce, "British Directors" and Young, "Reflections on an 'Africanised' *Tempest*."
9. David Schalkwyk, *Hamlet's Dreams: The Robben Island Shakespeare* (London: Bloomsbury, 2013), 128–30.
10. Greg Doran and Rupert Goold, "Power and Glory: How to Tackle Shakespeare's Revolutions," *The Guardian*, 20 June 2012, http://www.theguardian.com/culture/2012/jun/20/gregory-doran-rupert-goold-shakespeare. Such claims about the suitability of certain plays to the South African or African context based on essentialized notions of race, culture and world view are not new; see Thurman, *South African Essays on 'Universal' Shakespeare* 11–15) and "After Titus".
11. Phillip French, "*Coriolanus*—Review." *The Observer*, 22 January 2012, n.p. Online: http://www.guardian.co.uk/film/2012/jan/22/coriolanus-film-review-ralph-fiennes.
12. Daniel Garrett, "War Becomes A Man: A Modern Interpretation of Shakespeare's *Coriolanus*," *The Compulsive Reader*, 21 August 2012, http://www.compulsivereader.com/2012/08/21/war-becomes-a-man-a-modern-interpretation-of-shakespeares-coriolanus-starring-ralph-fiennes-and-gerard-butler/.
13. Quoted in Roger Young, "Zulu Surf Films" (an interview with Sara Blecher). *Mahala*, 20 July 2011, http://www.mahala.co.za/culture/zulu-surf-films/.

14. For a poetic response to this stigma and an indication of the varied associations that swimming—in the sea in particular—may carry for black South Africans, see Koleka Putuma's "Water" in her collection *Collective Amnesia*.
15. Blecher, *Otelo Burning*. All quotations from *Otelo Burning* are based on the film's English subtitles, translated from isiZulu.
16. Formerly, the province of Natal and the Bantustan or black "homeland" of KwaZulu, located along the north-eastern coast of South Africa.
17. It is widely accepted that the National Party (NP) government aggravated the ANC-UDF-IFP conflict in order to undermine collective black resistance to apartheid.
18. The removal of racial difference in the relationship between Othello/Otelo and Iago/Mandla to some degree echoes a casting and conceptual decision made by Eubulus Timothy in his 2005 South African film version of *Othello*, in which both Iago (Hakeem Kae-Kazim) and Othello (Sello Maake ka Ncube) were black. This experiment would be reproduced in a very different context—Lucian Msamati's Iago opposite Hugh Quarshie's Othello in Iqbal Khan's 2015 production for the Royal Shakespeare Company.
19. Blecher in Young, "Zulu Surf Films," n.p.
20. "We were going to get the funding anyway. It's not as if the NFVF required us to use *Othello*." Blecher, Interview with the author.
21. David Johnson, "Beyond Tragedy: *Otelo Burning* and the Limits of Post-apartheid Nationalism" (Journal of African Cultural Studies, 26.3, 2014), 349.
22. Johnson, "Beyond Tragedy," 350.
23. See Orkin, *Shakespeare against Apartheid* and *Drama and the South African State*; Johnson, *Shakespeare and South Africa*; Distiller, *Shakespeare, South Africa, and Post-Colonial Culture* and *Shakespeare and the Coconuts*; Hofmeyr, "Reading Debating"; Wright, "Introduction: South African Shakespeare"; Willan, "Whose Shakespeare?" and "'A South African's Homage' at One Hundred"; Desai, *Reading Revolution*; and Schalkwyk, *Hamlet's Dreams*.
24. I discuss some of the consequences for South Africans of acknowledging Shakespeare's "inextricable intertwinement" in "hegemonic power structures"—the fact that he is "mired in history"—in Thurman, "Editorial" and *South African Essays on 'Universal' Shakespeare*, 11–15.
25. Johnson, "Beyond Tragedy," 350.
26. Blecher, Interview with the author, 11 October 2013.
27. Whyle, Interview with the author, 30 September 2013.
28. Whyle was one of the founders of the Take Away Shakespeare Company in the 1990s.

29. See Gordon, "Iago and the *swaart gevaar;*" Holmes, "A World Elsewhere" and Pearce, "British Directors in Post-Colonial South Africa."
30. In Parsons and Mason (eds), *Shakespeare in Performance*, p. 28. Mason is referring to gender in *The Taming of the Shrew*, but the tag applies equally to race in *Othello*.
31. Denel Honeyball, "A Racy New Othello at POPArt Theatre". *Artslink*, 5 May 2013, http://www.artlink.co.za/news_article.htm?contentID=32733
32. John Carlin, "Only Shakespeare could have written of the tragic story of Oscar Pistorius." *The Independent*, 15 February 2013, http://www.independent.co.uk/news/world/africa/john-carlin-only-shakespeare-could-have-written-of-the-tragic-story-of-oscar-pistorius-8497532.html. It is worth noting that Carlin echoes French's assertion that the connections between Shakespeare and South Africa would have been beyond the playwright's comprehension: Pistorius' life-story is "a tale that would have defied even Shakespeare's powers of imagination."
33. John Kani, *Apartheid and Othello*, in "Living Shakespeare" series, edited by Virginia Compton (London: British Council, 2016), 11.
34. In Precious Maputle, "*Desdemona*: A UJ Dance Deconstruction of *Othello*." *Artslink*, 22 February 2013, http://www.artlink.co.za/news_article.htm?contentID=32222. Shakespeare's position in both high school and university curricula, which means that a common model for productions of his plays in South Africa entails performance by university drama students for high school audiences, carries both advantages and disadvantages; see Thurman, "After Titus."
35. Douglas Lanier, "Post-Racial Othello" (2010 Lindberg Lecture, University of New Hampshire, 29 June 2012), http://www.youtube.com/watch?v=ScroEtGwmOQ.
36. This point was raised by an audience member in the discussion following Lanier's lecture.
37. Victoria Bladen, "*Othello* on Screen: Monsters, Marvellous Space and the Power of the Tale," in *Shakespeare on Screen: Othello*, edited by Sarah Hatchuel and Nathalie Vienne-Guerrin (Cambridge: Cambridge University Press, 2015), 38.
38. Ayanna Thompson in Gene Demby and Shereen Marisol Meraji, "All That Glisters is not Gold," *Code Switch* (NPR), 21 August 2019, https://www.npr.org/transcripts/752850055.
39. Thompson, "All That Glisters is not Gold."
40. Blecher explains that the idea of "burning" in the title is more directly linked to the devastating juxtaposition of Ntwe's necklacing with Otelo's victory at the surfing competition, which New Year describes as follows: "Otelo was on fire that day. It was like he owned the waves. The sea and Otelo were one." Blecher, Interview with the author, n.p.

41. Whyle, Interview with the author.
42. Blecher in Young, "Zulu Surf Films," n.p. Phrased differently, "It's essentially about the relationship between freedom and greed. When you're free politically, you then have the freedom to be greedy – and we in South Africa must guard against this." Blecher, Interview with the author, n.p.

Works Cited

Bladen, Victoria. "*Othello* on Screen: Monsters, marvellous space and the power of the tale". In *Shakespeare on Screen: Othello*, edited by Sarah Hatchuel and Nathalie Vienne-Guerrin, 24–42. Cambridge: Cambridge University Press, 2015.

Blecher, Sara, dir. *Otelo Burning*. Johannesburg: Cinga Productions . Film [DVD], 2011.

Blecher, Sara. Interview with the author, 11 October 2013.

Demby, Gene and Meraji, Shereen Marisol. "All That Glisters is not Gold". *Code Switch* (NPR), 21 August 2019. Online (transcript): https://www.npr.org/transcripts/752850055.

Desai, Ashwin. *Reading Revolution: Shakespeare on Robben Island*. Pretoria: Unisa Press, 2012.

Distiller, Natasha. *Shakespeare and the Coconuts: On Post-apartheid South African Culture*. Johannesburg: Wits University Press, 2012.

Distiller, Natasha. *Shakespeare, South Africa, and Post-Colonial Culture*. Lampeter: Edwin Mellen, 2005.

Fiennes, Ralph. *Coriolanus*. Valley Village: Hermetof Pictures/Magna Films. Film [DVD], 2011.

Gevisser, Mark. *Thabo Mbeki: The Dream Deferred*. Johannesburg: Jonathan Ball, 2007.

Gordon, Robert. "Iago and the *swaart gevaar*: The Problems and Pleasures of a (Post)colonial *Othello*." In *Shakespearean International Year Book* 9, edited by Graham Bradshaw, Tom Bishop and Laurence Wright. Abingdon: Ashgate, 2009.

Hofmeyr, Isabel. "Reading Debating/Debating Reading: The Case of the Lovedale Debating Society, or Why Mandela quotes Shakespeare." In *Africa's Hidden Histories: Everyday Literacy and Making the Self*, edited by Karin Barber, 258–77. Bloomington: Indiana University Press, 2006.

Holmes, Jonathan. "'A World Elsewhere': Shakespeare in South Africa." *Shakespeare Survey*, vol. 55 (2002): 271–84.

Johnson, David. *Shakespeare and South Africa*. Oxford: Oxford University Press, 1996.

Johnson, David. "Beyond Tragedy: *Otelo Burning* and the Limits of Post-apartheid Nationalism". *Journal of African Cultural Studies*, vol. 26, no. 3 (2014): 348–51.

Johnson, David. "Coriolanus in South Africa". In *The Cambridge Guide to the Worlds of Shakespeare* (XVII: Shakespeare as Cultural Icon), edited by Bruce R. Smith et al, 1235–41. Cambridge: Cambridge University Press, 2016.

Kani, John. *Apartheid and Othello.* "Living Shakespeare" series, edited by Virginia Compton. London: British Council, 2016. Online: https://literature.britishcouncil.org/assets/Uploads/06.-shakespeare-lives-south-africa-john-kani-digital-download.pdf.

Lanier, Douglas. "Post-Racial Othello". 2010 Lindberg Lecture, University of New Hampshire. 29 June 2012. Online: http://www.youtube.com/watch?v=ScroEtGwmOQ.

Lanier, Douglas. *Literary Quarterly* 4.1 (2010). Online: http://www.sentinelpoetry.org.uk/slq/4-1-oct2010/interviews/tinashe-mushakavanhu.html.

Mushakavanhu, Tinashe. "Shakespeare in Mzansi: A South African Perspective". *Sentinel.*

Orkin, Martin. *Shakespeare against Apartheid.* Johannesburg: Ad Donker, 1987.

Orkin, Martin. *Drama and the South African State.* Manchester: Manchester University Press, 1991.

Parsons, Keith and Mason, Pamela (eds). *Shakespeare in Performance.* London: Salamander Books, 1995.

Pearce, Brian. "British Directors in Post-Colonial South Africa." In *Shakespeare in Stages: New Theatre Histories*, edited by Christine Dymkowski and Christie Carson, 264–76. Cambridge: Cambridge University Press, 2010.

Pearce, Brian. "Review: *Coriolanus* (dir. Debbie Lutge)." *Shakespeare in Southern Africa*, vol. 21 (2009): 83–84.

Putuma, Koleka. *Collective Amnesia.* Cape Town: uHlanga Press, 2017.

Roux, Daniel. "Shakespeare and Tragedy in South Africa: From *Black Hamlet* to *A Dream Deferred*". *Shakespeare in Southern Africa*, vol. 27 (2015): 1–14.

Schalkwyk, David. *Hamlet's Dreams: The Robben Island Shakespeare.* London: Bloomsbury, 2013.

Seeff, Adele. *South Africa's Shakespeare and the Drama of Language and Identity.* London: Palgrave Macmillan, 2018.

Thurman, Christopher. "Sher and Doran's *Titus Andronicus* (1995): Importing Shakespeare, Exporting South Africa". *Shakespeare in Southern Africa*, vol. 18 (2006): 29–36.

Thurman, Chris. "Editorial". *Shakespeare in Southern Africa*, vol. 24 (2012): 3–5.

Thurman, Chris. "After *Titus*: Towards a survey of Shakespeare on the post-apartheid stage". In *New Territories: Reconfiguring Theatre and Drama in Post-apartheid South Africa*, edited by Greg Homann and Marc Maufort, 75–104. Brussels: Peter Lang, 2015.

Thurman, Chris. *Guy Butler: Reassessing a South African Literary Life*. Scottsville: University of KwaZulu-Natal Press, 2010.

Thurman, Chris (ed). *South African Essays on 'Universal' Shakespeare*. Burlington: Ashgate, 2014.

Timothy, Eubulus. *Othello: A South African Tale*. Johannesburg: The Other Theatre Company. Film [videotape], 2011.

Uys, Pieter-Dirk. *MacBeki—A farce to be reckoned with*. Darling: Peninsula/Junkets, 2009.

Whyle, James. Interview with the Author, 30 September 2013.

Willan, Brian. *Sol Plaatje: A Biography*. Johannesburg: Ravan Press, 1984.

Willan, Brian. "Whose Shakespeare? Early black South African engagement with Shakespeare". *Shakespeare in Southern Africa*, vol. 24 (2012): 3–24.

Willan, Brian. "'A South African's Homage' at One Hundred: Revisiting Sol Plaatje's contribution to the *Book of Homage to Shakespeare* (1916)." *Shakespeare in Southern Africa*, vol. 28 (2016): 1–19.

Wright, Laurence. "Introduction: South African Shakespeare in the Twentieth Century". In *Shakespearean International Year Book* 9, edited by Graham Bradshaw, Tom Bishop and Laurence Wright. Abingdon: Ashgate, 2009.

Young, Sandra. "'Let Your Indulgence Set Me Free': Reflections on an 'Africanised' *Tempest* and Its Implications for Critical Practice." *Social Dynamics*, vol. 36, no. 2 (June 2010): 315–327.

CHAPTER 5

Shakespeare in Bits and Bites in Indian Cinema

Poonam Trivedi

The 'bit'/'byte' is a ubiquitous figure in our world of digital communication. It is familiar as the primary unit of information, memory, and storage. But while we routinely add up the megabytes and gigabytes capacities of our computing devices, we usually neglect to note the presence of the 'Shakebyte:' the equally ubiquitous circulation of Shakespeare's plays and poetry in bits and pieces, which function to newly configure data from Shakespeare and create virtual memory banks that are increasingly attracting the attention of the young generation. It is a sobering fact that more and more people are coming to know and experience Shakespeare first through such bits and fragments and it's time this kind of encounter was given critical attention.

Bits of Shakespeare circulate incessantly. Citations, references, allusions, echoes, adaptations, appropriations, re-creations, and intertextualities with Shakespeare are to be found everywhere: in newspapers, magazines, journals, fiction, poetry, theatre, television, visual and digital arts, and

P. Trivedi (✉)
University of Delhi, New Delhi, India

A. A. Joubin and V. Bladen (eds.), *Onscreen Allusions to Shakespeare*, Global Shakespeares, https://doi.org/10.1007/978-3-030-93783-6_5

increasingly in films. What is surprising is that even in a country like India, with twenty-two official languages and with only ten per cent of the people—at a generous estimate—knowing and speaking English, bits of Shakespeare and Shakespeare in bits proliferate. Not a day passes without some citation or allusion to him cropping up in print, periodical, or online publications. Much of it, of course, is an unselfconscious usage of Shakespeare's words and phrases which have been absorbed in the English language and circulate as handy references in the Indian press.

While it is almost impossible to fully quantify and theorize such Shakespearean 'bits' that float around in the print medium, those in the visual and digital medium that have been consciously 'bitten' off/torn out of the corpus to serve a new, seemingly cavalier, purpose demand closer attention. We find that like the digital 'bit,' the literary bit or fragment (in the words of programming language) embeds a binary capacity. It is significant in what it abstracts out of the whole and what new dimensions it invests in it. We need to take a leaf out of digital technology to fully appreciate the fragment as a modular section that has its own life cycle and can receive its own inputs and may be detachable from the whole. Such new emergent forms of referencing Shakespeare, particularly in mass media, form anomalous entities: usually short, startling pieces that do not have the spread or scope of adaptation. The thousands of re-mediations of Shakespeare uploaded on You Tube, for instance, are fast becoming a pop archive of the Shakespeare fragment. All of these have posed a challenge to critical epistemologies. In some cases, they are valorized as subaltern, levelling the high in terms of the low in what Douglas Lanier has described as 'Shakespop.'[1] In other cases, these You Tube re-mediations are problematized by Richard Burt; Burt terms them 'Schlockspeare' and theorizes them in terms of 'loss,' a form of use that cannot and should not be dismissed as inauthentic but which results in a what Burt calls a 'paradoxical hyperunproductivity' which frames Shakespeare in terms of 'archaism' and 'obsolescence' because of the speed with which it is updated and replaced.[2]

In the Indian context, however, such libertine use of Shakespeare marks a turning point in the cultural engagement with what was once a colonial icon.[3] The proliferation of quotations, allusions, and references to Shakespeare—not just full-scale adaptations of whole plays in films e.g. *Maqbool* (*Macbeth* 2004), *Omkara* (*Othello* 2006), and *Haider* (*Hamlet* 2014)—is a recent trend that shows that Indians are no longer inflected by the reverential attitude inculcated by colonialism. Rather, there is now an individualized freedom of approach, to abstract sections, to play around with, and appropriate Shakespeare for comment and critique. An earlier instance of a free and virtually plagiarizing and plundering use of Shakespeare in the Indian cultural space was seen when the first modern theatre, the Parsi theatre (c.1870–c.1930), was trying to establish itself and there was a huge demand for stories. This theatre became infamous for not only borrowing widely from Shakespeare but also for mashing up character, scene, and dialogue with other plays from different traditions. Today's utilization of Shakespeare, especially in Indian films, reveals a more purposeful and dynamic shift, reflecting the changed political circumstances. Of late, brief references to Shakespeare in the form of names e.g. 'Much Ado About Nothing,' and 'Troilus and Cressida' in *Dil Chahata Hai* (directed Farhan Akhtar, 2001), or citation of lines in *36 Chowringhee Lane* (directed Aparna Sen, 1981) have cropped up,[4] but this essay will attend to more substantive instances of 'bitten off' or modular Shakespeare in Indian films that have remained unnoticed by critics, come upon us as a surprise, and in which there is a tangential, parodic, or unacknowledged relation to the source. Each of these represents differing modes of referencing Shakespeare: *Eklavya: The Royal Guard*, directed by Vidhu Vinod Chopra, 2007, *Matru ki Bijlee ka Mandola* (Matru's Bijlee changes her Mind) directed by Vishal Bharadwaj, 2013, and *Bodyguard*, directed by Siddique, 2011, tracing an evolving cultural trajectory of Shakespeare citations in Hindi cinema.

'Shall I Compare Thee…': Surrogacy and Shakespeare

The first example of a Shakespeare 'bit' is from Vidhu Vinod Chopra's stylish and lush but noir film, *Eklavya*, which is an exposé of the decadence of erstwhile Rajput rulers. Chopra is one of the leading director/producers and script writers in the Hindi film industry today who has made several path-breaking films that have won both critical and popular success. His métier can be held to be popular films with a message, though *Eklavya* is more serious than others. Those who know Chopra's style will not be surprised at his use of Shakespeare; he references *Romeo and Juliet*, in an allusive layered manner, in his earlier film *1942: A Love Story* (1994). In *Eklavya*, the Shakespearean bit is a seemingly straightforward quotation of Sonnet 18, which is later repeated in the film, but which subtly takes on many interconnections potent with meaning. The film opens with the sound of the words of the sonnet, 'Shall I compare thee ....'[5] Surprisingly, and unusual in a Hindi film, the recitation is in the original English, immediately establishing an elite context. The camera closes in on to the King, Rana Jayawardhan (Boman Irani), who is seen comforting his ailing wife by reading out the favourite poem of their courtship days, 'Shall I compare thee...' and showing her the rose, preserved within the pages of the book, which she had given him in return. The somewhat delirious Queen (Sharmila Tagore) is moved and calls out, however, not to the King, but for her secret lover, Eklavya, who happens to be a loyal guard. This puzzles the King; he does not call Eklavya, closes the book and moves to caress her face, and gives her some water. The Queen disregards these gestures and continues to call out for Eklavya, whereupon the King is enraged, his tenderness turns into jealousy, and, Othello like, he strangles her in bed in an orgasmic fury. Love sonnet and tragedy are collapsed; courtship and death, love and betrayal are telescoped, legitimizing each other. Later we learn that the king was impotent and that his loyal retainer cum guard Eklavya (Amitabh Bachchan) had been enjoined by the Queen mother to father two children with the Queen to safeguard the succession. The King had been unaware of this until the Queen's insistent cry for Eklavya on her death bed reveals this surrogacy (he had been led to believe that it was instead a sage who had fathered his heirs). The romantic sonnet ironically exposes the King's life long impotence and pretence and inadvertently provokes murderous jealousy, which precipitates a series of counter revengeful murders. It is least suspected that lines from Shakespeare's sonnet, recalled and read aloud in a gesture of care and love nostalgia to console the dying Queen, in the opening sequence of the film, will become the pivot on which the whole intricate narrative will hang: if there was no sonnet, there would be no revelatory yearning for Eklavya, then no murder, no counter bloodshed, and no reprisals. Yet the story does not spin out in a linear fashion; the reverberations of the words of the sonnet are subtle and potent, linking the many turns and twists of the plot. As a matter of fact, this film is drenched in Shakespearean allusions and references, mainly from *Hamlet*, *King Lear*, and *Macbeth*, and of course, the *Mahabharata*, analysed perceptively by Robert White; while most of these can be called 'spectral,'[6] morphing Shakespeare to suit the involved narrative of the film, the repeated recitation of lines from Sonnet 18 in the original English, provoking memory and information from the storage of the past, insistently presents itself as a Shakespearean fragment, a 'bite / byte.'[7]

There is always more than meets the eye in Chopra: this opening scene, of the King reciting Shakespeare to the Queen, is witnessed by their mentally challenged daughter, Nandini (Raima Sen), who is also present in the bedroom. Though seemingly preoccupied playing with a hand fan, she giggles at the intonation of 'and thy eternal summer shall not fade,' only to be silenced by a glare from the King. The camera swivels to show her on a rocking chair, her image reflected in the mirror behind her, signalling a double witnessing. She is the one who voices the Queen's barely audible cry for her secret lover, Eklavya, to the King and she is the only one who witnesses the murder. The deployment of this 'bite' of Shakespeare's sonnet is replete with irony in the film: it is addressed to one who is dying, whose 'eternal summer' is about to 'fade,' but it becomes the trigger that preserves the memory of the beloved Queen not in art but in death. On the other hand, the message of the sonnet, of the preservation of the truth of love and beauty in art 'when in eternal lines to time thou grow'st ... So long lives this, and this gives life to thee'... eerily and inversely comes alive when the young prince, Harshvardhan (Saif Ali Khan), discovers the truth about his mother's death recorded in a painting made by his sister Nandini who is subsequently too traumatized to speak about it.

This opening sequence of the film is preceded by a prologue that narrates the story of Eklavya from the epic, *Mahabharata*, a story of unflinching devotion to duty: a low caste but skilled archer is asked by his guru to present the thumb of his right hand as tribute so that the Princes whom the guru has trained remain unrivalled. The epic narrative flows seamlessly into Shakespeare: devotion to duty and to the beloved blend until suddenly and shockingly they are inverted. If the *Mahabharata* story provides a structural frame to the larger narrative that is centred on a challenge to the dharma of a deeply loyal retainer of the royal family whose family has been protecting them for nine generations, Shakespeare's sonnet provides the inner connecting threads. Lines from the sonnet crop up again when the King is driving to the encounter that will liquidate Eklavya. With the come-uppance of the surrogacy and betrayal playing upon his mind, he recalls the Queen and the memory of the sonnet associated with her by repeating: 'Shall I compare thee to a summer's day….' He stops to tell Eklavya, who is also in the same vehicle, that the Queen loved this poem and died while listening to it; 'Shakespeare!' he pronounces, in between, and continues to recite the sonnet. Just when he gets to 'summer's lease hath too short a date,' bullet shots ring out. This recall and repetition of the sonnet by the King, especially with the emphatic underlining of the author 'Shakespeare,' is designed to cut down the surrogate lowly lover, Eklavya, to size: 'the Queen loved Shakespeare too' it implies, which I, the King, gave her. A deeper irony is underlined when in the ensuing gunfight, the King is assassinated: as the sonnet says, 'every fair from fair sometime declines.'

The main theme of the film is an investigation into the traditional oppression of the lower castes by the elite in Indian society, as exemplified by the Eklavya story, both in the epic and the film, which is internalized as duty/dharma. Chopra's deft and resourceful use of Sonnet 18 harnesses love poetry to this end. A classic example of ekphrasis, it poses an equation between surrogacy and Shakespeare, revealing how the cultural capital of Shakespeare's very name can be a means to undermine the lowly guard and how ultimately art triumphs, exhibited when the recitation of the sonnet evokes the secret true love for the lowly surrogate lover. Shakespeare's sonnet is used to dignify and redeem, as only juxtaposition with art can, a tale of centuries-old oppression, deceit, and treachery.

'Is It a Crime to Read Shakespeare in This Country?'

The second example, *Matru ki Bijlee ka Mandola*, presents a more complex intertextuality with Shakespeare of a tongue in cheek kind, in which the well-known temptation scene from *Macbeth* is playfully inverted into a mock conspiracy to murder the bridegroom on the wedding night. Since this film is directed by Vishal Bhardwaj, of *Maqbool, Omkara,* and *Haider* fame, and is a typical Bollywood comedy but laced with searing satire, both the elements—Shakespeare and Bollywood—need to be taken seriously. Occurring towards the latter half of the film, this 'bite' fleshes out the moment when the heroine, Bijlee (Anushka Sharma), the free-spirited daughter of a rich businessman, Mandola (Ranjit Kapur), realizes that she does not really love the rich young dolt she has agreed to marry and would rather team up with her childhood friend from the village, Matru (Imran Khan). Caught in this dilemma, she is found reading *Macbeth*. Joined by her friend/lover who begins to tease her, she throws the book at him, which he picks up and starts to leaf through. Reading Shakespeare's *Macbeth* together consoles the lovers: they identify their situation with the Macbeths. They are in a cleft stick and don't know how to proceed; fair and foul seem alike, and they seem to be hovering through the fog and filthy air of confusion and indecision. Then Shakespeare inspires them, suggesting a way out: discovering that they are being spied upon and overheard by the rejected bridegroom and his three cronies, the two friends transform into conspiring Macbeths, plotting a kill. But since this is a comedy, it needs must be a fantasy kill. Bijlee takes the lead, like Lady Macbeth, saying that she will first mix sleeping pills in the bridegroom's drink and when he lies unconscious, she will pull out the dagger from under the pillow, cut him to bits, and then shout murder! Matru adds that he will implicate the guards by drugging them and placing the dagger in their hands. Swept along in this fantasy of 'solely sovereign sway and masterdom' the young lovers dance and dream of sailing away together. This mock plot and mimic performance, of course, are meant to scare away the eavesdropping bridegroom and his witch-like cronies. Lady Macbeth's temptation of her husband into a tragic 'river of blood' from which there is no return in the play, is here parodied as a comic prank that will supposedly release the lovers from an unsuitable marriage.

This mock irreverence is, however, not the heart of the episode. Bhardwaj, the director, is too sensitive a humanist to merely dislocate Shakespeare, and the comic fantasy is not without wit and depth. This slick 'conspiracy' is configured as a journey of self-reflexivity and self-realization too. During the scheming in which the two friends come together in intimate tandem, Bijlee/Lady Macbeth turns towards a mirror, which reflects back and prompts her actions. After the excitement of the mock performance is over, Bijlee is flushed with the realization of her passion for Matru and returns to kiss him, sealing their bond as conspiring lovers in a game of a mock symbolic murder of the arranged marriage. Their 'reading of Shakespeare' from 'underwater,' as Matru later says to excuse himself, provides an understanding of themselves—mirrored and spied upon—in a kind of double vision, instigating them into action within and without. The entire scene happens to be set, incidentally, beside a swimming pool, but which is not a gratuitous embellishment.

Indeed, this episode is a 'reading' of Shakespeare, as the lovers confess doing, literally and intuitively, but parodically, from 'underwater.' Inverting the message of 'water' from the play where supposedly 'a little water clears us of this deed,' the pool of water in *Matru* is the obverse, a ducking into that brings Bijlee's drunken father to his senses earlier in the film. In this scene, the lovers can stand at the edge of the pool, precariously balanced on the diving board. Reading Shakespeare has cleared their minds and they have no need of a ducking in the pool. In this comic inversion of Shakespeare's *Macbeth*, water washes clean and clarifies, and is not 'incarnadined' with blood.

The film is a pungent exposé of the corruption in Indian society, and once Bijlee and Matru realize their love for each other during the temptation scene prank, they team up to successfully thwart attempts to bamboozle the villagers of their land. The Macbeth parody is not in vain or gratuitous. Many other, broader analogies with *Macbeth* may also be gleaned: another duo of a grasping politician mother and an avaricious father businessman, who scheme to destroy the flourishing farmland of the village and convert it into a glitzy mall are seen, supported by three foolish aides who hinder more than help. Since this is a comedy, through a series of turns and counter turns, they fail, outwitted by their younger ones. There is also a mandatory storm—'thunder, lightning and rain,' which destroys the farmer's harvest; instead of the 'raven,' a bright pink buffalo serves as an ill omen, and an apparition called 'Mao' advises the villagers on their resistance. There is even a battle between the henchmen of the politician and the villagers who camouflage themselves behind the leafy sugarcane in the fields to pelt the enemy with cow dung pats. Yet, this zany inversion and parody are not a mere post-modernist lark or an opportunist 'Shakespop' of random bits sprinkled for 'exotic or elitist' effect to impact the international box-office. It cunningly deploys Shakespeare to voice and strengthen a protest against the urgent political issue of land scams versus the development dynamics of globalization.

Vishal Bhardwaj has been praised by Mark Thornton Burnett as an auteur, 'director as author,' who has successfully negotiated 'interrelated artistic and commercial imperatives' in the huge dream factory that is Bollywood.[8] One of the marks of an auteur is a self-referential touch, which Bhardwaj reveals clearly in *Maqbool* and suggestively in *Omkara*. In *Matru ki Bijlee*, the entire episode is permeated with a bravura self-reflexive slant: not only is the name of Shakespeare pronounced several times, his image, pictured on the cover of the book, is glimpsed twice, along with a full bookshelf alongside the pool where Bijlee is sitting. It is very much the 'textual Shakespeare' that is being fore-grounded here and the episode functions as acts of reading, and re-writing. Pointers, like a ceremonial coconut with 'R J' embossed on it in the background at the end of scene when Bijlee's furious father pulls a rifle at Matru's throat, are strategically placed. As a matter of fact, befitting the comic mood, the episode concludes on a self-reflexive note that turns upon itself: when Matru, caught and confronted by Bijlee's irate father, offers the reading of Shakespeare as a defence, further enraging him, the dejected bridegroom tries to save the situation and retorts: 'Is it a crime to read Shakespeare in this country?' voicing an apologia and justification not only on behalf of the errant lovers, but more crucially for the director, Vishal Bhardwaj, who is unusual in his predilection towards Shakespeare with three full-length films in ten years. The double-edged nature of the parodic Shakespeare in *Matru* is neither a vulgarization, nor a scaling down of the bard, but a nimble appropriation for comedic inversions and a self-assertion of its own games with Shakespeare. As Douglas Lanier has put it, 'recent Shakespearean film parody is profoundly ambivalent in its transgression: it rearticulates principles of cultural decorum - Shakespeare's highness, pop's lowness – in the very act of temporarily violating them. ... to create a (new) space for Shakespeare in the empire of pop.'[9] In this post-modernist, whacky but relentlessly Bollywood-ish film with the Shakespearean fragment, Bhardwaj delights in playing around both with the bard and himself.

Chhaya or Shadow Shakespeare

The final example is of an unacknowledged bit of an interpolation of Shakespeare that is so absorbed and re-presented in an unobtrusive and delicate manner that most viewers have entirely missed noticing it. It is the use of the love test from *As You Like It* in a typical Bollywood romantic blockbuster, *Bodyguard*. The film presents the story of a dutiful guard (Salman Khan) engaged to protect a college-going daughter of a politician. Predictably, the young woman (Kareena Kapoor) first chafes at such surveillance, but then finds herself falling in love with her bodyguard. She successfully manages to woo him via the mobile phone, but in the guise of another persona, called Chhaya, meaning shadow/reflection. A meeting in a park is arranged, but the bodyguard, unschooled in such encounters with the fair sex, is understandably nervous. The heroine offers help: 'pretend that I am your sweetheart Chhaya, and rehearse what you will say to her,' she says, assuming the suggestive manner of Rosalind, disguised as Ganymede pretending to be standing in for Rosalind, to Orlando. He does take up her offer, and illusion and reality coalesce.

This fragment is unusual and different from the others in that it neither cites Shakespeare's name or his words, but freely incorporates a signature moment from the play to telling effect without changing its substance. It pops up unsuspected towards the latter half of the film and is completely indigenized and so integrated into the narrative that it resists identification. The other two examples, of lines from a sonnet and the mock inversion of part of a scene, while also skillfully intertwined in their new locales, foreground their appropriations, clearly naming 'Shakespeare'. This last one from *Bodyguard*, however, is so embedded that it is only the schooled viewer who is able to catch it. It may be seen as an example of what has been termed an 'accidental' appropriation, one that provokes 'wonder' and 'surprise' at the unexpected encounter with Shakespeare in an unlikely brawn and muscle Bollywood blockbuster.[10]

These three examples from *Eklavya*, *Matru ki Bijlee ka Mandola*, and *Bodyguard* present a new diversity of form and intent in the referencing of Shakespeare in Indian films. They neither mock nor burlesque the bard as many such instances are generally wont to do. Instead, they use and thereby reinstate the authority of Shakespeare, which in turn gives the fragment a narrative valency: the preceding analyses show how they are integral to the plots even while seemingly standing outside them. They prove that for Indians, as much as for anyone else, Shakespeare is a valuable resource that they feel free to creatively dip into. Hence the sweeping assertions by Richard Burt, in his article, 'All that remains of Shakespeare in Indian film,' which especially focuses on what he calls the 'Shakespeare-play-within-the-Indian-film genre,' that such 'Indian films are unable to map successfully parallel temporal shifts from colonial Shakespeare to post-colonial Shakespeare' and that they use 'Shakespeare's obsolescence as a means of entering into world cinema' are not supported by the larger evidence.[11] Dismembering the iconic bard and appropriating the bits and pieces to one's own purpose are obvious acts of post-colonial opposition. And none of the above films managed an international or diasporic success—they were not designed for them.

Critical and theoretical estimation of the Shakespearean bit/fragment/allusion, particularly of the intercultural, has been in a ferment; while fragmentation is usually celebrated now, the field is not without contestation. Richard Burt is a central figure in this: he was one of the first to speak for the fragmentary Shakespeare in the digital medium, for 'Schlockspeare,' as he terms it. He is also the only one who has given attention to the Shakespeare citations and spin-offs in

Indian films. He points out how the changed dynamics of film circulation through digitalization and globalization have not been matched in film criticism. He argues that we need to detach the digital both from the authenticity debate and from the historicist perspectives of location. With migration, diaspora and the transnationality of film, the opposition between the local and the global is breaking down, he insists. Hence for him, the 'local' in the Indian Shakespeare films is only 'an effect of cinematic framing' and since film is a transnational medium, the 'local' in his formulation is not so much a post-colonial speaking back but a 'global' speaking to. More interested in challenging post-colonial critical debates than in unpacking the local, he goes on to pronounce that in the Indian Shakespeare-play-within-the-film examples, the 'throwaway citation' is 'weak' with 'no sustained parallel between the characters in the film and the Shakespeare roles they perform or the lines they cite' and that 'the cinematic inset Shakespeare scenes... give us a diminished, fragmentary, even forgettable Shakespeare.'[12] Burt represents a position in extremis: while he is alert to rapidly changing forms of media and the necessity of critical regimes to keep up, he himself betrays an inability to deal with the modular binaries of a fragment, independent, yet connected. He reveals instead a liberal humanist nostalgia for a wholeness and completeness in his rejection of the Shakespearean fragment in Indian films. Albeit he focuses on different films than the ones discussed above, yet with views as Shakespeare as a 'vanishing mediator,' a 'kernel whose repression enables something else to be formulated'[13] he is bound to be unsympathetic to any 'expression' of the same kernel.

This reasoning further leads Burt to make other sweeping statements. In another essay, 'Shakespeare and Asia in Postdiasporic Cinemas: Spinoffs and Citations,' which again argues for the challenge to nation-states and identity politics by the diaspora, he comes to the conclusion that 'the difference between Hollywood and Bollywood is being dissolved' and that 'Bollywood is a sign of transnational hybridity.' He goes on to proclaim that 'Shakespeare has become almost inescapable in the Bollywood film' and the 'Indian filmmakers targeting international audiences find Shakespeare appropriation unavoidable.'[14] Burt's arguments have been reproduced at some length to underline the difficulties in achieving an interpretative balance. They need correctives: despite globalization, the local has not been obliterated; in fact, it can be argued that it is constitutive of the global. Vishal Bhardwaj's Shakespeare trilogy (*Maqbool*,

Omkara, and *Haider*), which has attracted substantial international attention, is deeply rooted in local cultures. Further, if diaspora has unsettled boundaries and created hybridities, Shakespearean migrations too must be conceded to have a similar effect.

Some hard facts too need reiterating here. Firstly, the term 'Bollywood' is a deeply contested media-driven convenience that is rejected by most stalwarts of the industry. The growth, development, styles, and genres of Indian films as a whole have been vastly different from Hollywood, despite the huge transnational influences. The Indian film industry is impelled to be responsive to indigenous tastes to be able to survive and be commercially successful. And it has continued in its own idiosyncratic modes, despite some crossover examples in recent times. Indian films as a whole have a steady market in the Middle-East, parts of Africa, South Asia, the Far East too, and of course amongst the Indian diaspora in UK, USA, Europe, and Australia. As far as the Indian Shakespeare film or film with references to Shakespeare is concerned, it is a niche area and not quite the 'inescapable mode' that Burt seems to think. The filmography appended to the collection of essays, *Shakespeare and Indian Cinemas: 'local habitations'* (2018)[15] lists 115 diverse films based on Shakespeare produced by the fourteen Indian language film industries over almost a hundred years, a number and a corpus more substantial than many other national cinemas, yet a minute fraction in an industry that churns out almost two thousand films a year. The Indian Shakespeare film merits serious scholarly attention.

To return to the remains of Shakespeare in Indian films, they bubble up because Shakespeare has been ingested and absorbed in the cultural and intellectual memory of India. While the Shakespeare film that adapts a whole play testifies to the love for the poet, the film with Shakespearean bits and bites emerges out of another level of cultural backup. It is somewhat akin to the Brazilian cannibal theory of translation developed by Harold de Campos,[16] which argued that a subject culture devours the colonizing culture as an act of homage, and translation unsettles the primacy of the original by reproducing it in plural and reconfigured terms. It creates a transfusion, placing the colonized on par with the colonizer, who now lives through the infusion of new energy via the translator. Shakespeare is what his readers and users make out of him. Without them he remains inert, within the covers of a book, without the bite.

Notes

1. Douglas Lanier, 'Will of the People: Recent Shakespeare Film Parody and the Politics of Popularization,' in *A Concise Companion to Shakespeare on Screen*, edited by Diana E. Henderson (Malden, MA.: Blackwell Publishing, 2006), 177.
2. Richard Burt, 'To E – Or Not to E -?: Disposing of Schlockspeare in the Age of Digital Media,' Introduction to *Shakespeare After Mass Media*, edited by Richard Burt (New York: Palgrave, 2002), 8, 17, 25.
3. For a quantification and theorization of the Shakespeare quotes in print and digital media in India, see Thomas Kullmann, 'Shakespeare on the Internet: Global and South Asian Appropriations,' in *Asian Interventions in Global Shakespeare: 'All the World's His Stage.'*
4. See the filmography for more information on Shakespearean fragments in *Shakespeare and Indian Cinemas: 'Local Habitations,'* 319–32.
5. William Shakespeare, Sonnet 18 in *The Norton Shakespeare*, edited by Stephen Greenblatt, Walter Cohen, Jean E Howard and Katherine Eisaman Maus (New York: Norton, 1997), 1929.
6. Maurizio Calbi, *Spectral Shakespeares: Media Adaptations in the Twenty-First Century* (London: Palgrave Macmillan, 2013).
7. See Robert S. White, '*Eklavya*: Shakespeare meets the *Mahabharata*,' in *Shakespeare and Indian Cinemas.* White observes that 'Chopra clearly sees Shakespeare as a complex and ambiguous symbolic force in Indian culture, neither fully accommodated nor fully alienated, neither obsolescent nor fully localised, but instead suggesting plural and hybrid forms and associations entirely in tune with Indian cinema itself,' 47.
8. Mark Thornton Burnett, *Shakespeare and World Cinema* (Cambridge: Cambridge University Press, 2013), 56.
9. Lanier, 195.
10. Christy Desmet et al., 'Introduction' to *Shakespeare Not Shakespeare* (London: Palgrave Macmillan, 2017), 4.
11. Richard Burt, 'All That Remains of Shakespeare in Indian Film,' in *Shakespeare in Asia: Contemporary Performance*, edited by Dennis Kennedy and Yong Li Lan (Cambridge: Cambridge University Press, 2010), 74, 73.
12. Burt, 'All That Remains of Shakespeare in Indian film,' 74–75, 76–77.
13. Burt, 'All That Remains of Shakespeare in Indian film,' 74.
14. Richard Burt, 'Shakespeare and Asia in Postdiasporic Cinemas: Spinoffs and Citations,' in *Shakespeare, the Movie II: Popularizing the Plays on Film, TV, Video and DVD* (New York: Palgrave, 2002).
15. See 'Introduction,' in *Shakespeare and Indian Cinemas: 'Local Habitations'* for an overview on Shakespeare in Indian cinema.

16. Else Ribeiro Pires Vieira, 'Liberating Calibans: Readings of Antropofagia and Harold de Campos' Poetics of Transcreation,' in *Post-Colonial Translation: Theory and Practice*, edited by Susan Bassnett and Harish Trivedi (London: Routledge, 1999).

Works Cited

Burt, Richard. "To E – Or Not to E -?: Disposing of Schlockspeare in the Age of Digital Media." Introduction to *Shakespeare After Mass Media*, edited by Richard Burt. New York: Palgrave, 2002.

Burt, Richard. "Shakespeare and Asia in Postdiasporic Cinemas: Spinoffs and Citations." In *Shakespeare, the Movie II: Popularizing the Plays on Film, TV, Video and DVD*, edited by Richard Burt and Lynda Boose. New York: Routledge, 2003.

Burt, Richard. "All That Remains of Shakespeare in Indian Film." In *Shakespeare in Asia: Contemporary Performance*, edited by Dennis Kennedy and Young Li Lan. Cambridge: Cambridge University Press, 2010.

Calbi, Maurizio. *Spectral Shakespeares: Media Adaptations in the Twenty-First Century*. London: Palgrave Macmillan, 2013.

Desmet, Christy, Natalie Loper, and Jim Casey, editors. *Shakespeare Not Shakespeare*. London: Palgrave Macmillan, 2017.

Kullmann, Thomas. "Shakespeare on the Internet: Global and South Asian Appropriations." In *Asian Interventions in Global Shakespeare: 'All the World's His Stage*, edited by Poonam Trivedi, Paromita Chakravarti and Ted Motohashi. New York: Routledge, 2020.

Lanier, Douglas. "Will of the People: Recent Shakespeare Film Parody and the Politics of Popularization." In *A Concise Companion to Shakespeare on Screen*, edited by Diana E. Henderson. Malden, MA: Blackwell Publishing, 2006.

The Norton Shakespeare edited by Stephen Greenblatt, Walter Cohen, Jean E Howard and Katherine Eisaman Maus. New York: Norton, 1997.

Thornton Burnett, Mark. *Shakespeare and World Cinema*. Cambridge: Cambridge University Press, 2013.

Trivedi, Poonam, and Paromita Chakravarti, editors. *Shakespeare and Indian Cinemas: 'Local Habitations.'* New York: Routledge, 2018.

Trivedi, Poonam, Paromita Chakravarti, and Ted Motohashi, editors. *Asian Interventions in Global Shakespeare: 'All the World's His Stage.'* New York: Routledge, 2020.

Vieira, Else Ribeiro Pires. "Liberating Calibans: Readings of Antropofagia and Harold de Campos' Poetics of Transcreation." In *Post-Colonial Translation: Theory and Practice*, edited by Susan Bassnett and Harish Trivedi. London: Routledge, 1999.

White, Robert S. "*Eklavya*: Shakespeare Meets the *Mahabharata*." In *Shakespeare and Indian Cinemas*, edited by Poonam Trivedi and Paromita Chakravarti. New York: Routledge, 2018.

CHAPTER 6

What "Doth Grace for Grace and Love for Love Allow"? Recreations of the Balcony Scenes on Brazilian Screens

Aimara da Cunha Resende

"Tupy or not tupy, that is the question."[1] When this sentence appeared in Oswald de Andrade's *Manifesto Antropófago* (Anthropophagic Manifesto), in the wake of the Week of Modernist Art, held in São Paulo in 1922, the idea was to use one of Shakespeare's most famous sayings as an ironic illustration of what was meant by the Brazilian Modernists' concept of artistic anthropophagy. The Manifesto was published in the first number of *Revista Antropofágica* (Journal of Anthropophagy) in May 1928, when Oswald de Andrade dated it as: "Ano 374 da Deglutição do Bispo Sardinha" (Year 374 from the Swallowing of Bishop Sardinha).[2] Like Bishop Sardinha being eaten by the indigenous people the Portuguese found when they "discovered" Brazil, Hamlet's famous sentence was *swallowed* by the Brazilian modernist writer and had its English characteristics and canonical value conflated through *digestion*

A. da Cunha Resende (✉)
Federal University of Minas Gerais, Belo Horizonte, Minas Gerais, Brazil

A. A. Joubin and V. Bladen (eds.), *Onscreen Allusions to Shakespeare*, Global Shakespeares, https://doi.org/10.1007/978-3-030-93783-6_6

with a genuine Brazilian word taken from the Tupi language. The conflated saying then becomes, not the canonical "To be or not to be," but the foreign-looking "Tupy or not Tupy," now a new construct since *i*—present in the word *tupi*, the name of both a Brazilian indigenous tribe and its language—becomes *y* in the newly created word. Shakespeare's protagonist's doubt in relation to life and death is turned into the aim of Brazilian artists—Andrade's *concoction* ironically nudging the Eurocentric socio-political-artistic society of the twentieth century, not only in Brazil but all over the world.

Literary Anthropophagy and Brazilian TV Scraps from Shakespeare

Keeping in mind Andrade's theory of anthropophagic literature, later on extended to art in general, this text discusses some Brazilian appropriations for the screen, *scraps* of Shakespeare's plays. Andrade's theory has as its staple the custom among some of the Brazilian tribes to eat their conquered adversary so as to assimilate his qualities such as courage, strength, loyalty to his group. Inserted in mystical rituals, such eating, communally practiced by the victors, would make them better, as the eaters would have their former characteristics merged with the newly assimilated ones, turning them into stronger, more capable men and warriors. For this to be accomplished, the person to be eaten must have positive traits. This demand, in literary appropriation, carries with it the acceptance of high quality in the text to be appropriated, taking into account its canonical position though not considering it unique, untouchable.

According to the Brazilian Modernists, Brazilian art should not ignore the world's canonical works but assimilate them, digest their qualities, and dispense with their weaknesses. Native art would then represent its own culture, identified and nurtured in its roots as well as in canonical foreign works, offering a digested output despite, but also partially due to, the presence of foreign elements.

Shakespeare's *Romeo and Juliet* was *devoured* by the screen constructs here discussed which, as often happens in appropriations of the playwright especially by the little screen, uses only some of the best-known scenes in the source text. The production must use well-known *scraps* because the audience it caters for is mainly made of lower- and middle-class workers and housewives. After a day's work, such audiences look for light entertainment, that will bring relaxation through laughter and identification with situations and people in their everyday world, without concern for intellectual commitment.

Culture

I use the term *culture* as a signifying system of representation inherent in a certain social order or community, with its various forms of communication, production, and reproduction, that is, *all* its "signifying practices."[3] In every recreation of Shakespeare's work—whether translation, play, novel, quotations, opera or jazz piece, advertising text, comic magazine—there is the metamorphosing influence of the target culture and the individualized stance of its appropriator. This kind of deviation is partly responsible for Shakespeare's *immortality*: re-readings of his work not only secure his status in the canon but also allow his texts to be adapted to new forms and temporally replaced constructions. Media that had not been used before to transmit his plays or poems have taken their place among the only sites previously accepted as proper to the rendering and/or discussion of his canonized plays: the stage and the critical survey.

Shakespeare's ubiquitous presence throughout time and space may be seen as the result of an imperialist imposition of cultural values, but it is also due to the multifarious viewpoints, the rich conjunction of differences and similarities, and the relativistic stance that permeates his work, reflecting/refracting mankind. As Gary Taylor says, "He embodied mutability."[4] Such mutability can be measured by the innumerable offshoots that abound all over the world in various countries and in many different languages.

The global afterlife of Shakespeare transcends the binary of domestic and foreign works. It has given rise to artistic creativity and a wide range of uses of Shakespeare's works. In his discussion of the contemporary need of understanding the importance of tolerance towards diversity, Claude Lévi-Strauss states:

> The need to preserve the diversity of cultures in a world threatened by monotony and uniformity certainly has not escaped international institutions. They also understand that to reach such an aim it will not suffice to give life to local traditions and offer some truce to the past. Diversity is what must be safeguarded, not the historical content stamped on it by each

> period of time and which no epoch is able to perpetuate beyond itself. It is therefore necessary to encourage the secret potentialities, awaken every vocation for communal life that history has kept in store; it is also necessary to be ready to face without surprise, repugnance, or revolt whatever these new social forms of expression may offer that has not been used. Tolerance is not a contemplative spreading of indulgences between what has been and what is. It is a dynamic attitude that consists in foreseeing, understanding and promoting that which wishes to be. The diversity of human cultures is behind us, around us, before us. The only requirement we may have in relation to it (a requirement that creates corresponding duties for each individual) is that it will come true through forms in which each one becomes some sort of contribution to the greater generosity of the others.[5]

Rewritings in languages entirely alien to Shakespeare's native English have given new voice to Shakespeare's and our contemporary cultural values. "Dissemination of his work in foreign languages," says Anston Bosman, "began in his lifetime, when so-called English players travelled the Continent, assembling multi-national troupes, mounting polyglot productions and seeding translations in European vernaculars."[6] He echoes Lévi-Strauss:

> The Shakespeare we confront today has been globalized beyond the confines of any single language or territory. As migrants and media exchange his works back and forth across national borders, a simple opposition between 'domestic' and 'foreign' Shakespeare grows ever less convincing, and to set down his fortunes country by country is to tour the empty pavilions of an abandoned world's fair.[7]

Globalized *Romeo and Juliet*

Among Shakespeare's plays, *Romeo and Juliet* has been one of the most intensely adapted texts, one of the preferred sources for unaccountably diversified appropriations or anthropophagic recreations. Mark Thornton Burnett writes:

> The play strikes a chord with cultural systems and nation-states characterized by an uneven relation to modernity and, seen within such a framework, its specifically early modern dimensions do not appear incongruous. Defining moments in *Romeo and Juliet* are smoothly accommodated within the particular storylines of world cinema where context

> means issues of individual will and community connection are invariably put to the fore.[8]

The balcony scenes in this play have attracted artists on different fields and at various times all over the world. As an iconic text, these scenes have also populated Brazilian screens, large and small. But cultural constraints have also left their marks on these appropriations and have turned them into what Bruce Smith calls *residual* constructs.[9] Shakespeare is, and is not, there. As an icon, he can be discerned by a knowing audience; and as a residual construction, he appears diffused, unrecognized, for an unknowing audience. "For an adaptation to be successful in its own right," Linda Hutcheon asserts, "it must be so for both knowing and unknowing audiences."[10] She further states that:

> Nevertheless, it is probably easier for an adapter to forge a relationship with an audience that is not overly burdened with affection or nostalgia for the adapted text. Without foreknowledge, we are more likely to greet a film version simply as a new film, not as an adaptation at all. The director, therefore, will have greater freedom—and control.[11]

Quoting John Ellis, she continues: "If the adapted work is a canonical one, we may not actually have direct experience of it, but may rely on 'a generally circulated cultural memory.'"[12]

Shakespeare in Brazil

His presence in Brazilian culture is therefore a matter of hybridism rather than of sacred permanence. Discovered in the same century as Shakespeare was born, far from England, Brazil had no links with English or British art and education, and Brazilian artists have never had any obligation to maintain the sacralized aura of the Shakespeareana found in Anglophone countries. Added to this, the traits found in Brazilian national identity would necessarily invest the products inspired by or appropriating Shakespeare's work with a *new habitation* and also often a new *name*.

Any discussion of significant Brazilian appropriations of *Romeo and Juliet* must start from the fact that in them one finds not only the crossroads of culture,[13] but also the crossroads *within* a culture, due to the miscegenation found in Brazil's population and the realization that the subject implies awareness of its vast territorial extension and extremely varied geographic, economic, educational, and folkloric conditions.

Products for the Brazilian cinema have not escaped this challenge, and, from time to time, new appropriations have appeared. With the advent of television, Shakespeareana was slowly being introduced into the Brazilian homes, especially in the *novelas* (a term I prefer to the American *soap opera*, as the two genres differ, *novelas* having their own defined structure). I say it was being introduced because, differently from what happens in English-speaking countries, the Bard is not known by the average Brazilian, and, as already said, those who watched novelas belonged at first to the lower socio-economic demographics and watched TV at the end of an exhausting work day, with the aim of relaxing, unconcerned with more erudite productions.

Discussing the link between ballads and Shakespeare's plays, Smith states: "Ballads did not *record* performances; they *perpetuated* them. They enabled performances to happen again and again as new performers learned the words and took up the story."[14] The same is true of the Brazilian appropriations discussed here.

The "residual," or part of it, especially the balcony scenes, is there, although it is likely that most of the people watching the production on the screen will not necessarily be able to recognize its source; they will, however, have an idea of what has happened, even if not entirely, which is perpetuated despite the uncertainty of precisely where, bringing the emotional experience the new construct aims to create. "It is a curious coincidence, to say the least, that films offer the same kind of intensely personal experience that ballads do, in a medium that is no less socially inclusive and crassly commercial."[15]

Besides the novelas—which I will discuss later on—there appeared on the Record network a series of shorts recreating the play. One of them appropriates the first balcony scene. Starring well-known comic actor and actresses (Ronald Golias as Romeo, Hebe Camargo as Juliet, and Nair Bello as the nurse), this appropriation aimed at making the audience laugh, unconcerned with Shakespeare's text. The comedy arose from the actor's behaviour, topical puns, previously established body language, and from the actresses' use of topical expressions and constant laughter. This sketch should be seen as typical of the appeal well-known performers and a *residual* construct have to audiences that are not particularly well educated or artistically trained and seek entertainment that makes them laugh and relax with no other corollary satisfaction.

This short film was broadcast in 1968.[16] In terms of the adaptation-appropriation continuum, it arguably constitutes appropriation, rather than adaptation. There is no continued plot, the two *households both alike in dignity* appear, but their *ancient grudge* never *break[s] to new mutiny*; there is only topical fun irrupting from a well-known story recreated by well-known performers to please an audience unaware of the cultural capital called Shakespeare. In TV shorts, comedy becomes a strong way to create such an experience in a new kind of audience; no more the *erudite* author or director catering to *cultured minds*, but the evanescent content and language of everyday life embodied in native performers bringing to the fore quotidian situations and easy laughter, often rooted in the satirical ridicule of politicians and people from the higher social stratum.

In the 1968 production, the first scene begins with the Nurse coming to the balcony and, looking at the sky, exclaiming, in typical popular language: "*Porca miseria*, what a lovely night! And the air is cool!"[17] She then calls out: "My little Julieta!" No answer is heard. She calls twice again, the third time repeating the expression in Italian, which subtly suggests the setting of the source text, "*Porca miseria*, why are you taking so long?" As the thirty-year-old Hebe Camargo playing a thirteen-year-old Juliet appears on the balcony, both actresses start laughing. They then talk about Romeo, and the Nurse tells Juliet what people are saying about him. In her story, she recaptures the body picture she draws in the primary text after she had been sent to him by Juliet: "Though his face be better than any man's, yet his legs excel all men's, and for a hand and a foot and a body, though they be not to be talked on, yet they are past compare" (2.4.38–41). In the TV offshoot, the Nurse speaks of the young man's bodily parts in these words: "Everybody is saying that he is very good looking, that he still has the same head, he still has the same size, he still has the same hair, he is still gorgeous. And do you know what they are saying? That his legs are the most beautiful legs in Verona." The issue of this Brazilian Romeo's legs will return later on, during the lovers' conversation.

Another *residual* moment in this short is the famous speech about *th'inconstant moon*: "Juliet: O, swear not by the moon, th'inconstant moon,/ That monthly changes in her circled orb,/ Lest that thy love prove likewise variable" (2.1.151–3), when Hebe/Julieta says to herself, not to Romeu: "I wish I were as swift as the wind to meet you. Oh, Romeo, my Romeo, I'm burning with my love for you, my beautiful Romeo! I beg the heavens, the heavens, not to let your love for me be like the moon that changes every month. This new love surprises me." In this passage, a lyrical moment in the source text is turned into a comic recreation, especially as the TV heroine laughs almost uncontrollably while speaking the enamoured words, to the point of Bello/Nurse holding her hands and telling her to calm down, to which she replies, still laughing: "I'm so nervous…" Here, the appropriating text also inverts the roles of the lovers since, in Shakespeare, Romeo, not Juliet, is the one to have the new love.

Romeu/Golias arrives in the yard under the balcony and as Julieta/Hebe comes, he asks her why she has taken so long to appear, and she replies that she was "inside." He moves a bit away from the balcony, saying: "I understand…But you did take long…" with the *double entendre* suggesting she was in the bathroom. The innuendo is later taken up again when, during their conversation, Julieta says she's going back inside. Romeu, surprised, immediately asks: "What, again, Juliet?" The idea is now very clear to the audience. Later on, Julieta speaks of her beloved's legs: "Your legs, Romeo…" But he abruptly stops her: "You know that too," to which she replies: "They're the most beautiful legs in Italy." But he does not seem to hear her and nervously moves around, saying: "I'll kill him! I'll kill that damned fellow! Somebody has seen me naked and is spreading it around." Julieta tries to calm him down as the soundtrack from Zeffirelli's highly successful film of the same year is heard in the background. One is never sure if there is anything wrong with his legs, but the suggestion of something wrong with the size of his penis looms in the air.

The scene ends with Romeu kissing a ribbon from one of Julieta's braids that he had seized when trying to climb up the balcony to kiss her. He seizes the ribbon and in an outburst of passion slides down with the ribbon still in his hand. Juliet, laughing, tells him to keep it as a souvenir. He caresses it and kisses it, and the scene is over.

In 1990, a full version of *Romeo and Juliet* was broadcast, this time by the SBT network, using the same performers. Written by Carlos Alberto de Nóbrega and directed by Hélio Lopes, this comic recreation of Shakespeare's tragedy explicitly acknowledges its debt to the playwright in its presentation as *The True Story of Romeo and Juliet, based on William Shakespeare*. Although the title stresses fidelity, this recreation retains the love story and the familial conflict—though the cause of the conflict, unknown in the source, is clear in the Brazilian appropriation—emphasizing the current political situation in Brazil, right after Fernando Collor de Mello won the election for President against the working-class candidate Luiz Inácio Lula da Silva. It has the two households clearly divided: the Capuletos are strong members of the Labour Party (PT), whose leader is Lula, and the Montéquios are followers of President Collor. As Julieta says, she can never hope to marry Romeu, for her father is a "friend of Lula's, a buddy of Erundina's, and a partner of Suplicy's." These three politicians were the leaders of the Labour Party at the time. The Nurse, for her part, reminds Julieta of the fact that Romeu's father "has lent *the man* his jet-ski to enjoy the lake on weekends, has lent *the man* his special clothes to break the sound barrier, and has introduced *the man* to Zélia."[18] *The man* she alludes to is Collor. Julieta cannot accept the fact that she and Romeu must part because of political hatred and tries to convince both her and Romeu's parents to change their positions.

There are many allusions to the political moment and, as usual, Golias's famous mime causes laughter in both the audience and the two actresses playing the heroine and her nurse. The balcony scene turns into two *serestas*[19] with two famous pop stars (Aguinaldo Rayol and Ronnie Von) doing the songs; it continues to the end with the political criticism for those able to perceive it, and simple entertainment with a lot of sexual puns for those who watch it without any interest in what is going on in politics: "...the meaning that individuals give to media products varies according to each one's bringing up and social conditions in such a way that the same message may be understood in various ways in different contexts."[20] Thus, Shakespeare's *Romeo and Juliet* in SBT's 1990 production uses the playwright's cultural value at a diminished level while at the same time comically focussing on politics and sex, the meaning of the message depending on who is watching the short.

Brazilian TV Novelas

In Brazilian TV novelas, Shakespeare's play had ever broader representations, first, through quotations ranging from parodies or suggestions of certain scenes, and eventually in 1980, in an appropriation of the whole play on Globo TV's *Caso Especial* ("Special Program"). This *Romeu e Julieta* was directed by Paulo Afonso Grisolli and adapted by Walter George Durst, with the young Fábio Júnior and Lucélia Santos as the main protagonists.

Created under the dictatorship, it subtly dared to allude to the system, in its indirect deployment of power, with the representation of the police and the Catholic Church. In this appropriation, the feudal enmity in the source text is transmuted into social-economical rivalry, not only in the unexplained (as in Shakespeare) animosity between the protagonists' families, but more violently in the behaviour of students in the two rival *repúblicas*,[21] some, like Caveira/Paris, attending the renowned Engineering School, and others, like Romeu, studying at the less important Pharmacy School.

Inserted in the appropriating text, Shakespeare's language sparkles, but always covered with national traits, as with the first words the lovers exchange: not a sonnet, but a blend of lines from its source, heard in the new scenery, a república for young women, first in the ballroom and later on in the backyard. Recreating Shakespeare's first balcony scene in a carnivalized form, it juxtaposes a sort of pastoral visual construction, masquerade, and the canonical text. The occasion was said to be a party for girls only, which would allow the young women who belonged to traditional families of the town to participate, since their parents would let them go, believing that it really was a girls only gathering. But the male students, wearing masks and women's clothes, manage to get in, with the consent of the female participants.

This is the lover's second meeting. They first meet during a religious procession, when, to win a bet against the young men from the rival república, Romeu suddenly enters the procession naked, to the utter dismay of the priest and abhorrence of the others in the religious event. His opponents lock the door of his república, preventing his escape. Noticing his predicament, Juliet takes the mantle covering the statue of the Virgin Mary being carried and throws it to him. Romeo covers himself, looks at her and just says: "God bless you." Later on, during the party at the girls' república, and wearing masks (the masks and fancy-clothes suggesting the party at the Capulets') they meet again, and after exchanging a few words of feigned anger, go to the inner garden where, after having used speeches taken from Shakespeare's text in the first balcony scene, they make love for the first time. Among other citations from the source text, a few lines spoken by the lovers at this moment are taken from the balcony scene. Romeo's first line after Benvolio and Mercutio leave him, and as he sees that Juliet appears on the balcony, "He jests at scars that never felt a wound" (2.1.44), is repeated in Grisolli's recreation as well as Juliet's: "What man art thou that, thus bescreened in night,/So stumblest on my counsel?" (2.1: 95–6). Later on, she says:

"My bounty is as boundless as the sea,/My love as deep; the more I give to thee,/The more I have, for both are infinite" (2.1.176–8).

The carnivalesque, joyful relativity, and mixture of genres in the crowning/uncrowning of a canonized text are beautifully created by Grisolli, as if to illustrate Mikhail Bakhtin's point, when he discusses the genres of the serio comical and places them in the realm of carnivalesque literature:

Characteristic of these genres are a multi-toned narration, the mixing of high and low, serious and comic; they make wide use of inserted genres—letters, found manuscripts, *retold dialogues, parodies on the high genres, parodically reinterpreted citations*; in some of them, we observe a mixing of prosaic and poetic speech, living dialects and jargons (and in the Roman stage, direct bilingualism as well) *are introduced, and various authorial masks make their appearance.* Alongside the representing word, there appears the *represented* word; in certain genres, a leading role is played by the double-voiced word. And what appears here, as a result, is a radically new relationship to the word as the material for literature.[22]

In the case of this 1980 production of *Romeu e Julieta*, I would add that the double voice is present not only in the dialogue of the "star-crossed lovers" in the backyard, during the party, but also in the visual aspects, since they wear carnival costumes and, even more, are intertwined with the scenery, where culture and nature mix and exchange aspects. It is in a surrealistic environment that the two lovers, masked and dressed in white fancy-dress, slowly move among tropical plants.

Shakespeare's play is also found in two novelas of the Globo TV network, *Pedra Sobre Pedra* (Stone over Stone), of 1992, and *Fera Ferida* (Wounded Beast), of 1993. These appropriations evoked the socio-political atmosphere of clans in rural Brazilian areas, when the *Coronéis* (Colonels)[23] had absolute sway over the majority of the population.

Pedra Sobre Pedra, written by Aguinaldo Silva, Ricardo Linhares, and Ana Maria Moretzsohn, under the general direction of Paulo Ubiratan, follows Shakespeare's story, as Marina/Juliet and Leonardo/Romeo live the same experience of love that her mother and his father had but were unsuccessful in, while their children end up happily married. After all, this is a novela and admits of no tragedy.

Dialogism is found here, when, before performing the roles of an Angel and the Virgin Mary, in a religious play after which Leonardo/Romeo and Marina/Juliet will be secretly wed by the local priest, they meet in a solitary hut, in the wilderness of the *Chapada*

Diamantina.[24] At this moment, the novela is invested with Shakespeare's prestige:

Leonardo:	I love you, you know that?
Marina:	(gently) No... You've never told me that before. Or have you? If you have, I have forgotten.
Leonardo:	Then I will shout it, very loud, so that the whole world can hear it! [shouts] I love Marina Pontes
Marina:	You're mad! What if someone hears you?
Leonardo:	The lark is the only one that hears, my Juliet, and it will not tell anyone.
Marina:	Two days... Two days and our *Romeo and Juliet* will have a happy end, against everything and everybody.[25]

As the lark that greets the morning in the allusive balcony scene is not a Brazilian bird, and the young lovers in the offshoot explicitly name Shakespeare's play, there is no doubt about intentional borrowing. Later on, before the religious performance, and still echoing the primary text, Leonardo/Romeo says to his beloved: I'm ready for the feast. Will I have only the role of the Guiding Angel, or will I also have that of… Romeo?[26]

In 1993, another novela appeared on Globo TV, with general direction of Paulo Ubiratan and again written by Aguinaldo Silva, Ricardo Linhares, and Ana Maria Moretzsohn: *Fera Ferida* (Wounded Beast). This production conflates *Hamlet* and *Romeo and Juliet*. Dealing with prototypes of dishonest politicians, corrupted and corrupting military leaders, and various types of rural areas in Brazil, it also recreates the balcony scene, this time inserting it at a moment when the two young lovers are leaving for a party offered to "Romeo/Hamlet," a new arrival in the small town where the girl lives. Here, part of Romeo's and Juliet's exchanges in the source text is appropriated. Flanel, the Brazilian Romeo/Hamlet in this case, does not wish to be recognized because his father had been murdered by the girl's father, who is now the mayor. The young Flanel had been taken from the town as a child and has now returned to avenge his father. But he falls in love with the girl, Linda Inês, and they are now leaving together for the party. Here, the Brazilian construct appropriates Juliet's speech in act 2, scene 1, but is mostly spoken by Flanel, not Linda Inês, who in fact has only two lines from it:

Linda Inês: As we have no priest, and I cannot yet sign my name as Mrs. Raimundo Fla/(here she stops). I had forgotten that that's not your real name...Don't you think we are close enough now for you to let me know your name, even though it may sound terrible?

Flanel: (speaking with exaggeration) "What's in a name?" It will be neither a hand, nor a foot, arm or face, or any part of one's body.

Linda Inês: Is your name perchance Romeo?...

Flanel: What's in a name? That which we call rose by any other name wouldn't smell as sweet? Thus Juliet, that is, Linda Inês, if she were not called Linda Inês, would not keep the perfection that is her own even without such a name?

At this point, some more lines are inserted and their conversation ends with Linda Inês saying: "Throw away your name and as a substitute for it that is no part of yourself have the whole of me."[27] They kiss, and the scene ends.

In the Brazilian cinema, two examples are noteworthy: the anthological scene in a 1949 *chanchada* (Brazilian musical comedy of the 1930s and 1940s that generally launched Carnival songs)[28] *Carnaval no Fogo,* directed by Watson Macedo, where only the balcony scene was performed as a parody that ridiculed the dominant cultural elite and protested against the prevailing presence of American films in the country. Two of the greatest Brazilian comic actors, Oscarito and Grande Otelo (the latter a Negro, an accomplished comedian and dramatic actor), are shown in the film rehearsing the balcony scene as a presentation to the director of the shows in the luxurious Copacabana Palace Hotel. The lines of the source text are parodied by these actors, poking fun at highbrow intellectuals and film critics who were openly opposed to the chanchadas. But in this reflexive process of transposition, the cultural icon William Shakespeare was introduced to the lower classes with fun, and artistically validated to be placed among the canonical works of performance. The predominant cultural values were once more put to the test.

Fran Teague's statement about musicals also applies to screen appropriations such as this one:

> The relation each musical has to its Shakespearean base is crucial: the show employs Shakespeare for the sake of incongruity, prestige, or whatever, but simultaneously erases him to create enough aesthetic distance for success.
> [...] Shakespeare becomes a beard, a subterfuge that permits the show to get on with what it really wants to do (i.e. amuse and sanction naughtiness) by misdirection.[29]

In *Carnaval no Fogo*, Serafim and Anselmo, respectively, performed by Oscarito and Grande Otelo, are menial workers at the hotel, and Serafim wants to become an actor in its permanent drama group. As the rehearsal begins, Romeu/Oscarito enters the yard and literally speaks the words found in Shakespeare: "He jests at scars that never felt a wound" (2.1.44). Carnivalization then transgresses the canon, in a transvestite Juliet at a time when there were no longer boy actors playing women, and in the focus on race, since this Juliet is a black man. The new construct appropriates the lines from the primary text without concern for "fidelity," when, before the heroine appears at the balcony, Romeu/Oscarito delivers Shakespeare's hero's speech in his reply to Juliet's question on how he had arrived there: "With love's light wings did I o'erperch these walls,/ For stony limits cannot hold love out" [2,1:109–10]. He then returns to the moment, in the primary text, when Juliet "enters above": "But soft, what light through yonder window breaks?" [2,1:45]. At this point, everyday language is introduced: "Will it be Juliet? Or won't she come?" He then whistles, and another whistle is heard offstage, responding to his, to which he exclaims: "It is she! It can only be she! Oh, my love, oh, my beloved!" and he continues, still reproducing the source: "Arise, fair sun, and kill the envious moon,/Who is already sick and pale with grief..." [2,1:47–8]. Julieta appears, exclaiming: "Ay me!" From this moment on, colloquial language and contemporary context take over, interspersed with the reproduction of words from the source text. In an ironical criticism of the American 1948 film *Johnny Belinda*, with Jane Wyman, and directed by Jean Negulesco, whose heroine is dumb, which was a hit in Brazil at the time, Romeu, still romantically reproducing the source text, says to Julieta: "She speaks. Speak again, bright angel." Grande Otelo/Julieta, not knowing what to say, asks him: "But what am I gonna say, Romeo?" and he nervously replies: "Say anything! Don't just stand there imitating Belinda!"

The well-known lines, in act 2, scene 2, about *th'inconstant moon*, are also recreated here, when Romeo proposes to swear by the moon:

"Lady, I will swear by the splendor of the moon..." In this appropriation, in Juliet's dismissal of the moon as a witness, carnivalization permeates the source lines "O swear not by the moon, th'inconstant moon,/That monthly changes in her circled orb,/ Lest that thy love prove likewise variable" [2,1:152–4]. The canonical words are transmuted to the double meaning implicit in Macedo's production: "Don't swear by the moon, th'inconstant moon that is always changing quarters"; the word *quarto* (quarters) is used for "circled orb." As in Portuguese *quarto* means both "the quarter moon"—"waning quarter" and "waxing quarter"—and "bedroom," the *double entendre* engenders a bawdy reply. There are several such moments in this scene, but space does not allow me to comment on them.

After years of success with his comic books and his characters such as Mônica and Cebolinha, Maurício de Souza decided to create his own version of *Romeo and Juliet*. In 1978, the play *Mônica e Cebolinha no Mundo de Romeu e Julieta (Mônica and Cebolinha in Romeo's and Juliet's World)* was produced. After its huge success, in 1979, the Bandeirantes TV network turned it into a film to celebrate Children's Day.

It states in the credits of the film that it is a play "by William Shakespeare, adapted by Yara Maura" under the "supervision of Maurício de Souza" and starts with a group of dancers substituting the chorus, singing a samba whose lyrics tell of the immortal love story. In this parody, Mônica becomes "Monicapuleto," Cebolinha is "Romeu Motéquio Cebolinha"; the nurse, embodied in Magali, Souza's gluttonous girl character, is called Amagali (joining *ama*, the Portuguese word for nurse, and the girl's name, Magali). All the other characters from Mônica's gang also have their names transmuted into hybrid constructions.

Cebolinha is a naïve boy who cannot pronounce the "r"—he changes it for "l"—and is easily duped; Mônica is an overbearing little girl that terrifies every boy who knows her with her notorious toy rabbit which seems to have something hard and heavy inside it, and she instantly beats her "enemies" with it if they interfere with her plans or contest her ideas.

The balcony scene is comically enacted with Monicapuleto coming to the balcony and exclaiming: "Oh, Romeo, Romeo! Romeo!!! Where are you?" The boy answers from the yard, but she cannot spot him and keeps asking, to which he "soliloquises": "Is she blind?" The girl finally sees him and tells him to climb a kind of rope made from plants, which he is unable to do. She then impatiently orders him to come up to her room, to which he replies: "How can I come up, bossy lady? Do you think I am Spider Man?" in a link with other comics. In his attempt to climb, and with Monicapuleto shaking the vegetal rope, he falls and becomes upset. As she thinks he is talking too loud and may awaken her father, she tells him so, but he does not hear and she speaks louder and louder: "With such noise you'll wake my father." The word in Portuguese for "wake," *acorda*, sounds like the word *corda* (rope). When he hears that, Cebolinha remembers that he can use the rope and asks Monicapuleto to throw it to him. But as she takes too long lowering it, and he keeps telling her to lower more and more, they wake her father, who, offstage, asks who is there. Cebolinha then imitates a bird warbling. Monicapuleto's father says it is the lark heralding the morning, to which Cebolinha, still pretending to be a bird, explains: "No, it is the nightingale, bird of the red dawn." Julieta's father says he may then sleep five minutes longer. Realizing they can no longer talk, the girl tells Romeu/Cebolinha to meet her next morning at the church. To his question: "But why the church?" she replies: "For us to get married." Puzzled, the boy asks: "But who was talking about getting married?" She answers: "*We* were." And goes inside, closing the door behind her.

Shakespeare is overtly referred to here, both visually, with the image of a large book with his name on its cover, and verbally, when, at Monicapuleto's refusal to have a tragedy interfering with her wedding, Cebolinha says to her: "Shakespeale is like that, Mônica. Evelything is vely lomantic, vely beautiful, but vely sad…".

As this is a film for children, it is expected to have a happy ending, which occurs when Monicapuleto decides not to die or let her husband die. With the help of the infallible rabbit, she forces everyone around her to agree on her decision and the film ends with everybody happily dancing. Like Maurício de Sousa's characters, all the lovers here discussed, as Brazilians, might rather dance the samba than have their lives crossed by the stars.

From the *scraps* here discussed, as examples of Brazilian transmutations,[30] when Shakespeare's *Romeo and Juliet* enters people's homes in the various parts of this continent-sized country by way of television programmes meant solely for entertainment, it nevertheless subtly reproduces the generally unknown source text, but recreates it in such a way that the hybrid constructions bring with them the national trait of *joyful relativity* characteristic of carnivalized literature.[31] You may then ask: "Is this Shakespeare?" or "Where is Shakespeare"? I would reply that the English playwright, now global cultural capital, due to his exuberant, multiple voices, resonates in these new constructs, and so anthropophagously becomes, so to speak, a *Twentieth Century Brazilian Shakespeare*. Together, irony and laughter reproduce both the source text and the everyday life of the audience of the foreign culture. Unaware of the play's deep issues, of its subtle considerations of arguable values found in both Shakespeare's time and country and in those of contemporary Brazil, this audience may be able to introject them and give them a new voice. After all, do we really need a *brand*, is the canon so untouchable? Shakespeare is present despite the new robes, and the new production can maintain his main objectives: to entertain and subliminally provoke deeper thoughts through a re-enactment of life, with interlinked love and war. Although not signed by the master, does not the new construct bring to the fore the issues he probably desired to be considered? So... "What's in a name"?

Notes

1. Oswald Andrade, "Manifesto Antropófago," in *Vanguarda Europeia e Modernismo Brasileiro* (Petrópolis: Vozes, 1973), 232.
2. Andrade, "Manifesto Antropófago," 232.
3. On the concept of culture, see Raymond Williams, *1981, 1982.*
4. Gary Taylor, *Reinventing Shakespeare* (Oxford: Oxford University Press, 1989), 4.
5. Claude Lévy-Strauss, *Raça e História*, translated by Inácio Canelas (Lisboa: Editorial Presença, 1996), 66–67.
6. Anston Bosman, "Shakespeare and Globalization," in *The New Cambridge Companion to Shakespeare*, 2nd edition, edited by Margreta de Grazia and Stanley Wells (Cambridge: Cambridge University Press, 2010), 286.
7. Bosman, "Shakespeare and Globalization," 286.
8. Mark Thornton Burnett, *Shakespeare and World Cinema* (Cambridge: Cambridge University Press, 2013), 196.
9. Bruce R. Smith, "Shakespeare's Residuals," in *Shakespeare and Elizabethan Popular Culture,* The Arden Critical Companions, edited by Stuart Gillespie and Neil Rhodes (London: Thomson Learning, 2006), 93–217.
10. Lynda Hutcheon and Syobhan O'Flynn, *A Theory of Adaptation*. 2nd edition (London and New York: Routledge, 2013), 122.
11. Hutcheon and O'Flaerty, *A Theory of Adaptation*, 121.
12. Hutcheon and O'Flaerty, *A Theory of Adaptation*, 122.
13. Patrice Pavis, *Theatre at the Crossroads of Culture*, translated by Loren Kruger (London: Routledge, 1992).
14. Smith, "Shakespeare's Residuals," 194–95.

15. Smith, "Shakespeare's Residuals," 217.
16. Due to loss of archives, the name of both author and scriptwriter is unknown.
17. This and all other translated quotes into Portuguese are mine.
18. Zélia Cardoso de Mello, Minister of Economy during Collor's government (1990–1992). She was responsible for the notorious "Plano Collor" that confiscated Brazilian people's savings for the government to use for eighteen months and to be paid back later on. Such procedure brought tremendous bankruptcy in the country and ended up with Collor's impeachment in 1992.
19. *Serestas* were part of Brazilian folklore, when young men sang on the streets in front of their beloveds' windows. The first song, interpreted by Aguinaldo Rayol in the role of Paris, is the love theme of Zefirelli's film.
20. John B. Thompson, *A Mídia e a Modernidade*, translated by Wagner de Oliveira Brandão (Petrópolis: Vozes, 2002), 42.
21. "República" is the name given to students' boarding houses.
22. Bakhtin, *The Dialogic Imagination: Four Essays by Mikhail Bakhtin*, edited by Michael Holquist, translated by Caryl Emerson (Austin: University of Texas Press, 1985), 108 (italics in the original).
23. The "Coronéis" were wealthy landowners who had absolute control over the local communities where they had their lands.
24. Area of a Mountain Chain in Minas Gerais.
25. Gonzaga Blota, *Pedra Sobre Pedra*, Chapter 149, *Globo TV*, 1992.
26. Blota, *Pedra Sobre Pedra*, Chapter 151.
27. Carlos Araújo, *Fera Ferida*, Chapter 123, *Globo TV*, 1993.
28. On "chanchadas," see Augusto (2001), and Demasi (2001).
29. Fran Teague, "Shakespeare, Beard of Avon," in *Shakespeare After Mass* Media, edited by Richard Burt (New York: Palgrave, 2002), 221–24.
30. I use here Roman Jakobson's term (1959), later on taken by Umberto Eco, *Quase A Mesma Coisa (Dire Quase La Stessa Cosa)*, 2007.
31. See Mikhail Bakhtin, *Problems of Dostoievsky's Poetics*, 1981.

Works Cited

Andrade, Oswald. "Manifesto Antropófago." In *Gilberto Mendonça Teles, Vanguarda Europeia e Modernismo Brasileiro*, 226–32. Petrópolis: Vozes, 1973.

Augusto, Sérgio. *Este Mundo É Um Pandeiro: a chanchada de Getúlio a JK*. São Paulo: Companhia das Letras, 2001.

Bakhtin, Mikhail. *Rabelais and His World*, translated by Helene Iswolsky. Bloomington: Indiana University Press, 1984.

Bakhtin, Mikhail. *Problems of Dostoevsky's Poetics*, edited and translated by Caryl Emerson. Minneapolis: University of Minnesota Press, 1985a.

Bakhtin, Mikhail. *The Dialogic Imagination: Four Essays by Mikhail Bakhtin*, edited by Michael Holquist, translated by Caryl Emerson. Austin: University of Texas Press, 1985b.

Bosman, Anston. "Shakespeare and Globalization." In *The New Cambridge Companion to Shakespeare*, 2nd edition, edited by Margreta de Grazia and Stanley Wells, 285–301. Cambridge: Cambridge University Press, 2010.

Burnett, Mark Thornton. *Shakespeare and World Cinema*. Cambridge: Cambridge University Press, 2013.

Eco, Umberto. *Quase A Mesma Coisa*, translated by Eliana Aguiar. Rio de Janeiro-São Paulo: Editora Record, 2007.

Demasi, Domingos. *Chanchadas e Dramalhões*. Rio de Janeiro: Funarte, 2001.

Hutcheon, Lynda and Syobhan O'Flynn. *A Theory of Adaptation*. 2nd edition, 121. London and New York: Routledge, 2013.

Hutcheon, Lynda and Syobhan O'Flynn. *A Theory of Adaptation*. 2nd edition, 122. London and New York: Routledge, 2013.

Lévi-Strauss, Claude. *Raça e História*, translated by Inácio Canelas. Lisboa: Editorial Presença, 1996.

Pavis, Patrice. *Theatre at the Crossroads of Culture*, translated by Loren Kruger. London: Routledge, 1992.

Romeu e Julieta (1968) by Hebe Camargo e Ronald Golias. YouTube, September 22, 2007. https://www.youtube.com/watch?v=HTr97lTecg4, accessed 27 March 2020.

Romeu e Julieta (1980) by Fábio Jr e Lucélia Santos. Youtube. https://www.youtube.com/watch?v=iwN2yrMd7Kg, accessed 28 March 2020.

Shakespeare, William. *Romeo and Juliet*, edited by Jill L. Levenson. Oxford: Oxford University Press, 2000.

Smith, Bruce R. "Shakespeare's Residuals: The Circulation of Ballads in Cultural Memory." In *Shakespeare and Elizabethan Popular Culture*, The Arden Critical Companions, edited by Stuart Gillespie and Neil Rhodes, 193–217. London: Thomson Learning, 2006.

Taylor, Gary. *Reinventing Shakespeare*. Oxford: Oxford University Press, 1989.

Teague, Fran. "Shakespeare, Beard of Avon." In *Shakespeare After Mass Media*, edited by Richard Burt, 221–41. New York: Palgrave, 2002.

Thompson, John B. *A Mídia e a Modernidade*, translated by Wagner de Oliveira Brandão. Petrópolis: Vozes, 2002.

Williams, Raymond. *Culture*. Fontana New Sociology Series. Glasgow: Collins, 1981. US edition: *The Sociology of Culture*. New York: Schocken, 1982.

CHAPTER 7

"*Mon Petit Doigt M'a Dit* ...": Referencing Shakespeare or Agatha Christie?

Nathalie Vienne-Guerrin

The aim of this chapter is to consider the specificities and difficulties of referencing and understanding the effect of allusions to Shakespeare's plays on film when there is a double layer of mediation and quotation.[1] I am going to focus on the case of a French film version of Agatha Christie's *By the Pricking of My Thumbs*, one of her detective novels that was published in 1968. This French film is entitled *Mon petit doigt m'a dit...*, an expression which is the equivalent of the English "by the pricking of my thumbs." It was directed by Pascal Thomas and released in France in April 2005. This film refers to Shakespeare's *Macbeth* but is presented through the filter of Agatha Christie's detective novel and its film adaptation. Our purpose is to explore this double layer of reference and to examine what a French audience may make of such a reference. What remains of Shakespeare when it is both concealed and revealed by Christie's work and its afterlives? How do Shakespeare and Christie,

N. Vienne-Guerrin (✉)
Université Paul-Valéry Montpellier 3, Montpellier, France
e-mail: nathalie.vienne-guerrin@univ-montp3.fr

A. A. Joubin and V. Bladen (eds.), *Onscreen Allusions to Shakespeare*, Global Shakespeares, https://doi.org/10.1007/978-3-030-93783-6_7

the two best-selling authors of all times,[2] share the seeds and roots of such a reference? This chapter will examine the meaning and scope of the Shakespearean reference in Agatha Christie's novel before presenting the remains of Shakespeare in the French 2005 film version. In assessing the treatment of Agatha Christie's Shakespeare in this French film, it will be useful to contrast it with another film that was broadcast on ITV in 2006 as part of a TV series known as *Marple*, starring Geraldine McEwan.[3] This will allow us to better identify the specificities of the Shakespearean tatters that are present in *Mon Petit doigt m'a dit*... and to study how they are integrated into a francophone context.

Looking for *Macbeth* in Agatha Christie's Detective Novel...

The source of the title of Agatha Christie's novel, *By the Pricking of my thumbs*, is identified as Shakespearean in the epigraph that opens the novel:

> By the pricking of my thumbs
> Something wicked this way comes
> Macbeth.[4]

It is not the only time Christie uses Shakespeare in her novels[5] and the titles of her works. Her novel *Taken at the Flood* (1948) owes its title to *Julius Caesar* and quotes the passage from the play in the epigraph[6]; her very successful play *The Mousetrap* (first played in 1952[7]) is a clear reference to *Hamlet*; the title of her novel *Absent in the Spring* (published under the pseudonym Mary Westmacott in 1944) is a quotation from Sonnet 98, while *Sad Cypress* (1940) echoes the fool's song, "Come away, death," in *Twelfth Night*; the song is printed at the beginning of the novel. In *Agatha Christie's Murder in the Making. Stories and secrets from her archive*,[8] John Curran excavates one of Christie's letters to *The Times* entitled "Cleopatra as the Dark Lady," in which she describes her view of Shakespeare:

> I have no pretension to be in any way an historian—but I am one of those who claim to belong to the group for whom Shakespeare wrote. I have gone to plays from an early age and am a great believer that that is the

> way that one should approach Shakespeare. He wrote to entertain and he wrote for playgoers.
>
> I took my daughter and some friends to Stratford when she was 12 years old (...). One young schoolboy gave an immediate criticism after seeing *Macbeth*— "I never would have believed that was Shakespeare. It was wonderful, all about gangsters, so exciting and so real". Shakespeare was clearly associated in the boy's mind with a schoolroom lesson of extreme boredom, but the real thing thrilled him.[9]

Christie transforms Shakespeare into material for thrillers and mystery novels.[10] In *Macbeth*, the lines that the novelist isolates are delivered by the second witch at the end of the cauldron scene in act IV, scene 1 and are immediately followed by the arrival of Macbeth who thus appears as the "something wicked (that) this way comes." This line, which conveys a sense of intuition and foreknowledge, is particularly adapted to the suspense that characterizes Christie's detective novels. The origins of the expression are uncertain. All editions refer back to Steevens' comment that "It is a very ancient superstition that all sudden pains of the body, and other sensations which could not naturally be accounted for, were presages of somewhat that was shortly to happen."[11] The *Macbeth* quotation appears on the back cover of the book published in 2001 by HarperCollins*Publishers*, suggesting both that *Macbeth* is needed to elucidate the title of Christie's novel and that this reference may attract potential readers. Putting the reference on the back cover is no doubt part of a marketing strategy to boost sales.[12] At the same time, it also draws the reader's attention to the importance of the *Macbeth* motif in the novel and feeds a degree of Shakespearean expectation. Seeing this Shakespearean reference on the back cover, readers will tend to assume that *Macbeth* is going to play an essential part in the novel.

This, in fact, seems to exaggerate or to magnify the Shakespearean presence in Christie's novel, since, beyond this epigraph, the novel only contains two explicit references to *Macbeth*. The first one is part of a dialogue between Tommy and Tuppence, the two main protagonists of the novel, a couple of amateur detectives. Tuppence, the wife, has the intuition that "something wicked" has happened at Sunny Ridge nursing home, where Aunt Ada, Tommy's old aunt, has just died. Tuppence underlines the idea that she can see and feel things that others do not pay attention to:

> [...] nobody will take any *notice at all*
> 'Except Mrs Thomas Beresford,' said Tommy.
> 'All right, yes,' said Tuppence. '*I've* taken notice –
> 'But why did you?'
> 'I don't quite know,' said Tuppence slowly. 'It's like the fairy stories. *By the pricking of my thumbs – Something evil this way comes* – I felt suddenly scared. I'd always thought of Sunny Ridge as such a normal happy place – and suddenly I began to wonder – That's the only way I can put it....'[13]

This constitutes a misleading allusion or what Mariangela Tempera called a "pseudo-quotation." Christie rewrites the original quotation mentioned in the epigraph into an approximate quotation that is both Shakespearean and non-Shakespearean.[14] The text here does not mention *Macbeth* but "fairy tales"[15] as the source of these two lines and misquotes Shakespeare's text by replacing the word "wicked" with the word "evil." It is as if the reference, having been properly quoted once by Christie in the epigraph, can now be handled more casually. Shakespeare's text is thus blurred by way of approximation and generalization. However, as the readers have the epigraph in mind, they feel that they hear the text of *Macbeth* without really hearing it; thus, Shakespeare becomes a ghostly presence.

The second reference to *Macbeth* in the novel is longer and more precise as it constitutes a micro "explication de texte" or literary analysis within the novel, providing an interpretation for Macbeth's famous reaction to Lady Macbeth's death when he says: "She should have died hereafter" (5.5.17). The quotation appears in a dialogue between Tommy and Dr Murray who is in charge of the health of the elderly people at Sunny Ridge, where too many women have recently died:

> 'This case of Mrs Moody, however, was somewhat different. She died in her sleep without having exhibited any sign of illness and I could not help feeling that in my opinion her death was unexpected. I will use the phrase that has always intrigued me in Shakespeare's play, *Macbeth*. I have always wondered what Macbeth meant when he said of his wife, "she should have died hereafter."'
>
> 'Yes I remember wondering once what Shakespeare was getting at,' said Tommy. 'I forget whose production it was and who was playing Macbeth, but there was a strong suggestion in that particular production, and Macbeth certainly played it in a way to suggest that he was hinting to the medical attendant that Lady Macbeth would be better out of the way.

> Presumably the medical attendant took the hint. It was then that Macbeth, feeling safe after his wife's death, feeling that she could no longer damage him by her indiscretions or her rapidly failing mind, expresses his genuine affection and grief for her. "She should have died hereafter."
>
> 'Exactly,' said Murray. 'It is what I felt about Mrs Moody. I felt that she should have died hereafter. Not just three weeks ago of no apparent cause.' (Christie 207)

Macbeth is here used to refer to the mystery of a patient's death and to suggest that murder or unnatural death is in the air. "She should have died hereafter" sounds like a motto illuminating all suspicious deaths in all detective novels. This quotation throws into relief the kinship between *Macbeth* and the detective story in which it is embedded: the two stories are based on mysteries that need to be solved, a similarity that explains that *Macbeth* has notably been used in a *Columbo* episode entitled "Dagger of the mind."[16]

By invoking *Macbeth* as an intertext for Christie's novel, Shakespearean readers may gain the impression that they see *Macbeth* everywhere and have to deal with what Christy Desmet termed a "drama of recognition."[17] *By the Pricking of My Thumbs'* opening paragraph concludes with "It looked as though it might rain but wasn't quite sure of it" (Christie 13) which recalls the "Thunder, lightning and rain" (1.1) of *Macbeth*. When reading Tommy saying "Being a woman you're more ruthless" (Christie 22), a Shakespearean reader may think of Lady Macbeth's lack of pity in the play. The obsessive repetition of the enigmatic question "Was it your poor child?" (Christie 40, 255, 337) seems to bring us back to the presence of children in *Macbeth* that has been harped upon for so many years, notably since the publication of L. C. Knight's article "How many children had Lady Macbeth?" in 1964.[18] This obsession with the absent or lost child that L. C. Knights found in *Macbeth* seems to find its counterpart in what François Rivière, a specialist of Agatha Christie, sees as her obsession with the lost child.[19] The allusion to a "prophecy of some kind" (34) and the recurrent motif of the poisoned milk (37) seem to echo Shakespeare's script. In Christie's novel, milk is omnipresent and it is the milk of human un-kindness (1.5.16).[20] Having been put on the track of a Shakespearean intertext by the paratext (title, epigraph and cover) that Gérard Genette describes as the "thresholds of interpretation" ("seuils"),[21] the readers then become detectives looking for any trace of Shakespeare in Agatha Christie's novel. Through this filter, such a banal word as "Knock" (51) becomes an allusion to the porter scene, or such a common phrase as "it's like ghosts" (52, 171) recalls the banquet scene in *Macbeth*. When we come to Chapter 7 entitled "The friendly Witch," we cannot but see the witches in the play, and yet Agatha Christie challenges our expectation by explicitly referring not to *Macbeth* but to the fairy story of Hansel and Gretel (106). "Dead children, too many dead children" (Christie 106) seems to call us back to the play, both to Lady Macbeth's murderous imagination and to the murder of Macduff's children. Quoting Marjorie Garber, we could say that Shakespeare "haunts" the novel as "a ghost who returns again and again to interrogate modern life"[22] and here to interrogate and comment upon Agatha Christie's novel. Thus, the main question that we ask in this volume, which applies even more to the film medium, is how can this ghostly presence and these "spectral" traces[23] be spotted and referenced? The basic problem is that ghosts exist only if you see them. While clear fingerprints are easy to store and reference, how can one retain, identify, stabilize and reference impressions?

This leads us to examine how the French film version of Agatha Christie's novel erases, captures, retains and restores these Shakespearean remnants.

Looking for Agatha Christie's Shakespeare in *Mon Petit Doigt M'a Dit...*

The film was directed by Pascal Thomas and stars Catherine Frot (Prudence, the French version of Tuppence) and André Dussollier (Bélisaire, the French version of Tommy), two very popular French actors.[24] It is considered as an adaptation of Agatha Christie's novel as appears from the film's opening credits, which read "D'après un roman d'Agatha Christie" (after a novel by Agatha Christie). When you listen to the comments on the film by director Pascal Thomas and director of photography, Renan Polles, in the supplement to the film on DVD, you notice that they never refer to Shakespeare but constantly to the process of adapting Agatha Christie's novel and notably to the choice of simplifying its very complicated plot so that the whole story can make sense. When you read reviews of the film, you see that the reference to Shakespeare's *Macbeth* is not thrown into relief but that the adaptation of Christie's novel undoubtedly prevails over the allusion to Shakespeare.

Yet the original trailer[25] gives the spectators an idea of the tone and atmosphere of the film. It first throws into relief the humour of a film that is usually described as a "comédie policière," a comic detective film. It opens with comic equivocation when we discover Catherine Frot (Prudence), in bed, saying to her husband "je suis une femme comblée" ("I am in paradise"). The next shot reveals the double entendre and that she playfully means that it is not for sex that he is the best but for ironing. The trailer is based on a comment delivered in voice-over by the husband, Bélisaire, about his wife, Prudence, and insists on the mysteries of the story and on his wife's intuition.[26] What is striking is that the 85 seconds of the trailer contain the only explicit reference to *Macbeth*, thus allowing the spectators to understand the meaning of the title, as if Shakespeare were the key to the whole story. Here is the script of the trailer:

> I've got a wonderful wife. She is... how could I say this?... full of curiosity..., invention... and intuition.... What she likes most is mystery..., crime..., poisoning..., disappearances..., and travels by train.... To help her in her investigations, she's got one major asset...
> *[Shot of Prudence saying:] I've had the same revelation as the witches in* Macbeth...
> It's her thumb.
> *[Shot of Prudence saying:] By the pricking of my thumbs something wicked this way comes/ (Bélisaire translating) Mon petit doigt m'a dit, quelque chose de mauvais vient par ici.*
> At the start of the whole story – by the way, how did it all start? ...

The trailer is the equivalent of the back cover of the book. It magnifies the Shakespearean intertext and alerts us to Shakespearean allusions in the film.

In the ITV version, the characters refer to *Macbeth* in the very first minutes of the film. During the opening credits, the spectators see Tuppence (Greta Scacchi) fetching a book before leaving her home with her husband, Tommy (Anthony Andrews). Once they are outside, about to leave for Sunny Ridge, we have the following dialogue:

> Tuppence. Can't you drive? I want to read my book.
> Tommy (seeing the book cover, saying in disgust). *Macbeth*?
> Tuppence. *Macbeth*.
> Tommy (laughing with contempt). I was in *Macbeth* in my prep. school. (Playing bombastically) "Tomorrow, and Tomorrow and tomorrow,/ Creeps in this petty pace from day to day..."

Tuppence. I heard you were marvellous.
Tommy. Who from?
Tuppence. You.
Tommy (after starting the car). "By the pricking of my thumbs, something wicked this way comes."

From the first minutes of the film, this explicit reference elucidates the title derisively. This sequence follows a cold opening which shows two kids standing behind a window, watching what looks like a child-witch hunt and commenting: "They won't find him. He should be in the witches' house by now. Do you know the story of the witch, Ethan? My dad says she used to take children from the village, back in the olden days." This is followed by another clear reference to *Macbeth*, when Tommy and Tuppence leave Sunny Ridge and are waved good bye by three old women. Tommy, giggling, asks Tuppence: "Look at that. What does that remind you of? Act one, scene one: 'When shall we meet again,/ In thunder, lightning or in rain?'" (clip or/and image). Later on, Miss Marple and Tuppence discover a doll behind a mantelpiece and say: "Miss Marple. This is a warning. Tuppence. Something wicked this way comes." The ITV film wants to elucidate the title of Christie's novel as soon as the film starts, and the Shakespearean root is made material and objectified by the book that is handled by Tuppence at the beginning of the novel and by the very explicit allusions to the text of *Macbeth*.

In the French film version, the *Macbeth* sequence lies in these few words delivered by Prudence: *J'ai eu la même révélation que les sorcières de Macbeth*, "*By the pricking of my thumbs something wicked this way comes*" and immediately translated by her husband as "*Mon petit doigt m'a dit, quelque chose de mauvais vient par ici.*" The spectators are given both the original text in English and its translation into French in a kind of duet sequence which shows the intimacy between husband and wife who obviously share the same sophisticated literary culture. The quotation sounds strange in the francophone background of the film but the incongruity fits a character who is presented as full of originality and eccentricity.[27] Obviously, the director wanted to quote Shakespeare's precise words but as Agatha Christie's story is transposed into a French context[28] and as the audience of the film will be French, one needed to make sure that Shakespeare's words would be understood. In the context of the film, this quotation is a marker of the high culture of the characters and hearing it in English suggests that "Shakespeare's language is essential to Shakespeare."[29] This *Macbeth* quotation is the only one in the whole film where the "she should have died hereafter" we found in the novel is not explicitly mentioned.[30] The reference to *Macbeth* only occurs after the first 28 minutes of the film, and yet it irradiates and haunts the whole film.

Prudence's voice delivering the quotation is heard again in a fantastic ghostly sequence later in the film.[31] Bélisaire, worried about his wife's disappearance, hears her voice while looking at himself in a mirror. The sequence is part of the fantastic dimension of the film that includes strange dream sequences and cultivates an atmosphere of mild folly.

Yet the mode of irradiation is mainly musical in this film. The 85-second trailer also includes a song sung by a choir of children and the lyrics of that song are the Shakespearean "By the pricking of my thumbs,/ Something wicked this way comes."[32] The tune that can be heard in the trailer is an essential part of the film score composed by Reinhardt Wagner[33] which contributes greatly to the eerie, weird atmosphere that pervades a film that combines comic eccentricity and dark, nightmarish, ambience.

The first time you hear it, after seven minutes and 32 seconds,[34] is when the witch-like character, Tante Ada (Aunt Ada, played by Françoise Seigner), whistles it in an enigmatic way, and it seems that part of the suspense of the film will be to discover the meaning of that tune, in the same way as the suspense of *Macbeth* is based on the quest for the meaning of the witches' prophetic words. One can hear variations on the same tune again and again in the film, notably, around minute 22,[35] when Prudence examines a mysterious painting, looking for clues to find Rose Evangelista (the equivalent of Mrs. Lancaster in the novel). The tune has spread from Aunt Ada's whistling to Prudence's whistling, and it is associated with the enigma that is at the heart of Christie's plot.

When you hear it again, around minute 35,[36] you feel that, like a rumour, the tune is disseminated throughout the film as it goes from one mouth to another and builds the whole atmosphere of the film. Twenty minutes later, it is made more spectacular[37] as the tune is a key that opens a secret part of Aunt Ada's "harmonium." It is again associated with the mystery of the film; it is a clue that needs deciphering in the same way that the witches' words need to be interpreted. Then, the audience hear the tune in one of the final sequences in the open air where it is played by a little orchestra at a fair where we discover stands of "game of slaughter" (jeu de massacre) and the race of witches ("courses des sorcières") and the wheel of fortune.[38] The music of the fair turns "foul" in the next sequence[39] when we switch from the festive performance of the music to a thrilling atmosphere made of the combination of strange images of children and eerie music. It is only in this sequence, at the very end of the film, that the lyrics of the song are introduced and that we discover that they are Shakespeare's words. Thus retrospectively, the recurrent musical motif becomes Shakespearean and all the musical moments that we have just isolated and referenced become evanescent Shakespearean allusions. This example shows how when it comes to studying Shakespeare in tatters, we deal with ghostly figures, Shakespeare being there without being there. The end of the film, by putting lyrics on the tune that we have recurrently, almost obsessively, heard, provides a key and constitutes a first stage in the *anagnorisis* or recognition that is orchestrated in the final sequences.[40] When we recognize the lyrics, the tune takes on a new meaning in the same way as the witches' words take on a new meaning at the end of *Macbeth*, inviting the audience to re-consider the whole story. The lyrics that are *in fine* added to the tune thus allow the spectators to put the pieces together and to reconstitute a new picture and a new story.

Once we have identified the Shakespearean motto of the film, we feel we are, again, as with Christie's novel, invited to find Shakespeare here, there and everywhere. Like Prudence, we imagine that the red bottles received by her husband in a parcel are "blood" (du sang) and when Bélisaire identifies these bottles as bottles of Swiss wine, we may have the feeling that our visions of Shakespearean figments are as ridiculous as Prudence's anxious intuition. In the film, Prudence sees witches everywhere before realizing that these witches are the products of her interpretation. Yet, the dagger that we see at the end of the film is not a dagger of the mind. The Shakespearean motto of the film is an invitation to proceed to a Shakespearean reading of the film: in a comment on the film, Pascal Thomas refers to the symbolism of dark nativity that the film cultivates, through images of statues of the Virgin, through the presence of an important bestiary, notably the donkey and the "billy goat" that he sees as a symbol of evil, an embodiment of the devil. Pascal Thomas reveals in the DVD commentary that if he put the goat in his film, it is just because he loves that animal. It is only afterwards that he realized the coherent symbolism that was running throughout the film.

Once we identify and put the Shakespearean "tatters" together, it seems clear that we can offer a Shakespearean reading of the whole film and that Shakespeare provides tools to understand, read and interpret the film. At the end, while dancing at the fair with her husband, Prudence is thoughtful and we are given access to her thoughts thanks to the use of a voice-over:

> Everybody seems so agreeable. What secrets and what dark thoughts are hidden behind these smiles and banal discussions? What monstrosity is hidden behind these sweet faces and landscapes? There is no peaceful village in this world.[41]

When we have *Macbeth* in mind, this comment cannot but remind us of one of the quotations of Shakespeare's play that has become a sort of motto: "Fair is foul and foul is fair." This cannot be considered as an explicit reference but it is certainly part of the fleeting, almost subliminal presence of Shakespeare throughout.[42] *Mon Petit doigt m'a dit...* is no doubt a film that appropriates Shakespeare through a quotation, as the reference to *Macbeth* is explicit. Yet as Shakespeare's name is not uttered, one cannot be sure that *Macbeth* will be identified as a Shakespeare play by all people in the audience. *Anagnorisis* will not be effective for every viewer but referencing such an allusion enables us to see how such a famous and popular writer as Agatha Christie can communicate (with) Shakespeare. *Mon Petit Doigt m'a dit...*, by including the Shakespearean quotation in English, pays tribute both to Christie and Shakespeare. In this film, the witch's words are transformed into a nursery rhyme that remains in your mind long after the film ends. The Shakespearean fragment is absorbed into a skein which combines *Macbeth*, Shakespeare, Christie...The suspension points that are in the title reveal that the quotation is just the beginning or exterior sign of a deeper dialogue with Shakespeare's play. A few words permeate the whole film through musical sequences that keep Christie's allusion and Shakespeare's words alive from the beginning to the end of the film. The ellipsis (...) is in fact perhaps the best way of revealing and hiding the ghostly presence of *Macbeth* in this film and it is also emblematic of the rich and endless forms and processes of quotation that one can observe when it comes to Shakespeare's works.

Notes

1. Many thanks to Sarah Hatchuel and Victoria Bladen for their help and suggestions. Many thanks to Mariangela Tempera for organizing a wonderful conference in Ferrara (2013) where a first version of this paper was delivered.
2. Jerome Taylor, "The Big Question: How Big Is the Agatha Christie Industry, and What Explains Her Enduring Appeal?" *The Independent*, Wednesday February 25, 2009, accessed September 15, 2020.
3. Stewart Harcourt, writer, *Marple*, Season 2 Episode 3, "The Pricking of My Thumbs," dir. Peter Medak. Aired 19 February 2006.
4. Agatha Christie, *By the Pricking of My Thumbs* [1968] (London: Harper-Collins*Publishers*, 2001, *Agatha Christie Official Website*), accessed 15 September 2020.
5. Lisa Hopkins, *Shakespearean Allusion in Crime Fiction, DCI Shakespeare* (London: Palgrave, 2016), 17–61.
6. "There is a tide in the affairs of men,/ Which, taken at the flood, leads on to fortune:/ Omitted, all the voyage of their life/ Is bound in shallows and in miseries./ On such a full sea are we now afloat,/ And we must take the current when it serves,/ Or lose our ventures" (*Julius Caesar*, 4.3.216–22). Contrary to the quotation from *Macbeth* in *By the Pricking of my thumbs*, this one is not identified in the epigraph.
7. It was adapted from a radio play, *Three Blind Mice*, written by Christie in 1947. It was Agatha Christie's son-in-law, Anthony Hicks, who suggested the new title. See http://www.agathachristie.com/christies-work/stories/The-Mousetrap/525, accessed September 15, 2020.
8. John Curran, *Agatha Christie's Murder in the Making. Stories and Secrets from Her Archive* (London, HarperCollins, 2011).
9. *The Times*, February 3, 1973, in Curran, 370.
10. John Curran notes that "Agatha Christie was a lifelong fan of William Shakespeare" and he spots Shakespeare's presence in the titles of Christie's novels as well as in their plots. *Macbeth*, for example, "provides some of the background of *The Pale Horse*" and the line "Who would have thought the old man to have had so much blood in him" is quoted in *Hercule Poirot's Christmas*, following the discovery of a body. Curran, 366.
11. See note Arden 2, edition by Kenneth Muir, 109; John Brand, *Observations of the Popular Antiquities*, vol. 3 (London: Bell & Daldy, 1872), 179.
12. The same commercial strategy appears on the Agatha Christie website, which is presented as the "official home of the best-selling author of all time," where the Shakespeare quotation is thrown into relief: http://www.agathachristie.com/christies-work/stories/by-the-pricking-of-my-thumbs/153, accessed September 15, 2020.

13. Christie, *By the Pricking of My Thumbs*, 79.
14. Christy Desmet, Natalie Loper, Casey eds. *Shakespeare/Not Shakespeare* (New York: Palgrave Macmillan, 2017).
15. There are notably references to Hansel and Gretel and fairy tales in Christie, *By the Pricking of My Thumbs,* 106; 295.
16. Sarah Hatchuel, and Nathalie Vienne-Guerrin, "'Is This an Umbrella Which I See Before Me?': *Columbo* Goes to Scotland Yard," in *Shakespeare on Screen*: Macbeth, edited by Sarah Hatchuel and Nathalie Vienne-Guerrin, 397–410 (Rouen: Presses Universitaires de Rouen et du Havre, 2013).
17. Christy Desmet, "Dramas of Recognition: *Pan's Labyrinth* and *Warm Bodies* as Accidental Shakespeare," in *Shakespeare/Not Shakespeare*, ed. Christie Desmet, Natalie Loper and Jim Casey (New York: Palgrave Macmillan, 2017), 275–91.
18. L.C. Knights, "How Many Children Had Lady Macbeth? An Essay in the Theory and Practice of Shakespeare Criticism," in *Explorations* (New York: New York University Press, 1964), 15–54. See also, Rutter, "Remind Me: How Many Children Had Lady Macbeth?" (esp. 45–53).
19. See DVD supplement. See also François Rivière, *Agatha Christie, La Romance du Crime* (Paris: Éditions de La Martinière, 2012).
20. On the milk motif in Christie's novels, see Hopkins, 30–36.
21. Gérard Genette, *Paratexts: Thresholds of Interpretation* (Cambridge: Cambridge University Press, 1997, originally published in French as *Seuils*. Paris: Éditions du Seuil, 1987).
22. Marjorie Garber, *Shakespeare's Ghost Writers*: *Literature as Uncanny Causality* (First published in 1987 by Methuen. New York: Routledge, 2010), xv (preface).
23. Maurizio Calbi, *Spectral Shakespeares: Media Adaptations in the Twenty-First Century* (New York: Palgrave Macmillan, 2013).
24. The two actors played Tommy and Tuppence (Prudence and Bélisaire) in two other adaptations of Agatha Christie's detective novels, directed by Pascal Thomas, *Associés Contre le Crime* (2012) and *Le Crime est notre Affaire* (2008).
25. 8audreyrose, "Mon petit doigt m'a dit 2005 Trailer.flv," 8 October 2011, https://www.youtube.com/watch?v=X3SSVBlCkRE, accessed 15 September 2020.
26. "J'ai une femme formidable. Elle est, comment vous dire, curieuse, inventive, intuitive. Ce qu'elle aime le plus, c'est le mystère, les crimes, les empoisonnements, les disparitions, et les voyages en train. Pour l'aider dans ses enquêtes, elle a son atout majeur, si j'ose dire.

    J'ai eu la même révélation que les sorcières de Macbeth, c'est son petit doigt, *By the pricking of my thumbs something wicked this way comes/ Mon petit doigt m'a dit, quelque chose de mauvais vient par ici.* Quand cette histoire a commencé, d'ailleurs comment a-t-elle commencé cette histoire ? *Mon subconscient essaie de m'envoyer un message. Oh que je n'aime pas ça.* Un mystère d'Agatha Christie."

27. Catherine Frot is known for playing eccentric characters. She is notably famous for her part in *Un air de famille* (dir. Cédric Klapish, 1996) in which she plays Yolande who is offered a necklace by her husband and describes it as a dog collar. She also played the part of a very independent and original woman in *La Dilettante* (dir. Pascal Thomas, 1999).
28. Pascal Thomas reveals in the DVD comment on the film that what motivates him to make films is "to preserve images of a France that is disappearing" ("fixer une France qui disparaît").
29. For a discussion on the linguistic, verbal dimension of appropriation and citation, see Lanier, *Shakespeare and Modern Popular Culture*, 62.
30. It is erased but when you know Christie's book, you can recognize it in the dialogue between the doctor and Bélisaire, in the boat sequence.
31. Time code 1.8.38–1.9.13.
32. Interestingly, one finds a choir sequence with lyrics from *Macbeth* including "Double double toil and trouble" and "something wicked this way comes" in *Harry Potter and the Prisoner of Azkaban* (2004, dir. Alfonso Cuarón): http://www.youtube.com/watch?v=6I1P1Vml8WM, accessed September 15, 2020. Thanks to Alfredo Michel Modenessi for signalling this sequence to me.
33. Available at: https://itunes.apple.com/fr/album/mon-petit-doigt-ma-dit.../id76971739, accessed September 15, 2020.
34. Pascal Thomas, dir, *Mon Petit Doigt m'a dit*. (2005; Ah! Victoria! Films), Time code: 7.32–8.01.
35. Thomas, *Mon Petit Doigt m'a dit*, time code: 22.27–22.43.
36. Thomas, *Mon Petit Doigt m'a dit*, time code: 35.50–36.21.
37. Thomas, *Mon Petit Doigt m'a dit*, time code: 56.31–57.03.
38. Thomas, *Mon Petit Doigt m'a dit*, time code: 1.22.06–1.23.44.
39. Thomas, *Mon Petit Doigt m'a dit*, time code: 1.25.58–1.26.48.
40. Aristotle notably defined *anagnorisis* as "a change from ignorance to knowledge" (Aristotle, *Poetics*, ed. Penguin, 1996, 6.4, p. 18).
41. In French: "Tout le monde a l'air si convenable. Quelles arrière-pensées, quels secrets et peut-être quelle noirceur derrière ces sourires et ces propos anodins. Quelle monstruosité se cache derrière la douceur des visages et des paysages. Il n'y a pas de village tranquille."
42. This Shakespearean allusion is included in the "Shakespeare on screen in francophonia database" http://shakscreen.org/. This database records and analyzes Shakespeare adaptations and allusions on cinema and television screens in French-speaking countries, accessed September 15, 2020.

Works Cited

8audreyrose, "Mon petit doigt m'a dit 2005 Trailer.flv," 8 October 2011, https://www.youtube.com/watch?v=X3SSVBlCkRE. Accessed 15 September 2020.

Aristotle. *Poetics*. London: Penguin, 1996.

Brand, John. *Observations of the Popular Antiquities of Great Britain*, vol. 3. London: Bell & Daldy, 1872.

Calbi, Maurizio. *Spectral Shakespeares: Media Adaptations in the Twenty-First Century*. New York: Palgrave Macmillan, 2013.

Chillington Rutter, Carol. "Remind Me: How Many Children Had Lady Macbeth?" *Shakespeare Survey* 57 (2004): 38–53. Rpt. in revised, expanded form as "Precious Motives, Seeds of Time: Killing Futures in *Macbeth*." In *Shakespeare and Child's Play: Performing Lost Boys on Stage and Screen*, 154–204. London and New York: Routledge, 2007.

Christie, Agatha. *By the Pricking of My Thumbs* [1968]. London: Harper-Collins*Publishers*, 2001. *Agatha Christie Official Website*. Accessed 15 September 2020.

Curran, John. *Agatha Christie's Murder in the Making. Stories and Secrets from Her Archive*. London: HarperCollins*Publishers*, 2011.

Desmet, Christy, "Dramas of Recognition: *Pan's Labyrinth* and *Warm Bodies* as Accidental Shakespeare." In *Shakespeare/Not Shakespeare*, edited by Christie Desmet, Natalie Loper and Jim Casey, 275–91. New York: Palgrave Macmillan, 2017.

Desmet, Christy, Natalie Loper, and Jim Casey, eds. *Shakespeare/Not Shakespeare*. New York: Palgrave Macmillan, 2017.

Dorval, Patricia, and Nathalie Vienne-Guerrin, eds. "Shakespeare on Screen in Francophonia Database." http://shakscreen.org/. Accessed 5 July 2021.

Garber, Marjorie. *Shakespeare's Ghost Writers: Literature as Uncanny Causality*. First published in 1987 by Methuen. New York: Routledge, 2010.

Genette, Gérard. *Paratexts: Thresholds of Interpretation*. Cambridge: Cambridge University Press, 1997. Originally published in French as *Seuils*. Paris: Éditions du Seuil, 1987.

Hatchuel, Sarah, and Nathalie Vienne-Guerrin. "'Is This an Umbrella Which I See Before Me?': *Columbo* Goes to Scotland Yard." In *Shakespeare on Screen*: Macbeth, edited by Sarah Hatchuel and Nathalie Vienne-Guerrin, 397–410. Rouen: Presses Universitaires de Rouen et du Havre, 2013.

Hopkins, Lisa. *Shakespearean Allusion in Crime Fiction. DCI Shakespeare*. London: Palgrave, 2016.

Knights, L. C. "How Many Children Had Lady Macbeth? An Essay in the Theory and Practice of Shakespeare Criticism." In *Explorations*, 15–54. New York: New York University Press, 1964.

Lanier, Douglas. *Shakespeare and Modern Popular Culture*. Oxford: Oxford University Press, 2002.
Rivière, François. *Agatha Christie, La Romance du Crime*. Paris: Éditions de La Martinière, 2012.
Shakespeare, William. *Macbeth*, edited by Kenneth Muir. Arden 2, Methuen, 1951.
Taylor, Jerome. "The Big Question: How Big Is the Agatha Christie Industry, and What Explains Her Enduring Appeal?" *The Independent*, Wednesday February 25, 2009. http://www.independent.co.uk/arts-entertainment/books/features/the-big-question-how-big-is-the-agatha-christie-industry-and-what-explains-her-enduring-appeal-1631296.html. Accessed 15 September 2020.

Filmography

Cuarón, Alfonso, dir. *Harry Potter and the Prisoner of Azkaban*. 2004; Warner Bros.
Gillis, Jackson, Richard Levinson, William Link, writers. *Columbo*. Season 2 Episode 4, "Dagger of the Mind." Directed by Richard Quine. Aired 26 November 1972, in broadcast syndication. NBC.
Harcourt, Stewart, writer. *Marple*. Season 2 Episode 3, "The Pricking of My Thumbs." Directed by Peter Medak. Aired 19 February 2006.
Klapish, Cédric, dir. *Un air de famille*. 1996; Téléma.
Thomas, Pascal, dir. *Associés Contre le Crime*. 2012; Les Films Français.
Thomas, Pascal, dir. *La Dilettante*. 1999; Ah! Victoria! Films.
Thomas, Pascal, dir. *Le Crime est notre Affaire*. 2008; Les Films Français.
Thomas, Pascal, dir. *Mon Petit Doigt m'a dit*. 2005; Ah! Victoria! Films.

CHAPTER 8

Shakespeare's *Julius Caesar* in Federico Fellini's *Roma*

Mariacristina Cavecchi

Shakespeare has played an important role in forging Italian national identity and Julius Caesar, herald and founder of the Roman Empire, has undoubtedly been a key figure in Italian history and culture.[1] It is therefore natural that quotations from Shakespeare's *Julius Caesar* should figure conspicuously in Italian non-Shakespearean films. Indeed, references to Shakespeare's *Julius Caesar* are to be found in films by distinguished Italian filmmakers such as Dino Risi, Luciano Salce, Federico Fellini, Alberto Bevilacqua and the Taviani brothers, even though, as Mariangela Tempera suggests in her reconstruction and analysis of the quotations from Shakespeare's Roman plays in Italian cinema, "it is not always easy to unequivocally identify Shakespeare as the source of a reference".[2]

Federico Fellini's *Roma* (1972) exemplifies "the Shakespeare/ 'not Shakespeare' conundrum"[3] by including a very short and rather bizarre

M. Cavecchi (✉)
Università Degli Studi Di Milano, Milan, Italy
e-mail: cristina.cavecchi@unimi.it

A. A. Joubin and V. Bladen (eds.), *Onscreen Allusions to Shakespeare*, Global Shakespeares, https://doi.org/10.1007/978-3-030-93783-6_8

cameo of a fragment from a play about the Roman leader Julius Caesar. That this fragment, in fact, derives from a production of Shakespeare's *Julius Caesar* is asserted both by Tempera, who records the film in her archive,[4] and by cinema scholar Joanna Paul, who, in her analysis of Fellini's film, writes of "a production of Shakespeare's play in the theatre".[5] Watching the film, I was so excited at the idea of working on an appropriation of Shakespeare by one of the most internationally acclaimed Italian filmmakers that I light-heartedly and at first uncritically took (or mistook?) the quotation to be undoubtedly from Shakespeare. However, the *Julius Caesar* play referred to may not be by Shakespeare. Yet, this discovery does not materially change how "Shakespeareans" (the category of viewers that includes scholars, students and fans of Shakespeare on screen) interact with it and the film. What I am suggesting is that the meanings of *Roma* and of its *Julius Caesar* segment are shaped and determined to some extent by the expectations of this specific kind of viewer, which, I would argue, might be considered as a particular subgroup of those "perverse spectators" described by Janet Staiger in her work on the practices of film reception.[6] The Fellinian quotation is an example of how such passing references, so marginal to the films' narrative, are often interpreted by "Shakespeareans" as offshoots from Shakespeare's plays and made sense of in the light of their ponderous literary background. Whether or not it derives from Shakespeare, Fellini's rapid reference puts the Italian tribe of Shakespeareans on alert, immediately and almost automatically reminding them of Shakespeare's crucial role in the process of negotiating questions of national identity and in articulating the contradictory relationship between Italian culture and its troublesome Fascist history.[7] This reference is an example of the complicated reception dynamics at work when we watch a Shakespeare-related fragment in a non-Shakespearean film. As Douglas Lanier suggests, our recognition (or false conviction) that the quotation comes from Shakespeare often induces more general associations.[8] Indeed, the reference to *Julius Caesar* in Fellini's film functions in this manner, as it may cause the viewers to build a whole network of intertextual references which, however, risks being a mere "chimaera, born out of our desire to see elements of Shakespeare in nearly every narrative".[9]

Does Fellini Refer to Shakespeare?

Fellini's film is conceived as a pastiche of different views of Rome derived from the filmmaker's own memories, previous Italian films and images of the contemporary city. Not only does the filmmaker construct his Rome by physically rebuilding it in Cinecittà Studio 5, but he also visually recreates it primarily from his own experiences, so that he becomes "an integral part of the fabric of his cinematic city".[10] It is Fellini himself who, in a written introduction to the film explains that, for him, it is a palimpsest of images and reminiscences that go back to his long-gone childhood:

> When I was at school, Rome was Julius Caesar and Nero, a decadent and corrupt society, peopled by Epicureans, corpulent and gluttonous businessmen and invincible warriors. She [Rome] was the she-wolf, suckling Romulus and Remus, Mussolini, the huge mass meetings in Piazza Venezia, the popular image of "alla amatriciana" spaghetti and Frascati.[11]

Thus, in the first sequence of the film, with his usual irony and parodic touch, Fellini shows the role assigned to Roman history in the education of children in Fascist Italy and acknowledges the fact that the figure of Julius Caesar became part of the cultural propaganda programme of Italian Fascism.[12] As Nancy Isenberg observes, Mussolini deployed "a Caesarian model of politics and leadership to make of his rule a modern Roman Empire and of his persona a Modern Caesar".[13] Fellini ridicules the tribute paid to Julius Caesar and ancient Rome by the Fascist regime indirectly, making very subtle use of the points of view of extremely peculiar and eccentric characters. He even mocks Fascist cinema and its regime-encouraged effort to offer "a heroic universe that would revive the epic values of Imperial Rome".[14]

Thus, a fatigued and perspiring history teacher takes his students across the Rubicon, the river which Caesar crossed in 49 BC with the famous cry of "Alea iacta est" ("The die is cast"); he makes them take off their shoes and wade into the water, following in the footsteps of the Roman leader, as it were, and shouting "On to Rome! On to Rome!"—a clear parody of Mussolini's "March on Rome", which took place in late October 1922 and was intended "to replicate one of the greatest legends associated with Julius Caesar".[15] Soon afterwards, in the classroom, under the gaze of Mussolini's portrait on the wall, the teacher's history lesson is abruptly interrupted: as he is telling his class about the legend of the Capitoline geese, describing them as "umili palmipedi che con il loro schiamazzo svegliarono i guerrieri i quali [...] salvarono Roma" ("our humble web-footed friends, who, with their excited quacking woke the soldiers that [...] saved Rome from the enemy"), his bombastic and overblown tone is suddenly deflated by his students bursting into laughter at the sight of some geese outside the windows. Similarly, manner, in the refectory of a religious college, the projection of some slides showing the most important Roman monuments is interrupted by the sudden appearance, amongst the slides, of a risqué photograph of a semi-naked woman posing provocatively, much to the amused joy of the students and to the ashamed despair of the priest, who tries to cover the screen, urging the children not to look, as those "fleshy buttocks"[16] are "the devil". It may be interesting to point out that the series of slides of the Roman monuments shown to the students (the bronze sculpture of the Capitoline Wolf inspired by the legend of the founding of Rome, the Basilica of Santa Maria Maggiore, the tomb of Cecilia Metella on the Appian Way, the Arch of Constantine, Saint Peter's, "the greatest of all the temples of our Mother Church") includes the "Altare della patria", or Vittoriano. Built in honour of Vittorio Emanuele, the first king of unified Italy, this monument faces Piazza Venezia, which became famous between September 1929 and July 1943, on account of the palazzo standing there which housed Mussolini's office. Notoriously, it was from the balcony of this palazzo that the Duce harangued the crowds and from there that the "*dictator* and followers bellowed their approval of 'Mussolini's Roman Empire'".[17] As historian Richard Bosworth writes in his book on Rome, "everything about Vittoriano's site and bulk shouts its desire to represent the 'Third' Rome, its intention to connect the monarch's story with a glorious and imperial past and so to pave the way to as grand and imperial a future".[18] The decision to include the Vittoriano amongst the Roman monuments and the fact that the students burst into applause when they see this particular slide are therefore quite meaningful elements and seem to underscore the effort made by the institutions—both the school and the church—to bring up a whole generation, which they consider to be the true heirs of the Roman empire.

From the classroom to the streets: the sketch which immediately follows takes place in a square in Fellini's hometown Rimini, where an old, homeless Romagnole, referred to in the film's screenplay as "Giudizio",[19] makes outrageous comments on a damaged statue of Caesar and ironically links the figure of the Roman leader with that of Mussolini when he addresses two passing children with the rhyme: "Bambini, vi piace Mussolini? Come Cesare il Romano fa il saluto con la mano" (Hey, kids, do you like Mussolini? Like Caesar, the Roman, he [Mussolini] salutes with this hand). The statue—a parodic replica of those statues of Caesar that Mussolini ordered to be placed in symbolic locations[20]—is broken on its left side and is described in mocking terms by an old lunatic (or a fool, in the Elizabethan sense, that is, he who represents free speech and an unjaundiced view of reality). Caesar's damaged head and arm are explained through another coarsely debunking rhyme in Romagnole dialect: "Mèza tèsta lè fasèsta, lè faséstà mèza tèsta. Là pasè e' Rubicòn lé arvanzè cum un quaiòn!" ("Half - head is Fascist, the Fascist is half head. He crossed the Rubicon and just stood there like a jerk") (Fig. 8.1).

The ironic description of this statue of a half-Fascist Caesar by one who "appears to be the only anti-Fascist left in town"[21] is soon afterwards completed as the man explains that the missing hand was chopped off to stop him masturbating: "Bambini, vi piace Mussolini? Giulio Cesare romano fa il saluto con la mano... Mè, ch'a tir la carèta, a m faz 'na pugnèta!"[22]—an obvious scoff at Mussolini's self-mythologization as the embodiment of both political power and erotic potency.[23]

Fig. 8.1 Fellini—The damaged statue of Caesar

From the streets to the theatre, Fellini "compounds this humiliation by recreating the ancient military leader's assassination as tawdry theatrical spectacle".[24] After making fun of Caesar's statue, the filmmaker next ridicules the theatrical character. The actor who takes the role of the Roman leader, played by Fëdor Fëdorovič Šaljapin, is rhetorical and bombastic on stage, but even after the heavy red curtain falls following his "anche tu, Bruto, figlio mio" and the camera moves on to catch him offstage, he continues to behave in an extremely affected manner. Seen through his reflected image in the mirror of a bar in Rimini, he appears as a blasé actor in a black coat and a Borsalino hat, with a carnation in his buttonhole, lapping up the congratulations for his moving interpretation; one of the customers exclaims: "Commendatore, scusi eh, ma ieri sera ci ha fatto piangere tutti. È stata una festa dell'arte" ("Commendatore, pardon me, but last night you made us all cry. It was a feast of Art"). This last remark is also quite telling, in that it shows to what degree in Fascist Italy the audience could be sympathetic to the dying Julius Caesar. It is an attitude that was obviously the result of the common political, cultural and theatrical interpretation of the role and stature of the Roman leader and also of the Shakespearean text.

It is worth noting that Nino Guglielmi, author of a Fascist *Julius Caesar* published 1939 for Edizioni Fascismo and dedicated to the "Founder of the New Roman Empire", wrote that "never in the history of the world – and especially in the history of Italy, of Rome – have there been two periods so rich with references and analogies as the Cesarean and the Mussolinian periods".[25] In the summer of 1935, two months before Italy's official invasion of Ethiopia, which turned the Duce into "a modern Caesar whose legions had vast fields to conquer",[26] the Basilica of Maxentius, one of the most important monuments of the Roman Forum, close to the newly built Via dell'Impero (the Avenue of the Empire, today called Via dei Fori Imperiali), became the stage for a production of Shakespeare's *Julius Caesar* directed by Ferdinando Tamberlani. The Basilica of Maxentius was chosen as a stage for the play, which ran for five days and was sponsored by the Fascist organization "Opera nazionale dopolavoro" (the National Workers' Recreation Club).[27] It was felt that this space would immediately evoke a glorious past and serve to neutralize the subversive issues of the play, so that "the most politically dangerous scene, Caesar's assassination, played under the central arch, could only be read as a tragedy for all mankind".[28] The play seemed to reiterate Mussolini's appeal "not to the nostalgic contemplation of the past, but hard preparation for the future. Rome is our point of departure... our myth. We dream of a Roman Italy, that is wise and strong, disciplined and imperial".[29]

The following year, on 6 February 1936, an opera from Shakespeare's play, with libretto by Gian Francesco Malipiero, opened the season of the Teatro Carlo Felice in Genoa. Rather significantly, in this heavily truncated version of Shakespeare's text that aimed to please the Duce,[30] Caesar's death "was to be put into perspective, allowing for a vision that included the crisis of the republic and the prefiguration of an imperial future".[31] Mussolini himself, in fact, wrote a play called *Cesare*, in collaboration with Giovacchino Forzano, a prominent opera librettist and dramatist of the time.[32] The play premièred at the Teatro Argentina in Rome in April 1939, though, according to the authors' stated intentions, it was not meant to be compared to the Shakespearean play. Rather, it was conceived, as Silvia Bigliazzi points out, as "a vehicle for the regime's self-aggrandizement, a display of grandeur that reflected the greatness of the past and, by implication, suggested a present that was capable of recreating such splendour".[33] Mussolini and Forzano's play depicted Caesar as the "fondatore / alla vigilia dell'avvento Cristiano / dell'impero di Roma / che durò quattro secoli" ("the founder /on the eve of the Christian age /of the Roman Empire / which lasted for four centuries"), who falls "in nome di una menzogna"("in the name of a lie") by "assassin e traditori che Dante supremo giudice inchiodò negli inferi per sempre" ("assassins and traitors / whom Dante / supreme judge / confined in Hell / forever").[34]

As far as the fragment of *Julius Caesar* in Fellini's *Roma* is concerned, Tempera writes:

> In less than a minute, Fellini conveys a lot of information about the production. A very small company (only two assassins for this Caesar!) interprets a severely truncated version of the text, focused on a one-star actor—a very old actor with exaggerated makeup and reciting with overdramatic gestures, which recalls the style of the nineteenth-century Italian Shakespeareans.[35]

But if one analyses the sequence in greater depth, all our certainties about Shakespeare's paternity begin to waver. Is it really an excerpt from a Shakespearean production? As we watch it repeatedly, we start to suspect that, as always with Fellini, it is rather his recreation of a play about Julius

Caesar that creatively appropriates different elements from different plays, not only Shakespeare's tragedy. First of all, in the film Caesar speaks the famous line "Anche tu, Bruto, figlio mio!", which in Shakespeare was shortened to "Et tu, Brute?". Besides, unlike Shakespeare, the play in the film ends soon after Caesar's assassination, in a fashion rather reminiscent of Enrico Corradini's *Giulio Cesare*.[36] First written in 1902, revised and republished in 1926, Corradini's play focused on "the epic and extraordinary deeds of Caesar's life rather than on the consequences of his death", and it aimed to create a fascinating portrait of the Roman leader. It was staged in 1928 at the Greek Theatre of Taormina with Gualtiero Tumiati in the role of Caesar.[37] I would further suggest that there is something in Šaljapin's countenance that reminds one of Tumiati, and also that the stage designs are similar; in both versions, the protagonist is assassinated under a huge statue: in the Fellini film, Bruto appears from behind the pedestal of a gigantic statue (Fig. 8.2),[38] whilst in one of the photos of the 1928 production the Roman leader stands beneath the pedestal of a statue (Fig. 8.3)[39]; additionally, Corradini's 1902 script notes that "Caesar falls at the feet of the statue of Pompeius".[40]

For all these reasons, I am doubtful whether we can take for granted that Fellini's short performance of *Julius Caesar* derives from Shakespeare

Fig. 8.2 Alfredo Adami as Bruto appearing behind a statue in Fellini's *Rome*

Fig. 8.3 Gualtiero Tumiati as Julius Caesar—1928 Teatro Greco, Taormina

or is, in fact, a replica of a Shakespearean production. Indeed, *Othello* and *King Lear* are the only Shakespearean plays Fellini talked about. He never mentions *Julius Caesar* in the film script of *Roma*, nor anywhere else in his autobiographies or interviews.

Fellini acknowledged that he was introduced to the work of Shakespeare, and *King Lear* in particular, by his friend Ennio Flaiano, renowned author and screenwriter:

> Ennio Flaviano introduced me to Shakespeare. I would pick Flaiano up in my car and we'd drive to one of those rundown deserted bars that litter the beaches of Ostia. We'd order something to eat and drink and I would

> have him explain to me the subtlety of the great playwright's work, in particular *King Lear*.[41]

In the same interview, he even told an anecdote about his friend's comic appropriation of the Shakespearean tragedy:

> One day during our talks, Flaiano stood up and, to the sound of the crashing waves, recited the unforgettable lines: "Hark, did you hear the news? King Lear fell off a cliff. / O horrible! Were you very close to him? / Indeed, sir, close enough to push".[42]

Fellini also spoke of his passion for *Othello*, a tragedy that "inflamed [his] imagination".[43] He even had the idea for a film that would have been inspired by it, "to create a typical circus situation" with Othello represented as a White Clown—a character he introduces in his film *I clowns* (1970), where Maya explains that the white clown wears a "cappello a pan di zucchero" (a sugar loaf hat) and where some old "white clowns", such as Nino, Alex, Ludo, Louis Maïsse, the dwarf Roberto, Pipo, meet at the Café Curieux at Les Halles in Paris.[44] For his film based on *Othello*, Fellini thought he:

> would need to create a typical circus situation in which the clowns' makeup and costumes would require the following: Iago – an Auguste in white face and colourful rags, left leg chained to a tiny blackheart that he drags in the dust with ease. Othello – White Clown in black face and regal white costume, right leg chained to a giant white heart immobilizing him. By film's end, Othello is blown out of a cannon as the terrifying Green-Eyed Monster into the dying arms of Desdemona.[45]

On the other hand, Tempera is right when she writes that Fëdor Fëdorovič Šaljapin's rhetoric and overdramatic interpretation of Caesar seems to be in "the style of the 19th-century Italian Shakespeareans (Rossi, Salvini, etc.)".[46] Tommaso Salvini and Ernesto Rossi were the two great Italian actors who in the second half of the nineteenth century contributed to establish Shakespeare as one of the most honoured playwrights on the Italian stage and to link his work with the most famous actors of the times. Rossi was the only actor to stage *Julius Caesar* in the nineteenth century, in his translation,[47] despite being in serious financial difficulties and although the play lacked a suitable role for a "mattatore" (a spotlight chaser). The rhetorical style was also the main feature of the acting technique of Colaci, who took the role of Caesar in a 1905 production of the play intended as "a homage to the city of Rome through the celebration of a moment of its past".[48]

It is also true that Shakespeare's *Julius Caesar* was available throughout the Fascist period and could be read in a number of versions.[49] At the time, furthermore, Shakespeare was "a very well established cultural icon in Italy"[50] and thanks to Giovanni Gentile's 1923 school reform, the study of ancient Roman history was prescribed across the entire curriculum and Shakespeare's *Julius Caesar* included as a standard text in the middle school.[51] It is undeniable that the text is "problematic" and presents ambiguities that could clearly go against a Fascist interpretation, but it was studied only in extracts, and, with few exceptions,[52] Italian criticism, at the beginning of the twentieth century, began to establish a heroic interpretation of Roman history and of the figure of Caesar, who became "a man with high moral and intellectual qualities".[53] "Supplementary texts" on the subject of Caesar and Mussolini, circulating amongst students and teachers alike, also helped, as Nancy Isenberg demonstrates in her discussion of one such school book, "silence the 'disturbances' in Shakespeare's script".[54]

Shakespeare's *Julius Caesar* was, therefore, both well-known and popular in Italy, and it makes perfect sense that Fellini should consider this play as significant in his own (and in Italy's) past and that he should want to demonstrate how all the Roman props (the lictor symbol, the eagle) and theatrics (the Roman salute, the marching style, etc.) introduced into Fascism's self-fashioning and educational system should indeed induce students to read *Julius Caesar* and to see themselves as the direct heirs of ancient Rome with Mussolini as their Caesar.

Alea Iacta Est

Fellini's reference to the Roman play gains even more significance if we consider the paradigmatic way in which an "unmarked" Shakespearean (or supposed-to-be Shakespearean) fragment[55] can become the centre of a very complex dynamic and invoke further associations. In other terms, to quote Lanier, it becomes part of that "rhizomatic model", in which the Shakespearean text is "less a root than a node which might be situated in relation to other adaptational rhizomes".[56] As a matter of fact, the fragment moves from one text to another and from one medium (the theatre) to another (cinema), setting in motion a network of inter-textual links to other stage and film performances of *Julius Caesar* that turns out to be crucial to the construction of the Fellini's *Roma*. Fellini saw his film as a "flamboyant collision"[57] of images of the Eternal City drawn from literature, painting, tourism, films (including his own) following a process that is very similar to the literary process described by Antoine Compagnon in his book-length study on the history and theory of citation, *La seconde main ou le travail de la citation* (1979), as "déprédation and appropriation, or découpage et collage".[58] Fellini's quotation, in other words, can be considered as a clear exemplification of "le travail de la citation",[59] "un énoncé répété et une énonciation répétante",[60] in which, according to the French critic, "le sens d'une citation est infini, il est ouvert à la succession des interprétants".[61] The quotation is to be considered an agent of intertextuality, which engages the reader's or spectator's particular sphere of knowledge and that causes the reader or the spectator to interpret the "départ de sens" it produces.[62] Thus, the city of Rome is naturally conjured up through Fellini's own memories, but also through the spectators' recollections and associations, which are obviously dependent on their field of interest and knowledge and cannot be totally controlled by the filmmaker. It is possible that the spectators may fail to perceive or understand all of Fellini's inter-textual references, but, conversely, thanks to the pastiche nature of the film itself, they are encouraged to create their own connections. The short reference to *Julius Caesar* may therefore invite a Shakespearean cinephile to wonder whether there are possible links and connections between Shakespeare's Roman play and the other fragments constituting the film and eventually to recollect further intertextual allusions. He/she may feel called upon to parse the relationship of the Shakespearean reference to its host film, a process that Lanier considers to be "a source of pleasure for the audience".[63]

Because of its theatrical quality, the fragment from the performance of *Julius Caesar* in *Roma* can be immediately understood as a text of a "different regime",[64] and, as such, treated as a quotation. Spectators might therefore be induced to think both of *Julius Caesar*'s specifically Italian stage tradition and of other fragments from the play in Italian cinema, such as the Shakespearean cameo in Luciano Salce's *La voglia matta* (*A Mad Desire*, 1962), where a wealthy industrialist, "a commendatore", plays the role of Caesar during the theatre season at one of Roma's archaeological sites. The impressive beauty of the location jars with the amateurish acting of the large cast of actors, the inept interpretation of a Caesar continually in need of the prompter's services and with the vulgarity of the bourgeois audience; as Tempera suggests, "what on paper has all the makings of a magical evening (a great play performed in its ideal setting) turns into an easy target of ridicule".[65] The association is somehow legitimized by Fellini himself when in a Director's Notebook, made for NBC television, he explains that his imaginary Rome has more to do, in fact, with his memories of old Italian films than with the monuments: "Tramping around from ruin to ruin doesn't mean anything to me. My Rome is from the movies of my childhood".[66] Precisely because of the palimpsest-like nature of the film *Roma*, the quotation from the *Julius Caesar* play may function similarly and may, to a Shakespearean audience, suggest similar types of links to other films.

Interestingly, a Shakespearean audience might also have detected a Shakespearean *fil rouge* in Fellini's music hall sequence at the Barafonda Theatre. In *Roma*, the filmmaker recreates the theatrical world of the 1940's, when the audience used to insult the actors and thereby decree whether the performance was a success or a flop. The figure of the clumsy impersonator who is unable to make people laugh with his imitations and is therefore replaced on stage by the much more successful scantily dressed variety dancers is a stock character in many films of those years. Yet Fellini's sequence would immediately recall Dino Risi's 1960 *Il mattatore* (*Love and Larceny*), co-written by Fellini's good friend Ettore Scola, and its main character Gerardo Latini, the unsuccessful vaudeville performer, who is incapable of entertaining his audience. In Risi's film comedy, Gerardo Latini, who was played by Vittorio Gassman, Italy's most famous Shakespearean actor of the 1950s, is an impersonator whose performances are continuously interrupted by the audience's booing until he discovers that his acting abilities can be used far more successfully for less legitimate purposes, amongst which cheating people. It is perhaps worth noting that his only successful performance in the film is as an actor performing in prison, where he delivers Mark Anthony's funeral oration for Caesar, in prison uniform. In the yard, when a group of convicts ask him to perform a piece, he decides to play his dramatic pièce de résistance, Anthony's oration from Shakespeare's *Julius Caesar*. A demanding piece for a hard-to-please audience and yet, as he confesses in the voice-over, he is counting on the fact that "in any case [his] spectators could not leave the auditorium". Thanks to his over the top acting style, which includes physical contact with his spectators and a high degree of mimicry, he wins over the inmates, who naturally do not know either the play or the historical episode, so that when one of them asks the question, "Who is this

Caesar he is talking about?" another answers "He must be a friend of his", and the conclusion reached is that Brutus was "a real-son-of-a-bitch".

The fact that in the first part of *Roma*, Fellini tries to link Julius Caesar (the historical figure and the play) with the cult of Cesarism and Fascist propaganda may also produce other kinds of associations. Let us consider the sequence where Fellini-as-a-boy and his parents go to the cinema (probably a reproduction of the Fulgor cinema in Rimini, where the director first discovered films as a child[67]) and watch a clip from the old Istituto L.U.C.E.'s newsreel of the celebrations of 28 October (the date of the 1922 "March on Rome"). Produced by Unione Cinematografica Educativa with the precise aim "of spreading popular culture and general education [...] for national and patriotic propaganda purposes",[68] this kind of news footage rapidly became a tool for the "personal glorification of the Duce"[69] who could thus count on the building of "a monument to his own deeds"[70] on a daily basis. Once again, Fellini, who never allowed his characters to make explicit comments either in favour of or against Mussolini, expresses his mordant reproach of the celebration of Fascism by focusing on shots of people and situations that crush the myths of Fascism. Somewhat comically, therefore, the images of the gerarchi's leap across the circle of fire and of the parade of the "Balilla", the "Figli della Lupa" and "Fasci giovanili di combattimento" against the background of the martial profile of the Duce are projected on the cinema screen as a crowd is shown elbowing for seats. It is by juxtaposing the rhetorical propaganda of the newsreel proclaiming "Rome's faith in the brilliant destiny of our imperial motherland" and celebrating the (false) grandeur of the Italy portrayed on screen with the mean quarrelsomeness of the Italy represented by its citizens that the filmmaker reveals his critical and ironic attitude. Whilst he powerfully unmasks the representation of the splendour that was the very lifeblood of Fascism, we spectators are once more reminded of Shakespeare, with Joseph L. Mankiewicz's 1953 *Julius Caesar* coming to mind as another film, which interpreted the play in the light of Fascist history by drawing attention to some of the specific props of Fascism's public spectacles. Fellini's sequence might thus echo Mankiewicz's decision to use black-and-white photography to give his film the texture of the black-and-white newsreels that showed the growth and the collapse of recent dictatorships. In his personal and original fashion, Fellini seems to be in tune with the words of producer John Houseman, who had previously been involved in the anti-Fascist *Julius Caesar* of 1937, famously directed by Orson Welles as a warning against the current rise of dictatorships in Europe and the mob's enthusiasm for autocratic rule,

> *Julius Caesar*, when effectually performed before modern audiences, enjoys one clever advantage over most classic plays: the almost automatic emotion which this drama of political strife engenders in audiences, all of whom, in their time, directly or indirectly, by remote or immediate experience, have witnessed and suffered from analogous evils of political strife, demagoguery and mass violence.[71]

In Mankiewicz's intentions, the film's *mise-en-scène* was to be, in general, close to the Roman spectacle that sustained Fascist Italy, where ancient Rome (along with its eagles, salutes and triumphal processions) had been appropriated as Fascism's central political vision, and, indeed, Italian Fascism as a whole had been staged as a spectacular show with Mussolini playing the part of Caesar.[72] Houseman reports how inevitably the Forum scenes would evoke memories of Mussolini "ranting from his high balcony overlooking the wildly cheering crowd that would presently spit on his dead body as it hung by its feet outside a gas station".[73]

The intersection between (Shakespearean or not Shakespearean) *Julius Caesar*, spectacle and Fascism links Mankiewicz's evocation of the spectacle of Fascism with Fellini's use of spectacle; like the Fascists, Fellini returns to spectacle, but his massive crowd scenes are meant to oppose the official view by presenting freaks and outcasts instead of troops of athletic young men marching and saluting or performing feats of physical prowess. The link to Mankiewicz might be confirmed by Fellini's confessed admiration for the American filmmaker and by the fact that his film *The Barefoot Contessa* (1954) is acknowledged by Fellini as a major influence on his own *La dolce vita* (*The Sweet Life*, 1960). It is also legitimized by the notable resonance of Mankiewicz's *Cleopatra* (1963), the Hollywood epic shot in Rome and starring Elizabeth Taylor and Richard Burton, who reached the height of notoriety during their well-known love affair—a matter of great interest for the general public and the "paparazzi" and a source of inspiration for Fellini himself who was shooting *La dolce vita*.[74] Indeed, the spectators watching *Roma* are invited to make one more Shakespearean association when they view the surreal, dreamlike sequence where the pharmacist's nymphomaniac wife dances in a convertible, her hair loose in the wind, surrounded by men in togas (Fig. 8.4). Dressed in red and wearing a gilt crown of laurel, the

Fig. 8.4 Elisa Mainardi in Fellini's *Roma*

actress Elisa Mainardi reminds us of the Roman Empress Messalina, the third wife of Emperor Claudius, who had a reputation for promiscuity, but she also might recall Elizabeth Taylor, who, as Cleopatra in Mankiewicz' film, wore a similar red dress.

The Tunnel of Memories

I would like to conclude by focusing on the beautiful underground sequence in *Roma*, in which Fellini and his troupe accompany some engineers who are building Rome's metro line. Alessandro Carrera, author of the awarded book *Fellini's Eternal Rome: Paganism and Christianity in Federico Fellini's Films*,[75] writes that the montage alternates between shots of the tunnel excavating and of the 110 km of documents from the Archivio di Stato (State Archive), and he cites screenwriter Bernardino Zappi, who described the State Archive as "the cemetery of all the secrets of the country", where you find everything, from the murmurs at the table of King Vittorio Emanuele II to the reports written under Fascism; from the notes of paranoid Police officers ready to see conspiracies everywhere to the many unanswered letters of poor or mad people addressing ministers. When Carrera concludes that the State Archive, even if so surreptitiously framed, is "the only Fellinian place in which Rome is truly the capital of Italy", a nation that "to survive has to mythicize and at the same time humiliate its past",[76] he is also referring to the many unsolved mysteries of Fellini's cinema.

As one of the underground engineers explains, they must frequently stop digging since they often bump into archaeological finds, such as discovering an ancient villa. As the troupe and their guides enter a cavernous space, they look around, gazing in wonder on the mosaics, statues and frescos but then, slowly, the frescos begin to dissolve, attacked by the sudden gusts of fresh air, and even the sculptures crumble away in seconds. According to Joanna Paul, the sequence is powerfully symbolic of Fellini's attitude to the city in several ways:

> It is a city literally and metaphorically built on layers, on the material and imaginative presence of different historical moments. Antiquity's immediate presence on the surface is fragmentary and thus [...] visibly representative of its distance and incoherence. If we work hard and "dig" below the surface—literally, in this sense—we may hope to appreciate it as present and complete—*wie es eigentlich gewesen*, perhaps. But still, suggests Fellini, the distance, the gap between us and them, cannot be overcome. Such is antiquity's distance and its fragility that it disappears before we can really understand it – just like a dream, in fact.[77]

Perhaps we may interpret the scene differently and perceive it as symbolically referring to how our memory stores what we know, including our memories of Shakespeare. Like the archaeological finds, Shakespeare survives in a fragmentary fashion, which functions as a reminder of his oeuvre and his distance from us in such a way that our perception of his work and even of small tattered pieces of it is inevitably tied to our own expectations and lives. It is a process of recognition and questioning that is also a vital part of the aesthetic experience—a process prompted by the palimpsest-like quality of Fellini's film, but which, I suspect, is at work every time we unexpectedly come across a Shakespearean (or supposedly Shakespearean) fragment in films not directly connected with the Elizabethan playwright of Stratford, and therefore potentially "open" to many different interpretations.

Notes

1. Maria Wyke, *Julius Caesar in Western Culture* (Oxford: Blackwell, 2006).
2. Mariangela Tempera, "Staged by quick comedians: references to Shakespeare's Roman plays on screen," in *Shakespeare on Screen: the Roman Plays*, ed. Sarah Hatchuel and Nathalie Vienne-Guerrin (Mont-Saint-Aignan Cedex: Publications des universités de Rouenetdu Havre, 2009), 305. Tempera's is the only complete collection and analysis of the quotations from Shakespeare's plays in Italian cinema and I am therefore deeply indebted to her and to her amazing Shakespeare Centre Video library, which offers a huge archive of Shakespeare-related materials on video from all over the world and is the only video-archive of the material produced in Italy.
3. Douglas Lanier, "Shakespeare / Not Shakespeare: Afterword," ed. Christy Desmet, Natalie Loper, Jim Casey (Palgrave Macmillan, 2017), 293–303.
4. Federico Fellini's *Roma* (1972) is discussed in the above-quoted essay, which records films whose Shakespearean origin is "either self-evident or can be convincingly argued" (Tempera, "Staged by Quick Comedians," 305).
5. Joanna Paul, "Rome Ruined and Fragmented: The Cinematic City in Fellini's *Satyricon* and *Roma*," in *Cinematic Rome*, ed. Richard Wrighley (Leicester: Troubador Publishing, 2008), 114–5.
6. Janet Staiger, *Perverse Spectators: The Practices of Film Reception* (New York and London: New York University Press, 2000).
7. Shaul Bassi, *Shakespeare's Italy and Italy's Shakespeare. Place, "Race," Politics* (USA: Palgrave Macmillan, 2016); Paolo Caponi, *Otello in camicia nera. Shakespeare, la censura e la regia del ventennio fascista* (Roma: Bulzoni, 2018), 25–62.
8. Lanier, "On the Virtues of Illegitimacy: Free Shakespeare on Film," in *Shakespeares After Shakespeare. An Encyclopedia of the Bard in Mass Media and Popular Culture*, ed. Richard Burt, vol. 1, 132–7 (Westport, Connecticut and London: Greenwood Press, 2007), 136.
9. Lanier, "On the Virtues of Illegitimacy," 134.
10. Paul, "Rome Ruined and Fragmented," 115.
11. Fellini quoted in Paul, "Rome Ruined and Fragmented," 115.
12. Fellini's film released in the following year, 1973. In *Amarcord*, Fellini carries his bitter criticism further and remembers "the failure of an infancy deformed by the rhetoric of the schools, by Fascism and by the religious Manichaeism, closed to all exchanges with the outside world, nourished by myths and fears" (Aldo Tassone, "From Romagna to Rome: The Voyage of a Visionary Chronicler (*Roma* and *Amarcord*)," in *Federico Fellini. Essays in Criticism*, ed. Peter Bondanella (Oxford: Oxford University Press, 1978), 279).

13. Nancy Isenberg, "'Caesar's Word Against the World': Caesarism and the Discourses of Empire," in *Shakespeare and the Second World War. Memory, Culture, Identity*, ed. Irena R. Makaryk and Marissa McHugh (Toronto: University of Toronto Press, 2012), 83. See also Catharine Edwards, *Roman Presences: Receptions of Rome in European Culture, 1789–1945* (Cambridge: Cambridge University Press, 1999), 223.
14. Olivier Maillart, "Epic Consolation: The Fascist Adventure Film," in *Cinematic Rome*, ed. Richard Wrigley (Leicester: Troubador, 2008), 1–12; 8.
15. Isenberg, "Caesar's Word Against the World," 83.
16. Aldo Tassone, "From Romagna to Rome," 265.
17. Richard J.B. Bosworth, *Whispering City: Rome and Its Histories* (New Haven and London: Yale University Press, 2011), 133.
18. Bosworth, *Whispering City*, 134.
19. Bernardino Zapponi quoted in Fellini, *Roma di Federico Fellini*, ed. Bernardino Zapponi (Bologna: Cappelli, 1972), 214.
20. These were in addition to the bronze statue of the emperor (a copy of the one in the Palazzo Senatorio on the Campidoglio) placed on the Via dell'Impero in front of Caesar's Forum, the one that the Duce himself donated to the city of Rimini in 1933. See Ravara Montebelli in *Guida alla mostra documentaria Alea Iacta Est*.
21. Tempera, "Staged by Quick Comedians," 313.
22. Miro Gori, "Il dialetto di Federico," in *Federico Fellini: La mia Rimini*, ed. Mario Guaraldi and Loris Pellegrini (Rimini: Guaraldi, 2007), 333.
23. William Van Watson, "Fellini and Lacan: The Hollow Phallus, the Male Womb, and the Retying of the Umbilical," in *Federico Fellini: Contemporary Perspectives*, ed. Francis Burke and Marguerite R. Waller (Toronto, Buffalo, London: University of Toronto Press, 2002), 77.
24. Van Watson, "Fellini and Lacan," 77.
25. Nino Guglielmi, *Giulio Cesare: Quattro Momenti e Sei Quadri* (Roma: Edizioni Fascismo, 1939), 9.
26. Bosworth, *Whispering City*, 176.
27. It is Achille Starace who is credited with the idea of the Maxentius event. Starace was the President of the National Workers' Recreational Club and a supporter of Mussolini who led a squadron of Blackshirts in the famous 1922 March on Rome.
28. Marisa Sestito, *Julius Caesar in Italia* (Bari: Adriatica, 1978), 128.
29. Benito Mussolini quoted in Andrea Giardina, "Ritorno al futuro: La romanità fascista," in *Il mito di Roma da Carlo Magno a Mussolini*, ed. Andrea Giardina and André Vauchez (Bari: Laterza, 2008), 219.
30. Gian Francesco Malpiero, *Giulio Cesare in L'Armonioso Labirinto: Teatro da musica 1913–1970*, ed. Marzio Pieri (Venezia: Marsilio, 1992), 225–69.

31. Silvia Bigliazzi, "Julius Caesar 1935. Shakespeare and Censorship in Fascist Italy," Skenè Texts, 3, Supplement to *Skenè. Journal of Theatre and Drama Studies*, 2019, 38–40.
32. See Vico Lodovici, "*Cesare* di Forzano," *Scenario*, 8.5 (May 1939), 200–201.
33. Jane Dunnett, "The Rhetoric of Romanità: Representations of Caesar in Fascist Theatre," in *Julius Caesar in Western Culture*, ed. Maria Wyke (Oxford: Blackwell, 2006), 259–60.
34. Quoted in Bigliazzi, "Julius Caesar 1935," 41–2.
35. Tempera, "Staged by Quick Comedians," 314.
36. Enrico Corradini, *Giulio Cesare: dramma in 5 atti* (Milano: Mondadori, 1926), 311.
37. Ireneo Sanesi, "Enrico Corradini—*Giulio Cesare*, dramma in cinque atti," in *La critica. Rivista di Letteratura, Storia e Filosofia di-retta da Benedetto Croce* (1903), 104–18.
38. Zapponi, *Roma di Federico Fellini*, 215.
39. "Duilio Tumiati nel Giulio Cesare di Enrico Corradini al Teatro greco di Taormina," in *Cultura Italia. Un patrimonio da esplorare*, Last accessed 14 February 2022, http://www.culturaitalia.it/opencms/museid//viewItem.jsp?language=it&id=oai%3Aculturaitalia.it%3Amuseiditalia-work_65790.
40. Corradini, *Giulio Cesare*, 249.
41. Federico Fellini in Damien Pettigrew, *I'm born a Liar: A Fellini Lexicon* (New York: Harry N. Abrams Inc., 2003), 135.
42. Fellini in Pettigrew, *I'm Born a Liar*, 135.
43. Ibid., 136–7.
44. Tullio Kezich, *Federico Fellini. Il libro dei film* (Milano: Rizzoli, 2009), 198.
45. Fellini in Pettigrew, *I'm born a Liar*, 137.
46. Tempera, "*Staged by Quick Comedians*," 314.
47. Rossi's translation is included in Ernesto Rossi, *Studi drammatici e lettere autobiografiche* (Firenze: Le Monnier, 1885).
48. Sestito, *Julius Caesar in Italia*, 112.
49. Dunnett, "The Rhetoric of Romanità," 252.
50. Isenberg, "Caesar's Word Against the World," 86.
51. Galfré, *Una riforma alla prova. La scuola media di Gentile e il fascism* (Milano: Franco Angeli, 2000).
52. Amongst these exceptions is Benedetto Croce in his *Shakespeare*.
53. Sestito, *Julius Caesar in Italia*, 120.
54. Isenberg, "Caesar's Word Against the World," 88–90.
55. Lanier, "Shakespeare / Not Shakespeare: Afterword," 300.

56. Lanier, "Shakespearean Rhizomatics: Adaptation, Ethics, Value," in *Shakespeare and the Ethics of Appropriation. Reproducing Shakespeare: New Studies in Adaptation and* Appropriation, ed. Alexa Alice Joubin and Elizabeth Rivlin (Palgrave Macmillan, New York, 2014), 21–40.
57. Tassone, "From Romagna to Rome," 263. According to Landy, Roma is "a meditation on the cinematic image as the arbiter of a virtual 'reality' where the sense of place, the city with its evocations of ancient Rome – its frescos, statuary, architecture – is laden with memories of different moments in Italian history: cinematical historical spectacles from the silent era, early Roman art, Fascism and the 1970s". In Marcia Landy, *Italian Film* (Cambridge: Cambridge University Press, 2000), 138–9.
58. Antoine Compagnon, *La Seconde main ou le trevail* (Paris: Seuil, 1979), 18, 37.
59. Compagnon, *La Seconde main*, 36.
60. Ibid., 56.
61. Ibid., 61.
62. According to Compagnon, "la citation est un opérateur trivial d'intertextualité. Elle fait appel à la compétence du lecteur, elle amorce la machine de la lecture qui doit fournir un travail dès lors que, dans une citation, sont mis en présence deux textes dont le rapport n'est pas d'équivalence ni de redondance. Mais ce travail dépend d'un phénomène immanent au texte: la citation le creuse singulièrement, elle l'ouvre, elle l'écarte. Il y a quête de sens, que mène la lecture, parce qu'il y a écart, départ de sens: un trou, une différence de potentiel, un court-circuit. Le phénomène est la différence, le sens est sa résolution" (*La Seconde main* 44).
63. Lanier, "On the Virtues of Illegitimacy," 136.
64. Antonio Costa, "Nel corpo dell'immagine, la parola," in Giovanni Guagnelini and Valentina Re, *Visioni di altre visioni: intertestualità e cinema* (Firenze: Archetipolibri - Gedit Edizioni, 2007), 101.
65. Mariangela Tempera, "Political Caesar. *Julius Caesar* on the Italian Stage," in *Julius Caesar. New Critical Essays*, ed. Horst Zander (New York and London: Routledge, 2005), 333.
66. Federico Fellini quoted in Theodorakopoulos, "The Sites and Sights of Rome in Fellini's Films," in *The Sites of Rome*, ed. D.H. James Larmour and D. Spencer (Oxford: Oxford University Press, 2007), 354.
67. Pettigrew, *I'm Born a Liar*, 67.
68. Daniela Manetti, *Un'arma poderosissima, Industria cinematografica e Stato durante il fascismo, 1922–1943* (Milano: Franco Angeli, 2012), 51.
69. Manetti, *Un'arma poderosissima*, 51.
70. Gian Piero Brunetta, "Cinema," in *Dizionario del fascismo* (Torino: Einaudi, 2002), 286.
71. Houseman quoted in Wyke, "Film Style and Fascism: Julius Caesar," *Film Studies*, 4 (Summer 2004), 60.

72. Bosworth, *Whispering City*, 187–211; Maddalena Pennacchia Punzi, *Shakespeare intermediale* (Spoleto: Editoria & Spettacolo, 2021), 147–73.
73. John Houseman, *Unfinished Business- Memoirs: 1902–1988* (New York: Applause Theatre Books, 1989), 324.
74. See Bondanella, *The Films of Federico Fellini*, 68; Kashner and Schoenberger, *Furious Love* (Milano: Il Saggiatore, 2011), 40–41.
75. Alessandro Carrera, *Fellini's Eternal Rome: Paganism and Christianity in Federico Fellini's Films* (London: Bloomsbury, 2019).
76. Alessandro Carrera, "La Roma di Fellini: città eterna, città interna," in *Doppiozero*, January 20, 2020, Last accessed 14 February 2022, https://www.doppiozero.com/materiali/la-roma-di-fellini-citta-eterna-citta-interna.
77. Paul, "Rome Ruined and Fragmented," 115–16.

Works Cited

Bassi, Shaul. *Shakespeare's Italy and Italy's Shakespeare. Place, "Race," Politics*. London: Palgrave Macmillan US, 2016.

Bigliazzi, Silvia. "Julius Caesar 1935. Shakespeare and Censorship in Fascist Italy." Verona: Skenè Texts, Supplement to *Skenè. Journal of Theatre and Drama Studies* 3 (2019).

Bosworth, Richard J.B. *Whispering City. Rome and Its Histories*. New Haven and London: Yale University Press, 2011.

Brunetta, Gian Piero. "Cinema." In *Dizionario del fascismo*. Torino: Einaudi, 2002.

Burt, Richard, ed. *Shakespeares after Shakespeare. An Encyclopedia of the Bard in Mass Media and Popular Culture*. Westport, CT and London: Greenwood Press, 2007.

Caponi, Paolo. *Otello in camicia nera. Shakespeare, la censura e la regia nel ventennio fascista*. Roma: Bulzoni, 2018.

Carrera, Alessandro. *Fellini's Eternal Rome: Paganism and Christianity in Federico Fellini's Films*. London: Bloomsbury, 2019.

Carrera, Alessandro. "La Roma di Fellini: città eterna, città interna." *Doppiozero*, January 20, 2020. Last accessed 14 February, 2022. https://www.doppiozero.com/materiali/la-roma-di-fellini-citta-eterna-citta-interna.

Compagnon, Antoine. *La Seconde main ou le travail de la citation*. Paris: Seuil, 1979.

Corradini, Enrico. *Giulio Cesare: dramma in 5 atti*. Milano: Mondadori, 1926.

Croce Benedetto. *Shakespeare*. Edited by Gian N. Orsini. Bari: Laterza, 1960.
Dunnett, Jane. "The Rhetoric of Romanità: Representations of Caesar in Fascist Theatre." In *Julius Caesar in Western Culture*, edited by Maria Wyke, 244–65. Oxford: Blackwell, 2006.
Edwards, Catharine. *Roman Presences: Receptions of Rome in European Culture, 1789-1945*. Cambridge: Cambridge University Press, 1999.
Fellini, Federico. *Roma di Federico Fellini*. Edited by Bernardino Zapponi. Bologna: Cappelli, 1972.
Galfré, Monica. *Una riforma alla prova. La scuola media di Gentile e il fascismo*. Milano: Franco Angeli, 2000.
Gori, Gianfranco Miro. "Il dialetto di Federico." In *Federico Fellini: La mia Rimini*. Edited by Mario Guaraldi and Loris Pellegrini. Rimini: Guaraldi, 2007.
Guagnelini, Giovanni, and Valentina Re. *Visioni di altre visioni: intertestualità e cinema*. Firenze: Archetipolibri - Gedit Edizioni, 2007.
Guglielmi, Nino. *Giulio Cesare: quattro momenti e sei quadri*. Roma: Edizioni Fascismo, 1939.
Hatchuel, Sarah, and Nathalie Vienne-Guerrin, eds. *Shakespeare on Screen: The Roman Plays*. Mont-Saint-Aignan Cedex: Publications des universités de Rouen et du Havre, 2009.
Houseman, John. *Unfinished Business—Memoirs: 1902-1988*. New York: Applause Theatre Books, 1989.
Isenberg, Nancy. "'Caesar's Word Against the World': Caesarism and the Discourses of Empire." In *Shakespeare and the Second World War. Memory, Culture, Identity*, edited by Irena R. Makaryk and Marissa McHugh, 83–105. Toronto: University of Toronto Press, 2012.
Joubin, Alexa Alice, and Rivlin Elizabeth, eds. *Shakespeare and the Ethics of Appropriation*. Palgrave McMillan, 2014.
Kashner Sam, and Nancy Schoenberger. *Furious love. Liz Taylor, Richard Burton: la storia d'amore del secolo*. Milano: Il Saggiatore (2010), 2011.
Kezich, Tullio. *Federico Fellini. Il libro dei film*. Milano: Rizzoli, 2009.
Landy, Marcia. *Italian Film*. Cambridge: Cambridge University Press, 2000.
Lanier, Douglas. "On the Virtues of Illegitimacy: Free Shakespeare on Film." In *Shakespeares after Shakespeare. An Encyclopedia of the Bard in Mass Media and Popular Culture*, edited by Richard Burt, vol. 1, 132–7. Westport, CT and London: Greenwood Press, 2007.
Lanier, Douglas. "Shakespeare / Not Shakespeare: Afterword." In *Shakespeare / Not Shakespeare*, edited by Christy Desmet, Natalie Loper, Jim Casey, 293–303. Palgrave Macmillan, 2017.
Lanier, Douglas. "Shakespearean Rhizomatics: Adaptation, Ethics, Value." In *Shakespeare and the Ethics of Appropriation*, edited by Alexa Alice Joubin and Elizabeth Rivlin, 21–40. New York: Palgrave Macmillan, 2014.

Maillart, Olivier, "Epic Consolation: The Fascist Adventure Film." In *Cinematic Rome,* edited by Richard Wrigley, 1–12. Leicester: Troubador, 2008.
Malpiero, Gian Francesco. *Giulio Cesare in L'Armonioso Labirinto: Teatro da musica 1913–1970*. Edited by Marzio Pieri, 225–69. Venezia: Marsilio, 1992.
Manetti, Daniela. *"Un'arma poderosissima". Industria cinematografica e Stato durante il fascismo. 1922–1943*. Milano: Franco Angeli, 2012.
Paul, Joanna. "Rome Ruined and Fragmented: The Cinematic City in Fellini's Satyricon and Roma." In *Cinematic Rome*, edited by Richard Wrighley, 109–20. Leicester: Troubador Publishing, 2008.
Pennacchia Punzi, Maddalena. *Shakespeare intermediale. I drammi romani*. Spoleto: Editoria & Spettacolo, 2021.
Pettigrew, Damian. *I'm Born a Liar. A Fellini Lexicon*. New York: Harry N. Abrams Inc., 2003.
Ravara Montebelli, Cristina. *Guida alla mostra documentaria Alea Iacta Est. Giulio Cesare a Savignano sul Rubicone*. Cesena: Il Ponte Vecchio, 2010.
Rossi, Ernesto. *Studi drammatici e lettere autobiografiche*. Firenze: Le Monnier, 1885.
Sanesi, Ireneo. "Enrico Corradini - *Giulio Cesare*, dramma in cinque atti" - Roma, Rassegna Internazionale, 1902." In *La critica. Rivista di Letteratura, Storia e Filosofia diretta da Benedetto Croce*, 1, 1903. 104–18.
Sestito, Marisa. *Julius Caesar in Italia*. Bari: Adriatica, 1978.
Staiger, Janet. *Perverse Spectators: The Practices of Film Reception*. New York and London: New York University Press, 2000.
Tassone, Aldo. "From Romagna to Rome: The Voyage of a Visionary Chronicler (*Roma* and *Amarcord*)." In *Federico Fellini Essays in Criticism*, edited by Peter Bondanella, 261–88. Oxford: Oxford University Press, 1978.
Tempera, Mariangela. "Political Caesar. Julius Caesar on the Italian Stage." In *Julius Caesar. New Critical Essays*, edited by Horst Zander, 333–43. New York, London: Routledge, 2005.
Tempera, Mariangela. "Staged by Quick Comedians: References to Shakespeare's Roman plays on Screen." In *Shakespeare on Screen: The Roman Plays,* edited by Sarah Hatchuel and Nathalie Vienne-Guerrin, 305–28. Mont-Saint-Aignan Cedex: Publications des universités de Rouen et du Havre, 2009.
Theodorakopoulos, Elena. "The Sites and Sights of Rome in Fellini's Films: 'Not a Human Habitation But a Psychical Entity.'" In *The Sites of Rome*, edited by Larmour, David H. James and D. Spencer, Diana, 353–84. Oxford: Oxford University Press, 2007.
Van Watson, William. "Fellini and Lacan: The Hollow Phallus, the Male Womb, and the Retying of the Umbilical." In *Federico Fellini: Contemporary Perspectives*, edited by Francis Burke and Marguerite R. Waller, 65–91. Toronto: University of Toronto Press, 2002.

Vauchez, André and Andrea Giardina, eds. *Il mito di Roma da Carlo Magno a Mussolini*. Bari: Laterza, 2008.
Vico Lodovici, Cesare. *Cesare* di Forzano. Rev. of Cesare written by Giovacchino Forzano (and Benito Mussolini), *Scenario* 8, no. 5 (May 1939).
Wrighley, Richard, ed. *Cinematic Rome*. Leicester: Troubador Publishing, 2008.
Wyke, Maria, ed. *Julius Caesar in Western Culture*. Oxford: Blackwell, 2006.
Wyke, Maria. "Film Style and Fascism: Julius Caesar." *Film Studies* 4 (Summer 2004): 58–74.

CHAPTER 9

"Still Our Contemporary" in East-Central Europe? Post-Socialist Shakespearean Allusions and Frameworks of Reference

Márta Minier

The afterlife of Shakespeare in fragments—whether transparent and meaningful allusions or seemingly arbitrary references—is a compelling research subject, particularly where there is not only an intertextual but an intermedial reception to consider. Films that have Shakespearean fragments carry verbal and at times performative "guest-texts" that contribute to the dense, multi-layered fabric of big-screen or television films. Operating with the concept of intertextuality in a broad sense adheres to Julia Kristeva's 'original' use of the term in her *Revolution in Poetic Language*: "the transposition of one (or several) sign system(s) into another."[1] Intertextual reading strategies empower the reader/spectator. As Susan Bassnett summarizes,

M. Minier (✉)
University of South Wales, Cardiff, Wales, UK
e-mail: marta.minier@southwales.ac.uk

A. A. Joubin and V. Bladen (eds.), *Onscreen Allusions to Shakespeare*, Global Shakespeares, https://doi.org/10.1007/978-3-030-93783-6_9

> The creative role of the reader in making connections takes us from influence studies in the old-fashioned sense to intertextuality, to the idea that texts exist in an endlessly interwoven relationship with one another. Here, of course, the connectivity is more random, and depends as much on what a reader may or may not bring to the reading as what a writer inserts into the text in the first place.[2]

Perceiving intertextuality as a rhetorical practice not limited to linguistic or literary dimensions, Frank J. D'Angelo reminds us that in such a context 'reading' is to be used "in its broadest sense to include listening to and viewing nonverbal *texts* [or] *artifacts*."[3]

The present chapter examines two postmillennial films with a fragmentary Shakespearean presence that also share a strong connection with East-Central Europe: the Polish television film *Żółty szalik* (*Yellow Scarf*, dir. Janusz Morgenstern, 2000) referencing *Hamlet*, and the international biopic of a Polish-Jewish musician, *The Pianist* (dir. Roman Polanski, 2002), alluding to *The Merchant of Venice*. The latter is a big-budget film for global consumption—the work of a "cultural traveller"[4] auteur; the former is the product of a "small cinema"[5] or rather small television culture with relatively limited presence in global circulation. A "resistance and defiance film"[6] within the broader Holocaust genre, the latter demonstrates that Shakespeare "has a knack of showing up at fateful historical moments,"[7] whereas the former may be seen to construct the missing Christmas tale of Shakespeare that Max Beerbohm's "Shakespeare and Christmas" published in *A Christmas Garland* (1912) playfully laments not having. This writing is part of Beerbohm's parody of the style of flamboyant journalist, novelist and socialite Frank Harris and his *The Man Shakespeare and His Tragic Life Story* (1909). Both attest to Shakespearean texts' capacity to infiltrate 'contemporary' textures—to use this phrase so often used in association with a famous Polish theater critic, Jan Kott.[8]

Shared aspects, such as allusion to Shakespeare, the quasi-tragic or tragicomic hero and a Polish cultural and historical context, formulate a more than tenuous link between *Yellow Scarf* and *The Pianist*, yet—while focusing on the subtle Shakespearean presence in the films—we need to remain conscious of their respective places in the global market that alert us to an uneven balance in terms of the two films' potential to be part of a broader network of global cultural exchange and thus an expansive intertextual framework. It is undoubtedly difficult to sort "small national cinemas" into a convenient rubric because of "not only different production and exhibition patterns, but also dissimilar discursive contexts", to use Dina Iordanova's succinct phrasing.[9] Yet, importantly, a 'small cinema' in her definition is "linked to a minor language" and therefore is "likely to achieve limited circulation due to [...] linguistic constraints".[10] Janusz Morgenstern, while not as widely acclaimed as some, more obviously international, giants of Polish cinema such as Kieślowski, Wajda or Polanski, is still anthologized in English. His *Do widzenia, do jutra* (*Goodbye, See You Tomorrow*, 1960) appears in volume 1 of the three volume Polish Cinema Classics DVD series. This chapter will devote significant attention to the lesser-known film, and will elaborate more briefly and in a particularly tailored way on the otherwise much analyzed *The Pianist*.

Context

The wealth and longevity of Shakespeare's creative and critical reception in East-Central Europe have been documented extensively in English and even more so in the respective national languages. In his short but comprehensive monograph, *Shakespeare and Eastern Europe* (2000), Zdeněk Stříbrný provides a helpful overview, and recent years have seen some closer academic focus on artistic as well as critical responses to Shakespeare during the decades of socialism (see for instance Schandl 2008 and the inaugural issue of the *Romanian Shakespeare Journal* from 2013). The present chapter itself concentrates on screen productions emerging during the post-transition phase of the post-socialist stage of the history of East-Central European nations, from before the EU enlargement of 2004.[11] Even though the umbrella term 'East-Central Europe' has its problems (perhaps slightly less so than the somewhat polarizing 'Eastern Europe'), there is much in the cultural history and indeed the Shakespearean reception of these national cultures that validate the use of the term here. It ought to be borne in mind, however, that "the Eastern bloc was implicitly and sometimes explicitly conceptualized as a unified region" and "debunking notions of homogeneity, arguing [...] for the interconnectedness as well as the unboundedness of its various parts"[12] (Kürti and Skalník 2009) are a task for scholars working on cultures of this part of Europe.

As mentioned before, the case studies selected for this chapter take us to Poland. Indeed, as Marta Gibinska and Jerzy Limon emphasize in

Hamlet East–West about the reception of Shakespeare in Polish culture, Shakespeare has played a significant part in the intellectual history of the country. "Polish theatre history", they claim, "is largely the history of Shakespearean productions".[13] As Bogusław Sułkowski also asserts, "Hamlet links our culture with the European tradition and at the same time is a specifically Polish construct".[14] The close association of the Polish dramatic, literary and cultural establishment with Shakespeare continued from the Romantic period well into the socialist era and indeed into post-socialist times and settings where the national often meets the global, and the intertextual encounter is often intermedial as well.[15]

There are, of course, numerous contemporary reworkings of Shakespeare in East-Central Europe, as elsewhere, that are in a filmic mode and offer (almost) full-scale structural echoes or shadows of Shakespearean texts. These examples of looser adaptations may be considered 'analogies'—adaptations signaled by "a fairly considerable departure" from the source, in Geoffrey Wagner's terminology,[16] whereas in Dudley Andrew's term,[17] they may be viewed as cases of 'fidelity of transformation'—where the adaptation uses a "skeleton" derived from the source or stays close to the "original's tone, values, imagery, and rhythm", in a process of "finding stylistic equivalents". Ranging from Áron Gauder's Hungarian *Romeo and Juliet* story, *Nyócker* (*The District*, 2004) to the Polish theater-within-film production *Kolejnosc uczuc* (*The Sequence of Feelings*, 1993, dir. Radosław Piwowarski) also revisiting—with liberties taken—the dramatic template associated with Shakespeare's star-crossed lovers, these films amply demonstrate the presence of Shakespeare as a storyteller providing blueprints for the contemporary popular imagination.

Disregarding such looser or, in some cases, tighter systematic reworkings and focusing on the challenge of fragmentary Shakespearean intertextuality in East-Central European film, the present chapter will focus on two films that allude to or otherwise 'feed off' Shakespeare—one directly from Poland and one with a strong Polish connection. Rather than being merely scattered examples of the near-omnipresence of Shakespeare in East-Central Europe and some contemporizing tendencies in the practice of Shakespearean appropriation, viewed together these screen productions re-emphasize not only the significance of but the breadth of East-Central European recourse to Shakespeare.

The Contemporary Hamlet Figure in *Żółty Szalik (Yellow Scarf)*

The Polish television film *Żółty szalik* (*Yellow Scarf*, 2000) directed by a veteran of small and big screen, Morgenstern (1922–2011), makes a brief and easy-to-miss reference to *Hamlet*, but upon closer inspection the connection with Shakespeare's classic is much more than a customary reference to a Shakespearean "purple passage",[18] namely the "To be, or not to be" soliloquy. Some of the film's themes and characters evoke our memories of the play, and Hamlet's pondering over matters of existence in the great soliloquy lends gravitas to the protagonist who aims to tackle his severe alcoholism. The inclusion of the soliloquy in the film also provides him with the potential of being a modern-day tragic hero, while his petty situation and quixotic struggle fuse the tragic overtone with that of comedy.

Morgenstern, a very productive and versatile director and producer for the screen, is famous, among others, for such filmic explorations of Polish society as *Do widzenia, do jutra* (*Goodbye, See You Tomorrow*, 1960) and the French New Wave inspired *Jowita* (1967) in both of which love is "reduced to a social game".[19] Another signature direction of his, *Trzeba zabić tę miłość* (*To Kill This Love*, 1972), scrutinizes "the end of romantic attitudes to love among Poles".[20] As Janina Falkowska (2014) underlines, some of Morgenstern's television series from the heyday of the socialist era have been pressed into service in post-socialist nostalgic television, where a significant trend is rescreening 'golden-era' productions for the joy of the older generations. In Falkowska's appraisal of nostalgic trends in Polish screen culture after the fall of the Iron Curtain, "[t]he viewers can satisfy their longing for the past by watching" television series such as *Polskie Drogi* (*The Polish Ways*, 1976–77), *Kolumbowie* (*Columbuses*, 1970–72) and *Stawka wieksza niz zycie* (*More Than Life at Stake*, 1968–70) as well as work by other household names.[21] Morgenstern created this slight, yet, for our purposes significant, one-hour television film in a latter stage of his career (after 1990, he predominantly worked as an executive producer and less often as a director). With a moderate exaggeration, we might see it as a gentle directorial swan song about Hamletian existential questions against a rapidly changing backdrop shaped by globalization and an altercation between metanarratives.

The one-hour television film about a recovering middle-aged alcoholic company director was scripted by the novelist and essayist Jerzy Pilch

(1952–2020), "[o]ne of the wittiest and most provocative observers of the postcommunist Polish political and social scene".[22] Winner of the prestigious Nike award for contemporary Polish literature, his fourth and perhaps most successful novel, *Pod Mocnym Aniołem* (2000, literally: *The Strong Angel Inn*; in Bill Johnston's 2009 translation: *The Mighty Angel*), similarly engages with the theme of an alcoholic trying to kick his habit. This satirical and tragicomic 'drinking novel' is from 2000, as is *Yellow Scarf*. There is a subtle, non-intrusive autobiographical dimension to the script as for some of his writing Pilch took inspiration from his own long-term alcohol problem.[23] The film features the widely acclaimed Janusz Gajos in the main role (whom we might recall with warmth from Kieslowski's *White*). This is far from his only role with a Hamletic hue: he later played Claudius in a 2004 Polish television adaptation and was cast in a 1987 Polish version of Ivo Brešan's Acting *Hamlet in the Village of Mrdusa Donja*.

My reading will juxtapose a jocular piece of writing about Shakespeare and Christmas not only to the film under discussion but also to Eve Kosofsky Sedgwick's musings about Christmas in *Tendencies* (1998 [1993])in order to highlight how *Żółty szalik* represents urban Poland under global capitalism, during a process of social and ideological change, negotiating the metanarrative of Christianity, related communal folk customs and familial support network(s) for the individual with the swiftly changing and shifting zeitgeist shaped by a consumerist outlook on life.

Following the opening credits, the film begins with a powerful, dynamic and almost intrusive evocation of what Eve Kosofsky Sedgwick imaginatively labels "the Christmas phalanx" (5),[24] as we see a contemporary, all-too-familiar cityscape with Christmas illuminations fusing into a brief visual sequence showing a hospital corridor with an unidentifiable patient carried by a nurse on a stretcher—our first indication of the possible fate of the protagonist. Sedgwick's starting point for her thinking on "Christmas Effects" and on how one's relationship with Christmas may help articulate a sense of queerness is how church and state appear to institutionalize Christmas and force it upon society, despite the inadequacy of 'Christmas' to address all identities in the same way. In her sharp criticism: "They all - religion, state, capital, ideology, domesticity, the discourses of power and legitimacy - line up with each other so neatly once a year, and the monolith so created is a thing one can come to view with unhappy eyes".[25] Morgenstern's film, which constitutes part of the "Polish Holidays" cycle, gives us a snapshot of an urban Poland where Christmas is at the same time commercialized and communal, with a hint at the possibility of the latter aspect slowly becoming anachronistic and untenable. With gentle intertextual echoes of Dickens' "A Christmas Carol", the Everyman-style protagonist (who, in one of his many self-addressing screen 'soliloquies' appears to be calling himself Pilch, a name shared by the scriptwriter) meets all who matter to him between the day before Christmas Eve and the morning of Christmas day: his relentlessly dedicated (and probably besotted) secretary (mentioned as Saint Ewa by his mother, in an unmissable Judeo-Christian reference), his son and his son's fiancée, his ex-wife, his current girlfriend and finally—after meeting a whole gathering of social contacts at an office Christmas party—his mother who lives in the countryside. Needless to say, all these human interactions, except the last one which gives him hope, show us—and the Everyman character himself—how he keeps failing (and pulling himself together again, mostly with the help of supportive women). In between these encounters, there are a few other scenes containing dialogue and mostly episodes of solitude in which the alcoholic's yearning for spirits leads to the most existentialist and Hamletian soliloquizing—even struggling to remember the word for the opposite of 'no' in his worst delirium. In the same solitary scene, after the Christmas party, he attends against his secretary's and his girlfriend's advice, he questions the existence of God. His language is multi-layered, very allusive (both to popular and traditionally 'high' culture) and philosophical, expressive of his attempts to clutch at any straw. "May the Force be with you," he says to his son in the restaurant where they meet to exchange presents (and where he receives a yellow scarf as a Christmas gift), probably hoping that Star Wars lingo will help to bridge the generation gap. From the point of view of confusion and allusiveness, his language is strongly reminiscent of the language of the more and more troubled Hamlet. As Wolfgang Clemen argues, "The seven soliloquies spoken by Hamlet show Shakespeare at the peak of his powers with regard to the art of the soliloquy".[26] This is a trait *Yellow Scarf* can be seen to continue, even if inadvertently as far as directorial decisions are concerned. The quotation of some of the opening of Hamlet's great soliloquy takes place when, after visiting his ex-wife, the protagonist goes to a bar and meets another convalescing alcoholic—somewhat of an alter ego to him—suffering from withdrawal symptoms, treats him to a drink and chats to him. As the protagonist says "That is the question" (in answer to "when will it be well?") as part of this conversation, the fellow alcoholic starts reciting Hamlet's 'great soliloquy', which our Everyman acknowledges as a sign of intelligence.

Beyond the actual quotation, *Hamlet*'s influence can also be discerned in various character and plot features. These include the sharp focus on decisions and the protagonist's determination to stick to decisions, as well as his frustration over his Hamletic inertia, his failure when he does not keep his word or indeed, in Hamletian terms, when he delays delivering what he is meant to do. Of course, his dilemma—on a pragmatic level—is about whether to drink or not to drink, as he tries to stop himself from giving in to the temptation of consuming alcohol where in Witold Adamek's cinematography and Andrzej Przedworski's scenography the whole environment around him seems to consist of glasses, bottles, decanters, flasks or items reminiscent of them. As opposed to Hamlet, who hesitates over whether to act or not to act upon the ghost's imperative, *Yellow Scarf*'s protagonist has to avoid an action and chooses a non-action. As Hamlet, Janusz Gajos' character carries the burden of a formidable task from the very start of the action. His task, as Hamlet's mandate for revenge, is specific and apparently unavoidable—controlling his alcoholism—but, as Hamlet's, it is an inescapably lonesome and almost unreachable mission. While both mandates are initially private in their respective origins, their broader ramifications are boundless. Hamlet concerns himself not only with what he believes to be his father's murder but with the "time" that is "out of joint". The repercussions of the alcoholism of Morgenstern's quasi-tragic character are boundless: the issue affects all his relationships (with all the people from his festive visitations). While Hamlet has ghostly apparitions, Morgenstern's unnamed protagonist has almost ghostly visions of containers of alcohol. He finds one in an office lamp he lights up in the first scene of the film, which starts in a meeting room and continues in his office. He approaches this vision with respect and awe similar to Hamlet's in relation to his father's ghost. The often jarring images (and sounds) of alcohol containers, ice cubes and mirrors merge into a poetic system of motifs with the lights of Christmas, offices, shop windows, hospitals and so on. The iciness of these images is in contrast with the warm colors (mainly brown) associated with the mother and the girlfriend. The titular yellow scarf also fuses into this complex system of images. This postmodern-day Hamlet repeatedly receives as presents and then loses, or gets close to losing, various yellow scarves (a favorite object of his, especially in his favorite color). Similar to a lucky charm, the scarves and his attachment to them work as a *leitmotif* connoting the difficulties in holding himself together and having his teetotaling ambitions always in sight.

While the *Hamlet* intertext is central for our purposes, we need to note briefly some other strong intertextual connections, including the already mentioned medieval Everyman-styled quester and Dickens. The film also bears Pilch's distinct signature as there is a strong intertextual relationship between Pilch's aforementioned novel and the film script. The first chapter of *The Mighty Angel* is entitled "The Yellow Dress", and the motif of yellow remains a recurrent one in the novel. Its connotations have to do with the feminine principle, female warmth and the hope that may convey. The color appears on the striped dress of a desired woman that the first-person narrator sees at an ATM, who later becomes identified as budding poet Alberta Lulaj, and with whom he becomes immediately and helplessly infatuated. As the desired (and completely unfamiliar) woman disappears at the corner, with the enervated narrator unable to follow her, the scale of the loss is elevated to historical levels in this mockery of the great epic novel:

> I recalled the fall of the Berlin Wall and I was opposed to the fall of the Berlin Wall, for all those enthusiasts who had demolished the wall with their mason's hammers had taken the brunette in the yellow dress from me. I was opposed to Solidarity, because Solidarity had taken the brunette in the yellow dress from me; and Lech Walesa had taken the brunette in the yellow dress from me, and John Paul II as he cried: "Descend, Holy Spirit," had taken the brunette in the yellow dress from me, and the Holy Spirit, as it descended and altered the face of the earth, had taken the brunette in the yellow dress from me. My God, O Holy Spirit, I thought, if everything were now as it used to be, if communism hadn't fallen, if there were no free market economy, if numerous transformations had not taken place in the part of Europe where I was born, there wouldn't be any ATMs here now, and if there were no ATMs, everything would have worked out perfectly between me and the dark-haired beauty in the yellow dress.[27]

The Mighty Angel is an emphatically post-socialist story, with the narrator-protagonist struggling to come to terms with the lack of certainties the new era has brought in.

Żółty szalik itself is rather visibly a Christmas story, set in a traditionally predominantly Catholic but gradually secularizing society. The practice of breaking and sharing of *opłatki* (traditional Christmas Eve wafers)[28] as a Christmas greeting—part of the particularly powerful Christmas party scene—is a filmic cultural anthropology study in itself with its careful layering of old and modern, communal and consumerist. Christmas features prominently in the twin novel as well. From the novel's account of Christmas on the alcoholics' ward and the amicable encouragement Jerzy receives that Christmas is not far away, it appears that the festive season that has been in a hegemonic position over centuries in Western culture serves as the wry setting for a narrative dealing with solitude and addiction. The film has a narrative frame of the protagonist leaving his mother—the typical strong Polish mother figure of many post-socialist films for whom motherhood amounts to as much as being "even the ultimate purpose of [...] existence".[29] She can also be seen as a strong Gertrude figure, who—in a 'closet scene' with a reversed dynamic—aims to nurture her son back to life and re-establish a sense of belonging in him. The ending scene of the film is an extended one, where we understand the significance of him being nurtured, as if in a haven, by his mother. This involves physical (and at the same time, emotional) nourishment of a traditional kind, as their meticulously authentic multicourse Wigilia (Christmas Eve) meal starts with the obligatory *opłatek*-sharing (with its echoes of the Eucharistic feast) and we see *barszcz czerwony* (red borscht) with *uszka* (little stuffed dumplings; literally: 'little ears'), fish and boiled egg in aspic, braised sauerkraut, fruit compote and walnut cake. They also go to the *pasterka* (midnight mass) together before he returns to the gradually changing depersonalized city. What he insists on before leaving the warm maternal respite is that he should not lose his scarf. In the closing, longer framing sequence, he first leaves his scarf at his mother's, who almost religiously tries to persuade herself that leaving it with her is not the same as losing it, but then he remembers and returns for it, leaving us with a bittersweet but potentially cathartic 'Christmassy' message of hope for a difficult and delayed (re)birth—or just for the continuation of the same cycle of fits and starts. The Christian connotations of the postmodern-day Mary trying to (re)birth her son into an environment that is likely to suck him in immediately deepen the symbolism and intertextual archeology of this Everyman-meets-nativity-meets-Scrooge-meets-Hamlet screen drama.

> If you find, in the works of a poet whose instinct is to write about everything under the sun, one obvious theme untouched, or touched hardly at all, then it is at least presumable that there was at least some good

> reason for that abstinence. Such a poet was Shakespeare. It was one of the divine frailties of his genius that he must ever be flying off at a tangent from his main theme to unpack his heart in words about some frivolous-small irrelevance that had come into his head. If it could be shown that he never mentioned Christmas, we should have proof presumptive that he consciously avoided doing so. But if the fact is that he did mention it now and again, but in grudging fashion, without one spark of illumination - he, the arch-illuminator of all things - then we have proof positive that he detested it.[30]

Max Beerbohm, in his delightful parody of the thinking and mode of expression of Frank Harris, cites Shakespeare's apparently single reference to Christmas, which does indeed come from *Hamlet*, from Marcellus' conversation with Horatio and Bernardo:

> Some say that ever 'gainst that season comes
> Wherein our Saviour's birth is celebrated [...]
> (Act I, Scene 1)

There probably are other appropriations or reworkings that create that 'missing' Shakespearean Christmas drama, and the meaning of Christmas itself is different from what it meant in early modern England, at Harris' and Beerbohm's time and when Morgenstern made his film. (Kenneth Branagh's 1995 film, *In the Bleak Midwinter/A Midwinter's Tale* may be a case in point, but in that film *Hamlet* as a play is overtly at the center of the stage-on-the-screen production.) Morgenstern's 'Shakespearean' (post)Christmas story owes a significant indebtedness to *Hamlet*, which helps mold the script in its articulation of the central character's identity crisis against the backdrop of competing metanarratives and a serious addiction problem perhaps symptomatic of his tortuous personal positioning at a time signaled by changing values. "To watch the world with a sober eye? Oh my God!"—his Hamletic *de profundis* cry encapsulates a historical moment when corporate protocol meets time-tested festive rituals.

Articulating Cosmopolitanism Through Shakespeare in *The Pianist*

With its release only two years after Morgenstern's late gem, the Academy Award winning *The Pianist* (2002) also makes strategic use of a Shakespearean classic. *The Pianist* is also Polish related but largely transnational in its making as well as reception, directed by a cosmopolitan Pole, the Paris-born and Polish-raised Roman Polanski. Ronald Harwood's script adapts Polish-Jewish musician Władysław Szpilman's autobiographical writing about his experiences in Nazi occupied Poland during World War II. The film quotes another Shakespeare tragedy: perhaps unsurprisingly and provocatively, *The Merchant of Venice*.

The choice of Shakespearean text is pertinent. With a complex reception history, including stage history and filming, this "contentious comedy"[31] has been the subject of both anti-Semitic and philosemite interpretations (among others that do not place an emphasis on ethnicity or religion), and the play has been appropriated in many cultural and political contexts. As Horacio Sierra contends, "the plight of ostracized minorities and state-sanctioned discrimination are all too real" in our contemporary world as well, and there has been an overwhelming interest among scholars and creative artists in the twenty-first century.[32]

A memoir-based biopic, the big-screen production introduces us to a period of the life of concert pianist and composer Władysław Szpilman. There are, however, further layers to biography here. As Ewa Mazierska suggests, *The Pianist* is Polanski's most autobiographical film.[33] He himself survived in Krakow as a child when many other Jews were taken away, and he tapped into his early memories to access remnants of this experience when Harwood and he went on a writing retreat in France to finalize the script.[34] In terms of identity politics, the world of *The Pianist* is a relevant one for Ronald Harwood. While he was based in Britain for most of his career, he originally came from the Jewish diaspora in South Africa. *The Pianist* is not his only script about the life of a twentieth-century musician. *Taking Sides* (2001), his biopic script of the life of Wilhelm Furtwängler, based on his own 1995 play of the same title and directed for the big-screen by Hungarian director István Szabó, also deals with ethical conundra exactly in relation to German-Jewish relations during World War II, and the ethical responsibilities and choices of artists in a dictatorial context.

The screen time that the direct Shakespeare allusion is given in *The Pianist* is little, as in the case of *Yellow Scarf*, but for our purposes, the Shakespearean intertextuality is significant as it offers a further interpretative dimension to the reading of the film. It is the main protagonist Wladek's brother Henryk who reads *The Merchant of Venice* as the family are made to wait before they are pushed onto the trains taking them to their deaths (except the titular young musician, who is saved by an acquaintance). Henryk reads out this passage to Wladek, when—in a moment reminiscent of moments in *Hamlet*—Wladek is curious about what Henryk is reading. Then Henryk hands the book over to the protagonist:

> If you prick us, do we not bleed? If you tickle us, do we not laugh? If you poison us, do we not die? And if you wrong us, shall we not revenge?[35]

Wladek finds Shylock's famous "Hath not a Jew eyes?" speech from Act 3 scene 1 "[v]ery appropriate" to the situation, before handing the book back to his brother. The directions in the script are explicit about this gesture and about the visibility of the book on the screen. Harwood insists on spelling out the relevance of this historical text and asking the audience to ponder as he makes Henryk add that this is the reason why he chose to bring this book with him.[36] Henryk's quip concludes the scene, and the direct reference does not return later. Henryk is a man of letters, who is seen earlier selling books in the ghetto as an *adhoc* book merchant in order to support the family where he is one of two grown-up sons in addition to the two grown-up daughters, Halina and Regina. Dostoevsky's *The Idiot* is one of the books he succeeds in selling. Meaningfully, the scene when he reveals this comes from a part of the film close to the scene when Jews waiting for their turn at a crossing in the Warsaw ghetto are made by the guards to dance (and make idiots of themselves). The dialogue including the quotation from *The Merchant of Venice* has its role in the film's depiction of the relationship between the two brothers: a complex one in which love and sibling rivalry commingle. The *Merchant* allusion refers poetically, through the borrowing of a famous character's and author's voice, to the gravity of their inhumane treatment. Moreover, the citation of high cultural prestige also gives the family at the center of the film the moral and intellectual upper hand and seems to offer them the only possible comfort, apart from the company of each other (which they need to part with).

As mentioned, the script suggests that the cover of *The Merchant of Venice* by Shakespeare should be visible when the non-compromising Henryk shows Wladek what he is reading. The viewers are meant to recognize it, even if they do not identify the source when hearing the quotation. In the film, Shakespeare's image on the front cover is definitely visible as Wladimir looks at the cover (the title is not necessarily identifiable), so the director's emphasis is on Shakespeare as cultural capital, a highbrow text which signals the reader's education and good taste but is also adaptable—when in the 'appropriate' hands—to reflect on contemporary situations.

Specifying the Shakespeare reference here is certainly a choice made in the process of adapting the memoir, as "The Umschlagplatz" chapter (quoted below in Anthea Bell's beautiful, matter-of-fact prose) does not clarify what part of the Shakespearean *oeuvre* is being read:

> I hurried to meet Henryk, certain that his idiotically upright attitude was to blame for bringing him and Halina here. I bombarded him with questions and reproaches before he could get a word of explanation in, but he was not going to deign to answer me anyway. He shrugged his shoulders, took a small Oxford edition of Shakespeare out of his pocket, moved over to one side of us and began to read.[37]

Film scholar Ewa Mazierska describes Polanski with the help of what Isaac Deutscher defines as the 'non-Jewish Jew', who—in Mazierska's rewording—"transcends Jewry and Jewishness to live on the edge of various religions and national and cultural traditions".[38] In my reading of *The Pianist*, the specification of the Shakespeare reading for the screen drama solidifies the perception of cosmopolitanism, the broader intellectual belonging to European culture and world culture which the Szpilman family stand for (they crowd over the radio to listen to BBC news). It is to this culture that the surviving Szpilman makes his own contribution as an artist already as a young man as well as following the war. Shakespeare and his *Merchant* stand here for a shared language of the community of humans, for cultural heritage that is shared and revisited or appropriated at times of need.

Soon after the Shakespearean scene, the family share a single piece of caramel the father decides to buy from a young boy with twenty zlotys put together by the family. Shakespeare—food for the intellect that the two young men devoured moments earlier—may be seen as the same sort of 'luxury': a small act that nonetheless helps outlive the moment. This scene gains even more emphasis from the fact that we have seen the family enjoy a peaceful meal together in their home earlier in the film.

What about, one might ask, the considerably dark aspect of the play in question, where Shylock is humiliated, overpowered and punished? The overtone of that is, without doubt, in the atmosphere set up by the scene; the educated viewer knows how the play ends, despite Shylock's self-assured cry out against indignation in this pivotal speech. Yet, the scene on the whole emphasizes that very pride and the rhetorical demonstration of the injustice, with recourse to a European—and world—classic.

Conclusion

In her article, "Influence and Intertextuality: A Reappraisal" (2007), Susan Bassnett explains how her reading of Daphne du Maurier's *Jamaica Inn* and Dan Brown's *The Da Vinci Code* benefited from being read one after another (by her family when she was unwell). Her co-reading of these two texts galvanized by sheer personal circumstance is something I recall vividly when drawing my own intertextual reading of two, otherwise hardly connected films—*Yellow Scarf* and *The Pianist*. Shakespearean allusions, among other dimensions, connect the films to each other and to a broader intertextual network. The dimensions that link the two films beyond the Shakespearean and Polish connections include the subtle autobiographical one: both Pilch's script and Harwood's script can be linked to the respective authors' backgrounds, and Polanski's undertaking has strong autobiographical resonances.

Both *The Pianist* and *Żółty szalik* are tales of humanity with universal connotative layers beneath culture-specificity, and sharing food is curiously one element that ties the two films together. As Thomas O'Loughlin underlines in his broader, anthropologically based discussion of the Eucharist: "The meal is as much a fundamental element of humanity as shared rationality or language." Both films have scenes that shed light on this and suggesting a meaningful circumstantial co-reading of the kind Bassnett above pinpoints. Indeed, the unforeseen shared element of communal meals—in particular the office Christmas party and the family Wigilia in the countryside, both with their respective *opłatek*-sharing in *Żółty szalik*, and the caramel-sharing in *The Pianist*—render meal-sharing on the screen "an activity, an event, shared with a group that is bounded and bonded by that sharing" in a context where "[f]ood is more than food".[39] Both films show us shared sustenance in a physical, emotional but also a spiritual and intellectual manner, and Shakespeare is also part of that. While both Gajos's contemporary Hamlet-cum-Everyman-cum-Scrooge and Brody's Szpilman are solitary heroes (perhaps more of an anti-hero in the case of Morgenstern's film), they gain symbolic as well as physical nourishment from family meals and also from Shakespeare, a major intellectual quotidian within European culture.

As D'Angelo succinctly puts it, "If every text is an intertext, then every intertext is a context that issues invitations for readers or viewers to adopt a certain perspective for reading or viewing. Intertextuality can be said to create its own contexts in addition to the immediate rhetorical situation".[40] This intertextual reading of two East-Central European films with Shakespearean fragments has showcased not only that "Shakespeare has been [...] the cause of wit in others–and not only wit, but poetry, creative fantasy, and searching reflection as well"[41]—if we resort to rhetoric reminiscent of influence studies for a moment—but also how creative artists still contemporize Shakespeare, and how the smallest reference helps the reader-spectator toward an enriched interpretation, where identifying aspects of the Shakespearean intertextuality, alongside other intertexts, presents us with a more visibly multi-layered text or artifact.[42]

Notes

1. Julia Kristeva, *Revolution in Poetic Language*, trans. Margaret Waller (New York: Columbia University Press, 1984), 60.
2. Susan Bassnett, "Influence and Intertextuality: A Reappraisal," *Forum for Modern Language Studies* 43, no. 2 (2007): 138.
3. Frank J. D'Angelo, "The Rhetoric of Intertextuality," *Rhetoric Review* 29, no 1 (2009): 31.
4. Ewa Mazierska, *Roman Polanski: The Cinema of a Cultural Traveller* (London and New York: I.B. Tauris, 2007).
5. Lenuta Giukin, Janina Falkowska, and David Desser, *Small Cinemas in Global Markets: Genres, Identities, Narratives* (Lanham and London: Lexington Books (Rowman and Littlefield), 2014).
6. Aaron Kerner, *Film and the Holocaust: New Perspectives on Dramas, Documentaries, and Experimental Film* (New York and London: Continuum, 2011), 9; 59–78.
7. John Gross, *After Shakespeare: Writing Inspired by the World's Greatest Author* (Oxford: Oxford University Press, 2002), xii.
8. The question in the title of the chapter echoes John Elsom's 1989 book title, *Is Shakespeare Still Our Contemporary?*

9. Dina Jordanova, "Unseen Cinema, Notes on Small Cinemas and the Transnational," in Giukin, *Small Cinemas in Global Markets*, 216.
10. While this scenario may make for a somewhat pessimistic reading against the backdrop of global capitalism, I find it important to note that productions from 'small cinemas' can do some 'travelling': I first came across *Yellow Scarf* on Hungarian television, with Hungarian dubbing (Duna TV, 25 February 2002). I also first started reading film criticism about the film in Hungarian. The first helpful review was the assessment of playwright, novelist and Slavic literature graduate György Spiró (2002), who in his brief survey of the recent Polish film crop is critical of scripts but appreciative of acting talent, including that of Janusz Gajos in *Yellow Scarf*.
11. For an excellent anthropological overview of several countries in this region of Europe in this time period see Kürti and Skalník.
12. Peter Skalník and László Kürti, *Postsocialist Europe: Anthropological Perspectives from Home* (New York and Oxford: Berghahn Books, 2009).
13. Marta Gibińska and Jerzy Limon, eds. *Hamlet East–West* (Gdańsk: Theatrum Gedanense Foundation, 1998), 12–13.
14. Bogusław Sułkowski, "A Polish Reinterpretation of *Hamlet*," in *Hamlet East–West*, 171.
15. See for instance Courtney Krystyna Kujawińska, "Celebrating Shakespeare".
16. Geoffrey Wagner, *The Novel and the Cinema* (Rutherford, NJ and London: Fairleigh Dickinson University Press; Tantivy Press, 1975), 227.
17. Dudley Andrew, *Concepts in Film Theory* (New York: Oxford University Press, 1984), 100–101.
18. Alexander Shurbanov and Boika Sokolova, *Painting Shakespeare Red: An East-European Appropriation* (Newark-London: University of Delaware Press, Associated University Presses, 2001), 15.
19. Ewa Mazierska, *Masculinities in Polish, Czech and Slovak Cinema: Black Peters and Men of Marble* (New York and Oxford: Berghahn Books, 2008), 153.
20. Mazierska, *Masculinities*, 164.
21. See Falkowska, "New Cinema of Nostalgia in Poland".
22. Segel, Harold B., ed. *The Columbia Guide to the Literatures of Eastern Europe since 1945* (New York: Columbia University Press, 2003), 433.
23. Segel, 433.
24. Sedgwick, Eve Kosofsky, *Tendencies* (London and New York: Routledge, 1998 [1993]), 5.
25. Sedgwick, 6.
26. Wolfgang Clemen, *Shakespeare's Soliloquies*, trans. Charity Scott Stokes (London and New York: Routledge, 2010 [1987]), 119.

27. Jerzy Pilch, *The Mighty Angel*, trans. Bill Johnston (University of Rochester: Open Letter, 2009 [2000]), 5–6. Yellow crops up again when the narrator-protagonist visits the Catastrophe family.
28. The *opłatek* is a wafer made for Wigilia (the Christmas Eve ceremony and supper) to be broken and shared in the family as part of a tradition in Poland and some other Slavic cultures that goe back to medieval times. See also Swan, *Kaleidoscope of Poland*, 282.
29. Ewa Mazierska, "In the Name of Absent Fathers and Other Men: Representation of Motherhood in the Polish Post Communist Cinema," *Feminist Media Studies* 1 (2006): 81.
30. Beerbohm cited in Gross, *After Shakespeare*, 324.
31. Sierra Horacio, *New Readings of The Merchant of Venice* (Newcastle-upon-Tyne: Cambridge Scholars Press, 2013), 1.
32. Horacio, 1.
33. Mazierska, *Roman Polanski*, 16.
34. David Nicholas Wilkinson and Emlyn Price, *Ronald Harwood's Adaptations: From Other Works into Films* (Guerilla Books, 2007), 106.
35. Ronald Harwood, *The Pianist*, in *The Pianist & Taking Sides*, 1–115 (London: Faber and Faber, 2002), 54.
36. Harwood, 55.
37. Wladyslaw Szpilman, *The Pianist: The Extraordinary Story of One Man's Survival in Warsaw, 1939–45*, trans. Anthea Bell (London: Phoenix, 2000), 102.
38. Mazierska, *Roman Polanski*, 17.
39. Thomas O'Loughlin, *The Eucharist: Origins and Contemporary Understandings* (London: Bloomsbury, 2015), 62.
40. D'Angelo, 43.
41. Gross, xiii.
42. This article is dedicated to my Polish friends and acquaintances—Jacek, Ireneusz, Dorotka and many others. Among them special thanks to Alina Gorywoda, who advised me when I needed first-language Polish expertise as I was working on this chapter. I am also very grateful to Professor Ewa Mazierska for carefully reading and commenting on the chapter.

Works Cited

Andrew, Dudley. *Concepts in Film Theory*. New York: Oxford University Press, 1984.

Bassnett, Susan. "Influence and Intertextuality: A Reappraisal." *Forum for Modern Language Studies* 43, no. 2 (2007): 134–46.

Clemen, Wolfgang. *Shakespeare's Soliloquies*, translated by Charity Scott Stokes. London and New York: Routledge, 2010 [1987].

D'Angelo, Frank J. "The Rhetoric of Intertextuality." *Rhetoric Review* 29, no. 1 (2009): 31–47.

Elsom, John. *Is Shakespeare Still Our Contemporary?* New York: Routledge, 1989.

Falkowska, Janina. "New Cinema of Nostalgia in Poland." In *Small Cinemas in Global Markets: Genres, Identities, Narratives*, edited by Lenuta Giukin, Janina Falkowska, and David Desser, 17–30. Lanham and London: Lexington Books (Rowman and Littlefield), 2014.

Gibińska, Marta and Jerzy Limon, eds. *Hamlet East-West*. Gdańsk: Theatrum Gedanense Foundation. 1998.

Giukin, Lenuta, Janina Falkowska, and David Desser, eds. *Small Cinemas in Global Markets: Genres, Identities, Narratives*. Lanham and London: Lexington Books (Rowman and Littlefield), 2014.

Gross, John. *After Shakespeare: Writing Inspired by the World's Greatest Author*. Oxford: Oxford University Press, 2002.

Harwood, Ronald. *The Pianist*. In *The Pianist & Taking Sides*, 1–115. London: Faber and Faber, 2002.

Iordanova, Dina. "Unseen Cinema, Notes on Small Cinemas and the Transnational." In *Small Cinemas in Global Markets: Genres, Identities, Narratives*, edited by Lenuta Giukin, Janina Falkowska, and David Desser, 213–20. Lanham and London: Lexington Books (Rowman and Littlefield), 2014.

Kerner, Aaron. *Film and the Holocaust: New Perspectives on Dramas, Documentaries, and Experimental Film*. New York and London: Continuum, 2011.

Kott, Jan. *Shakespeare Our Contemporary*, translated by Boleslaw Taborski. W.W. Norton & Company: New York and London, 1964.

Kristeva, Julia. *Revolution in Poetic Language*, translated by Margaret Waller. New York: Columbia University Press, 1984.

Kujawińska, Courtney Krystyna. "Celebrating Shakespeare under the Communist Regime in Poland." In *Shakespeare in Cold War Europe: Conflict, Commemoration, Celebration*, edited by Erica Sheen and Isabel Karreman, 23–35. London: Palgrave Macmillan, 2016.

Kürti, László and Peter Skalník. *Postsocialist Europe: Anthropological Perspectives from Home*. New York and Oxford: Berghahn Books, 2009.

Mazierska, Ewa. "In the Name of Absent Fathers and Other Men: Representation of Motherhood in the Polish Post Communist Cinema." *Feminist Media Studies* 1 (2006): 67–83.

Mazierska, Ewa. *Roman Polanski: The Cinema of a Cultural Traveller*. London and New York: I.B. Tauris, 2007.

Mazierska, Ewa. *Masculinities in Polish, Czech and Slovak Cinema: Black Peters and*

Men of Marble. New York and Oxford: Berghahn Books, 2008.

O'Loughlin, Thomas. 2015. *The Eucharist: Origins and Contemporary Understandings*. London: Bloomsbury, 2015.
Pilch, Jerzy. *The Mighty Angel*, translated by Bill Johnston. University of Rochester: Open Letter, 2009 [2000].
Schandl, Veronika. *Socialist Shakespeare Productions in Kádár-regime Hungary: Shakespeare Behind the Iron Curtain*. Lewiston, New York: Edwin Mellen Press, 2008.
Sedgwick, Eve Kosofsky. *Tendencies*. London and New York: Routledge, 1998 [1993].
Segel, Harold B., ed. *The Columbia Guide to the Literatures of Eastern Europe since 1945*. New York: Columbia University Press, 2003.
Shurbanov, Alexander and Boika Sokolova. *Painting Shakespeare Red: An East-European Appropriation*. Newark-London: University of Delaware Press. Associated University Presses, 2001.
Sierra, Horacio. *New Readings of The Merchant of Venice*. Newcastle-upon-Tyne: Cambridge Scholars Press, 2013.
Spiró, György. "Színészek dicsérete: Új lengyel filmek." *Filmvilág*, 8 August 2002.
Stříbrný, Zdeněk. *Shakespeare and Eastern Europe*. Oxford: Oxford University Press, 2000.
Sułkowski, Bogusław. "A Polish Reinterpretation of *Hamlet*." In *Hamlet East-West*, edited by Marta Gibińska and Jerzy Limon, 171–76. Gdańsk: Theatrum Gedanense Foundation, 1998.
Swan, Oscar E. *Kaleidoscope of Poland: A Cultural Encyclopedia*. Pittsburgh, PA: University of Pittsburgh Press, 2015.
Szpilman, Wladyslaw. *The Pianist: The Extraordinary Story of One Man's Survival in Warsaw, 1939–45*, translated by Anthea Bell. London: Phoenix, 2000.
Wagner, Geoffrey. *The Novel and the Cinema*. Rutherford, NJ and London: Fairleigh Dickinson University Press; Tantivy Press, 1975.
Wilkinson, David Nicholas and Emlyn Price. *Ronald Harwood's Adaptations: From Other Works into Films*. Guerilla Books, 2007.

CHAPTER 10

Soviet and Post-Soviet References to Hamlet on Film and Television

Boris N. Gaydin and Nikolay V. Zakharov

Nowadays Romeo and Juliet seem to be the most popular Shakespeare characters on screen and TV in most countries of the world. Nevertheless, in Russia, Hamlet is the undisputed leader in this regard. Russians consider Shakespeare their own national poet, and Hamlet is one of the main iconic images that are deeply rooted in the very core of Russian culture.[1] If we say "Shakespeare" in Russian—'Shekspir'/'Шекспир'—we immediately think of the play *Hamlet* and its iconic hero.

The chapter was prepared within the framework of the project "Shakespeare in Contemporary Russian Culture: The National and Global" with support from the Council for Grants of the President of the Russian Federation (МК-1182.2017.6).

B. N. Gaydin (✉) · N. V. Zakharov
Moscow University for the Humanities, Moscow, Russia
e-mail: bngaydin@mosgu.ru

N. V. Zakharov
e-mail: nzakharov@mosgu.ru

A. A. Joubin and V. Bladen (eds.), *Onscreen Allusions to Shakespeare*, Global Shakespeares, https://doi.org/10.1007/978-3-030-93783-6_10

First appearing in Saxo Grammaticus' *Gesta Danorum* (twelfth century), Hamlet has been employed in a great range of original works by Russian authors, including: Alexander S. Pushkin, Fyodor M. Dostoevsky, Ivan S. Turgenev, Anton P. Chekov, Alexander A. Blok and Boris L. Pasternak. Russian culture has engaged with Hamlet in a broad range of applications, from art, such as Mikhail A. Vrubel's three paintings (Hamlet and Ophelia, 1883, 1884, 1888) to screen adaptation, in the landmark film directed by Grigori M. Kozintsev (1964).

Hamlet has a rich, intertextual screen history in Russia and there are numerous examples of the character of Hamlet being incorporated into various motion pictures and TV products (serials, TV shows, comic performances and advertising), giving the character polyvalence. Hamlet's capacity to encompass an extensive range of meanings has enabled scriptwriters, directors and actors to draw from the figure and his characteristics in a diverse spectrum of historical and situational contexts.

In this chapter, we will analyze a number of examples from Soviet and post-Soviet mass culture where one can find both obvious and cryptic allusions, ranging from brief comic citations to what we term "Hamletization." Hamletization suggests a process of appropriation encompassing allusions, appropriation of and/or references to characters, motives and/or aspects of plot. We will concentrate on appropriations appearing subsequent to Kozintsev's adaptation, considering examples from various films, TV shows and programs with evident or hidden references and analogies to Hamlet or parallels of plot or narrative content from the play.

In 1965 Innokenty M. Smoktunovsky played the title role of Yuri Detochkin in a Soviet crime comedy film *Beware of the Car* («Берегись автомобиля», *Beregis' avtomobilia*, aka *Uncommon Thief, or Watch out for the Automobile*, 1966), directed by Eldar A. Ryazanov and based on a screenplay by Emil V. Braginsky. Detochkin is a former taxi driver and now a Soviet insurance agent; an eccentric modern-day Robin Hood, he steals cars from swindlers and crooks and then sells them, giving the money to charity. Detochkin also plays the part of Hamlet in an amateur theater production. The acting coach for the production, Yevgeniy Aleksandrovich (Yevgeniy A. Yevstigneyev), says to the actors "Isn't it time, my friends, to hitch our wagon to William, you know, our Shakespeare?" The phrase (alternatively translated as "Isn't it time, my friends, to have a stab at William, you know, our Shakespeare?") has remained very popular in Russia and has become almost like a proverb that is used when somebody is encouraging others to do something difficult but special, in an ironic way. The actors agree. Subsequently, the protagonist is arrested, but the militiaman/detective Maxim Podberezovikov (Oleg N. Yefremov), who plays Laertes in the same production, allows Detochkin to participate in the opening night of the play. The conflict between the crime investigator and the good-hearted criminal is thus transferred to the stage as a duel between Hamlet and Laertes. Detochkin plays his role so persuasively that his real mother in the audience cries out "Yura, I'm here" when Hamlet is dying and says his last few words ("Mother, farewell" and "Wretched queen, adieu!" (5.2)). The boundaries between the play and spectating audience thus blur.

The intertextual references to *Hamlet* here imply a philosophical subtext. Detochkin is a naïve, openhearted and honorable person, Robin Hood and Hamlet rolled into one. He is trying to expose thievery, restore justice and thereby make the world a better place. The film's story is based on a "vagrant legend" about a contemporary outlaw who is carjacking from criminal elements. All efforts of the scriptwriters to find the real prototype were in vain. Ryazanov recollected: "until we began to write the script we wanted to make sure that the occurrence was real. ... We were making inquiries about this in the legal institutions, but we could not trace a similar judicial case. And finally we understood that it was a fictional story, a legend that had taken the form of a real event."[2] Interestingly, at the initial stages of the script there was an idea to do the film in the genre of a comic western, but they abandoned the idea, finding it was too difficult to depict Soviet society in its diversity. Ryazanov and Braginsky did not want to create a simplistic divide between "good" and "bad" characters. In this aim to present more nuanced and complex characterization, they followed Shakespeare's technique; the characters of the comedy are flesh and blood with all their virtues and imperfections. The creators stated: "Our hero is an honest man per se, but he is a trickster on his face. ... The interrogation officer who must be consistent, strong-willed and steadfast in duty ... actually turns out to be very facile, good-natured and compliant."[3] As the great Russian poet Alexander S. Pushkin once noted, "Molière's miser is only avaricious; Shakespeare's Shylock is avaricious, knacky, revengeful, philoprogenitive, witty."[4] Thus the aim of Ryazanov and Braginsky for character complexity adds another dimension to the Shakespearean appropriation, rendering it an example of neo-Shakespeareanism in Soviet cinematography.

Interestingly, Ryazanov does not mention Hamlet as a prototype of Yuri Detochkin: "Don Quixote, Chaplin's Charlie, prince Myshkin are the three composite sources of our protagonist."[5] Yet it is *Hamlet* that is staged in the film. It seems that the director's insistence in the process of negotiations with Smoktunovsky, who had just recently played the parts of Hamlet and Prince Myshkin in other productions, was not only a wish to cast a star in the title role but also to evoke the intertextual references that the actor's former roles create. The conjunction of the "effect of recognition" of Smoktunovsky's earlier work and the inclusion of *Hamlet* as a play-within-a-film presented a composite image of Detochkin to the viewers. Furthermore, the protagonist Detochkin's character traits include those of Hamlet. Similar to the Prince of Denmark, Detochkin, as the director points out, "seems to be abnormal, but in very deed he is more normal than many others. For he pays attention to those things that we often pass by indifferently."[6] Thus the hero of *Beware of the Car* demonstrates characteristics of Hamlet in that he has a keen sense of the imperfections of the world and is ready to fight against them, even if in a way that might be considered ambiguous from a moral point of view.[7] The conflict of the film centers on responding to evil and injustice through violence, creating intersections between the Soviet screen comedy and *Hamlet*, enriching its meanings.

Another example of a comic appropriation of *Hamlet* is the 3rd episode of the 14th issue of children's comedy TV show *Yeralash* entitled *Interesting Movie or Poor Yurik* («Интересное кино, или бедный Юрик»; *Interesnoe kino ili bednyi Iurik*, 1977), directed by Isaak S. Magiton, who co-wrote it with Vladimir M. Alenikov. In this episode, a boy recounts the content of a movie on at the "Lithuania" movie theater in Moscow. His account is not easily comprehensible; however, it is apparent that the film includes many sword fights. He also mentions a skull and changes "poor Yorick" to "poor Yurik," a pet form of Yuri, a common Russian name. His friend asks: "Which Yurik? Nikulin?",[8] to which the boy replies: "Not at all, whataya! Some foreigner!" The boy continues to retell the plot of the film, but his friend stops him and dashes away to the movie theater. We then see that they were discussing a "cool" film directed by Kozintsev with Smoktunovsky in the title role.

The mainstream Russian audience, like Shakespeare's early modern audience, has always liked spectacle and showmanship. They like to see life on stage and screen in all its diversity: fights, death, love and suffering. In this TV episode, we are presented with a child's perspective on Kozintsev's *Hamlet*. The boy seems to like this film primarily because of its visual appeal. Here Hamlet is mainly a hero with a sword in his hand bravely fighting with his enemies.

In the TV series *33 Square Meters* («33 квадратных метра»; *33 kvadratnykh metra*; season 3, *1999–2000*), the 11th episode *Hamlet, Prince of Dacha* («Гамлет, принц дачный»; *Gamlet, prints dachnyi*) constitutes another comic interpretation of *Hamlet*, with the script by Dmitry E. Zver'kov, Maksim A. Tukhanin and Ivan A. Filippov.

The series is about the everyday life of the Zvezdunov family. Andrei Zvezdunov (Andrei N. Bocharov), the son, has to repeat a year in school, because he could not answer a question on what *The Tragedy of Hamlet* was about. His father, Sergey Gennadievich (Sergey G. Belogolovtsev), scolds him, because, in his opinion, it is clear that *Hamlet* is about Hamlet. Sergey's mother-in-law Klara Zakharovna (Pavel M. Kabanov) mistakenly thinks that *Hamlet* is an "emotion picture"[9] about Smoktunovsky "where everyone dies." Sergey declares that in their family there is "no *Hamlet* — only 'Crocodiles'."[10] He starts looking for a copy of *Hamlet*. Their neighbor Tofik (Mikhail G. Shats) thinks that *Hamlet* is a book about a real man, an Armenian named Hamlet.[11] Sergey decides to look for the book in the library, but it is closed. He enters illegally, but he does not remember the author of the book. He asks Tofik, who says that he has no idea, retorting: "Am I Pushkin?" Sergey misunderstands and takes this literally, thinking that the Russian poet Alexander S. Pushkin is the author. Then Migro (Pavel M. Kabanov), captain of the local militia, arrests Sergey for breaking into the library. Andrei's mother Tatiana Yurievna Zvezdunova (Tatiana Yu. Lazareva) cries and tells Andrei that his father is a pilot and has flown off on a mission to the North Pole. Andrei is upset that he and his dad have not gone fishing. Suddenly he sees an image of his father in a photo. The "Ghost" laughs at him and tells him the truth. Andrei then thinks that it is Tofik who has put his father behind bars since Tofik is carrying on a flirtation with his mother, positioning Tofik as the Claudius figure. Andrei decides to have his revenge. In the end, Tofik/Claudius and Andrei/Hamlet compete in a badminton game for the honor to take Tatiana/Gertrude to the movie theater. Tofik has put laxatives into one of the wineglasses, which Tatiana drinks from this glass before running away. Andrei also drinks from the glass. Tofik celebrates his triumph, but all of a sudden, Sergey returns and makes him drink the "poison" too.

There are many other references to *Hamlet* in this episode. The characters use many (modified) lines from Shakespeare's text. The funny and foolish Andrei is put in Hamlet's position, but the events develop in accordance with the genre of "low comedy," so the tragic mode is transformed to a comic farce. Thus the conflict does not lead to the death of the characters; the struggle between Andrei/Hamlet and Tofik/Claudius does not aim for the "high" ideals of tragedy, but for achieving the "low" goals of comedy.[12]

This example is thus a good illustration of how the plot of *Hamlet* is appropriated just for entertainment. *Hamlet, Prince of Dacha* is a typical example of Hamletization. Here we can find only the outline of the classical plot, but "Hamlet" here has no philosophical or esthetic background. There is story fidelity but no thematic fidelity.[13] The characters are in situations analogous to those in Shakespeare's play, but only superficially: the content of the episode is disparate from the Bard's great tragedy.

In contemporary Russian mass culture, Hamlet is often used when the concept of acting is presented. It is evident that many Russians associate the profession of Melpomene's votaries with this iconic character. Therefore, when viewers see a person with a skull in their hand at stage or on screen reading the "To be or not to be" soliloquy, they more or less understand that this suggests theatrical art in general.

In 2002 the United Team of the twentieth century presented a student pop sketch *Hamlet* in the Club of the Funny and Inventive People (Клуб веселых и находчивых, КВН; Klub veselykh i nakhodchivykh, KVN).[14] Here Hamlet (Dmitry V. Brekotkin) is embedded within a very broad cultural context including fairytale and mythological heroes (The Three Bogatyrs, Old Man with Old Woman, Roly-Poly/Kolobok, Buratino—a Russian version of Pinocchio), characters of children's TV shows and animated cartoons (Khryusha the piglet, Stepashka the hare, Gena the crocodile, Cheburashka, etc.), Russian show business celebrities (pop singer Alla Pugacheva, comedian and showman Maxim Galkin), well-known political and public figures (Soviet leader Joseph Stalin, rhythmic gymnast and politician Alina Kabaeva). At first glance, there is an incompatibility to all these images, but it is mitigated by means of witty dialogue. The main purpose of these interlocutions is to make the viewers laugh. The actor playing the character of Hamlet faces the challenge of interacting with other actors playing characters who are aiming for laughs. While staying in character, Hamlet plays up to the other characters according to the rules of the genre, but he feels fear and discomfort and has to quit playing. The sketch shows how most Russians perceive the character of Hamlet—as a person with a skull in their hand who delivers pretentious soliloquies.

The 52nd episode of the popular family Russian TV series *Daddy's Daughters* («Папины дочки»; *Papiny dochki*) (3rd season, the premiere on STS TV channel, January 29, 2008; produced by Vyacheslav A. Murugov and Alexander E. Rodnyansky) contains an extract from Hamlet's soliloquy "To be or not to be" in Russian translation made by Nikolay V. Maklakov (1880; with minor alterations and abridgments). The youngest daughter Polina Vasnetsova (Ekaterina I. Starshova) or Pugovka (Button) is in a film. The director is searching for an actress for the speechless part of a maiden's ghost in the scene "Katya's Dream" and the young actress proposes to enroll one of her three sisters. The director decides to give her the right of choice. The elder sisters enthusiastically compete for the role, two of them trying to "bribe" Pugovka. Only the most intelligent sister, Galina Sergeevna (Elizaveta N. Arzamasova), chooses to compete fairly by showing her artistic talent and flair. She appears as Hamlet with a hat on her head and in a cloak made from a curtain. Her three sisters are amazed by her acting and applaud her. One of the sisters, Darya Vasnetsova (Anastasia S. Sivayeva), a Goth, is convinced that her gifted sister has written this soliloquy by herself. Galina Sergeevna corrects her mistake: "Mind you, this is Shakespeare! Hamlet's soliloquy! But all the same it is pleasant." The eldest sister, Maria (Miroslava O. Karpovich) enviously says that she does not like Galina's acting and that she can also "coil herself with a curtain and learn some lines from *Hamlet*..." However, the other sisters are skeptical of her claim and vote unanimously for Galina Sergeevna to feature in the film. Their debates are interrupted by an angry exclamation of their father who is dissatisfied that Pugovka has not tidied her toys. Apparently, Maria had promised to do this and attempts to avoid the task, stating: "Now do it yourself. Or there... ask Hamlet."

Hamlet is mentioned once again in the episode when Maria Vasnetsova comes to the film set earlier than her sister, Galina Sergeevna, attempting to take the role for herself. When she finds out that the role is speechless, she becomes outraged. The director replies disingenuously: "Well, have you been thinking that you will read Hamlet's soliloquy to us?"

There is also an allusion to the three witches from *Macbeth* at the end of the episode when Maria and Pugovka are watching the film footage. The eldest sister is very dissatisfied with the result and switches "this nonsense" off. Suddenly three other sisters appear dressed like ghosts, beseech her to put the TV on and ask her for an autograph.

This example is a classical sitcom. The effect of the incorporation of Hamlet's soliloquy into the story line is mainly based on the antithesis between the tragic and the comic. The viewers listen to a piece of "serious" Shakespearean text for a short period of time. The function of this text is ultimately to make them laugh, not to ponder over the issues of existence that Shakespeare's hero raises. This quality of antithesis makes the citation effective in this context.[15]

Another example that shows an image of an actor playing Hamlet is a sketch entitled *At the Theater's Principal* («У директора театра»; *U direktora teatra*) from a popular TV comic program *In A Small Town* («В городке»; *V gorodoke*; 2002–2006) with Ilya L. Oleinikov and Yuri N. Stoyanov in the title roles. An actor, Eduard Petrovich (Stoyanov), comes to the theater's principal, Gena (Oleinikov), and begins to complain that they have not bought fitting white tights for him and that he has to act Hamlet "like a putz"[16] in short stockings. The director promises that they will certainly buy tights for the actor. They shift the conversation to another topic relevant to the theater. The sketch ends with the same grumbling of the actor regarding his "Hamletian" costume.

There is another sketch from this program entitled *A Tragedy like a Tragedy* («Трагедия как трагедия»; *Tragediia kak tragediia*; section "Horror"). Here the image of Hamlet is also presented in the context of everyday theatrical life, but in a tragicomic key. The director (Oleinikov) resents that a scene has not been prepared and the rehearsal of *Hamlet* is to start in half an hour. Suddenly, an actor Zhuchkin[17] (Stoyanov) clad in a classical costume and with a skull in his hands comes up to the director and cries: "Poor Yorick!" The director is frightened because of the unexpectedness, but he collects himself and replies that the actor should not even dream of the part of Hamlet. Zhuchkin asks the director to give him a chance as he has "been coming to this tragedy" for all of his life. The director refuses expressly and asks where the actor has taken the costume and skull. The actor answers that he took the clothes from the wardrobe department and that the skull was a present from his brother who works at a pathoanatomical museum. The director states that as long as he holds the position of director, Zhorik Shumskiy will do Hamlet. The actor begs to give him an opportunity to play the part as an understudy. But Arkadiy Petrovich has already taken this position. The actor does not calm down and points at the skull saying: "This is not Yorick; this is Zhorik!.. Poor Zhorik! I knew him!"[18] He finds out that there is a hair remaining in the skull. The director sees this and is horrified. The actor exclaims: "Just so! I have also planned everything." He takes another skull from his bag: "…Oh! And poor Arkadiy Petrovich!.. I knew him!!! And so did you. Do you recognize him?" The director (stammeringly): "H–h-how could you do this?" The actor: "You heard me… I've been coming to this tragedy for all of my life! I have been coming, coming and finally I have come to." He grasps the director's chin and cries: "Poor Sigismund Emmanuilovich! I knew him!".

Another sketch in *Gorodok* that has some references to Shakespeare's *Hamlet* is *An Actor in the Theater Canteen* («Актер в театральном буфете»; *Akter v teatral'nom bufete*; aka "To Hamlet!"; «За Гамлета!»; *Za Gamleta!*). It depicts the daily life of a Russian provincial theater. An actor Gusev (Stoyanov) asks his colleagues to lend him some money, but all of them refuse to do so. He asks the bartender Vaniusha about the price of smoked sausages (implying that he cannot afford them in contrast to his more successful colleagues). He orders a cup of tea, refusing to drink vodka (although it is quite obvious that he rejects the offer with an effort), because he is to act the part of the fourth guard that night. He thanks the bartender for the tea, asks to charge the bill to his account and takes a handful of sugar cubes. Suddenly an assistant of the director (Oleinikov) comes running and asks the actor if he remembers the role of Hamlet. Gusev replies: "To be — not to be?.. Just so further…" The assistant sends him to put on make-up, because the director is desperate for an actor to stand in for Gromov who is ill and unable to play Hamlet that night. At first, Gusev hesitates but then joyfully crosses himself, saying: "Lord, my dream has come true! Good heavens! Hello, dream!" The assistant calms him down and asks him not to use "any ad-lib," but to do everything "meticulously" as Gromov does. Gusev agrees and changes his attitude in the twinkling of an eye: he demands some cognac, grabs a sandwich, eats it greedily and raises a toast: "As the phrase goes, to Hamlet! To be or nót to be! Yes? Ha!" He is rude to the bartender ("Choke over your lemon!") and to the assistant "Hey, get out of here! Huhza you are doing here, getting in my way?". The actor declares: "I'm doing Hamlet! Well guys, so what? To be or nót to be!" Then he elbows the colleague who had refused to lend him money and leaves the canteen.

In these examples, Shakespeare's iconic character symbolizes the star part of one's career. Most Russian actors would consider the role of Hamlet to be a landmark role that enables them to showcase their talents to the fullest degree. At the same time, the part can kill an actor's career prospects, depending on critics' reviews and audience opinions.

Another genre of comic television programs appropriating Shakespeare has a political subtext; these involve scenarios where real political figures are put into situations akin to those of Shakespeare's characters. The mixture of contemporary political affairs with Shakespeare's themes of power, treachery and corruption evidence the enduring relevance of Shakespeare's work. On January 28, 1995, an episode of *Puppets* («Куклы»; *Kukly*, a Russian TV show of political satire produced by Vasily Yu. Grigoryev, written by Victor A. Shenderovich) entitled *Hamlet* was shown on the Russian TV channel NTV. This satirical television program was a Russian version of the French satirical puppet show *Les Guignols de l'info* (*The News Puppets*). The episode presented President Boris N. Yeltsin as Hamlet. Hamlet-Yeltsin soliloquizes: "To be or not to be — that's the question." While drawing from aspects of *Hamlet*, the content of monologues and dialogues here reflects the contemporary political climate of the time. Hamlet-Yeltsin mulls over his situation and possible further actions, specifying surnames of real Russian political figures from the 1990*s* and mentioning the events in Chechnya. He opens a small volume of Shakespeare's *Hamlet* and reads: "Denmark is a prison." After this he declares: "Well, he [Shakespeare] has not lived in Russia even for a minute." Another well-known reformer of the period, economist Yegor T. Gaidar, appears as "Ophelia." Ophelia-Gaidar gives the decree of her/his appointment as the Prime Minister back to the "Prince" as well as other "presents" and "promises." Gennady A. Zyuganov, the First Secretary of the Communist Party of the Russian Federation, is presented as the 'Ghost' (literally "the Ghost of Communism"). He urges Hamlet-Yeltsin to have revenge for his "villainous murder," but his "son Boren'ka"[19] obviously does not want to do this. The "Ghost" attempts to remind him that he has also begun his career in the Communist Party. But Hamlet-Yeltsin replies: "But I'm like the Phoenix, I've burnt away and rejuvenated! ... That's it, dad, forsake your cares evermore." A cock cries. The "Ghost" has to fade away: "Adieu, son! ... Remember me!" A "market-oriented researcher" Grigory A. Yavlinsky appears as "Horatio." Hamlet-Yeltsin ponders: "Maybe I should really take vengeance for communism? Should I call Anpilov[20] and his friends and stand aside? ... It's too bad! I've not been able to decide for the fourth year in a row. Here it is, you know, Russian Hamletism! Doubts on the very throne..." Horatio-Yavlinsky responds: "We'll see whose the throne will be in a year when the people come to the polling stations" (*exeunt*). Hamlet-Yeltsin: "There are enemies round and round. Each and all wish me hell. Here, you know, I should be on my toes. Who is there behind the arras? Aha, got you, rat!" The "Prince" kills Vyacheslav V. Kostikov, his former spokesman, and decides to "bury him in the Vatican."[21] Then again through the arras Hamlet-Yeltsin kills Viktor V. Gerashchenko, the Chairman of the Central Bank of Russia ("An unexpected resignation!"). The Defense Minister Pavel S. Grachev emerges: "Save yourself, Prince!" He alerts that "the son of a lawyer" Vladimir V. Zhirinovsky (the leader of the Liberal Democratic Party of Russia) is coming and "going berserk." Laertes-Zhirinovsky appears with a sword in his hand: "Where is he? Yo-ho, bring him here! I'll tear everyone apart who'll interfere! And I declare as a liberal that soon there'll be no democrats here!" Hamlet-Yeltsin and Laertes-Zhirinovsky fight with swords and stab each other. Laertes-Zhirinovsky says: "Let us forgive the wrongdoings of each other, brother!" He dies. Hamlet-Yeltsin says: "Now, who will the electorate follow?" before falling dead. Prime Minister Viktor S. Chernomyrdin (Fortinbras) and Interior Minister Viktor F. Yerin (probably the First Ambassador) enter. Fortinbras-Chernomyrdin says: "Yes, by the way, we should place the combat troops on alert, and in the meanwhile I'll be the 'caretaker'." In the end he answers the questions "How long?" and "What next?": "What next? Far and by, generally speaking — silence!".

The Russian TV show *Puppets* had quite a large audience and, of course, its producers were trying to convey different political views, opinions and even fears regarding the future of the new Russian state after the collapse of the Soviet Union. In our opinion, it was hard to find a better disposition for a doubting Boris Yeltsin toward the end of his first term as the Russian President than that of the Prince of Denmark. And this could be not only because of Shakespeare's popularity, but also because of the long Russian tradition of comparing Russian leaders with Hamlet.[22]

The sketch *Hamlet* performed by Volodymyr O. Zelensky[23] (Kvartal-95 Studio) is a similar example of political satire and commentary on current events. The third President of Ukraine Viktor A. Yushchenko is shown in a Hamlet-like situation: "To be or not to be; that's the question! Who, who should I propose to be the Prime Minister? Who will take this appointment? Maybe Yulia Volodymyrivna[24]? Marusya will be offended! Or Petr, a seller of sweet death[25]?.. Or who? Or Viktor Fedorovych[26]? He is always open to..." The text of this monologue is difficult to understand without knowledge of the political situation in Ukraine in the 2000s. Nevertheless, it would have been interesting and comic for its Ukrainian audience. The form of "Hamlet's" soliloquy significantly amplifies its comic effect.

These examples suggest that the iconic character of Hamlet is often used when one needs to present (often in a comic and satirical light) an image of a vacillating and doubting politician. Another example is a short film *Hamlet* (2002) based on Leonid A. Filatov's eponymous play where Vladimir V. Putin is depicted as the Prince of Denmark and Boris Yeltsin as the Ghost. The film starts with the Ghost coming to Hamlet and asking him what is going on in the castle. The apparition, slightly drunk, notes that all his portraits have been removed. Then it says "In fact, I've asked you to take care of Russia!.." Hamlet replies: "You've asked to take care of Denmark!" Ghost: "Have you managed to save it?" Hamlet: "Partially. … But I'm doing my best." Then the Ghost says that Hamlet owes him a "lifelong debt" and mentions that some oligarchs have complained that Hamlet is too strict toward them. When Hamlet finally promises not to "whack" the tycoons, the Ghost disappears. Then Hamlet complains that everyone tries to give him advice, even his late father. Horatio says that Hamlet should consult with the people, but Hamlet replies that it is all in vain, because there are too many opinions ("One man was shouting angrily 'Give us order!..' / The other was crying furiously 'Freedom!'"). So, there are a "million paths" to take. He asks Horatio to give him advice, but the "court old-timer" says that Hamlet should "listen to the voice of his own fate" and that "all princes are pondering over one question." Hamlet (*hopefully*): "Which one?" Horatio: "To be or not to be?! It's a hard and long way to the top." Hamlet asks him to repeat the question. Horatio (*in surprise*): "You mean, you don't speak English?.." Hamlet: "I used to learn German when I was young." Then the Prince asks Horatio to translate the question, but his friend answers that he does not remember and advises Hamlet to ask his father. All these clues give us much evidence that Filatov's Hamlet is Vladimir Putin at the beginning of his career as the President of Russia and the Ghost is Boris Yeltsin.

Overall, the majority of references to Hamlet in Russian culture appropriate recognizable elements from the tragedy but significantly diverge from the content. The various examples evidence that *Hamlet* is an enduring aspect of Russian culture, their interpretation dependent on the social and historical contexts.

These instances of Hamletization are particular cases of Shakespeareanism and Shakespearization[27] or more accurately "Neo-Shakespeareanism" and "Neo-Shakespearization," registering that representations of Shakespeare and his legacy in modern cultural forms differ greatly in comparison with their early modern origins.[28]

What is apparent is that analysis of these *Hamlet* appropriations assist in understanding and providing a lens on modern Russian culture. The variety of Russian appropriations of *Hamlet*, comprising different fragmented allusions and references to the play in various post-Soviet films, TV programs and shows, are examples of Hamletization. Despite Alexey V. Bartoshevich's reflection that "our time, at least in Russia, is not for this play,"[29] *Hamlet* continues to generate interest among Russian screenwriters and audiences, regardless of changes in popular tastes, economic reforms and political environments.

Notes

1. See, for instance: Bardovsky, "Russkii Gamlet," 135–45; Gibian, "Russia," 728; Gibian, "Shakespeare in Russia"; Alekseev, ed., *Shekspir i russkaia kul'tura*; Rowe, *Hamlet: A Window on Russia*; Gorbunov, "K istorii russkogo «Gamleta»," 7–26; Levin, *Shekspir i russkaia literatura XIX veka*; Parfenov and Price, ed. *Russian Essays on Shakespeare and His Contemporaries*; Střibrný, *Shakespeare and Eastern Europe*; Zakharov, *Shekspirizm russkoi klassicheskoi literatury: tezaurusnyi analiz*; Bartoshevich, "Gamlety nashikh dnei," 209–16; Gaydin, *Vechnye obrazy kak konstanty kul'tury: tezaurusnyi analiz "gamletovskogo voprosa"*; Zakharov and Lukov, *Genii na veka: Shekspir v evropeiskoi kul'ture*; Zakharov, "Productions of Hamlet on the Post-Soviet Stage in Russia," 246–56; Zakharov, "Iconic Characters: Hamlet as Iconic Image in Russian Culture," 1336–38.
2. Ryazanov, *Grustnoe litso komedii, ili Nakonets podvedennye itogi* (Moscow: ProzaiK Publ., 2010). Hereinafter the translation of all Russian quotations was made by the authors.
3. Ryazanov, *Grustnoe litso komedii*, 48–49.
4. Pushkin, "Table-talk," 65. See more details, for example, in: Zakharov, "Shekspirovskii tezaurus v tvorchestve Pushkina," 75–77; Zakharov, "Shekspirizm Pushkina," 148–55; Lukov, "Pushkin: russkaia 'vsemirnost'"," 58–73.
5. Ryazanov, *Grustnoe litso komedii*, 49.
6. Ibid.
7. In the film, Yuri Detochkin jacks a car from a law-abiding auto enthusiast because of a mistake in his card index. This episode resonates with the point of view of some researchers who suppose that both Shakespeare's *Hamlet* and Cervantes's *Don Quixote* show the danger of the

idea that every human being is free to change the world according to their perceptions of right and wrong. See, for instance, Karen A. Stepanyan's opinion in: Vinogradov and Stepanyan, "Karen Stepanyan o Dostoevskom, chitavshem Servantesa, i poiskakh Boga v literature."

8. Yuri V. Nikulin was a prominent Soviet and Russian actor and clown.
9. It is not clear whether she means a motion-picture or a painting.
10. Here is a pun: he means both a copy of *Hamlet* and the character of Hamlet as well as the title of a satirical magazine *Crocodile* and his sarcastic attitude to his relatives.
11. Hamlet actually is a very popular name in Armenia.
12. See, for instance: Mokulsky, "Komediia," 407.
13. On the distinction between story fidelity and thematic fidelity, see Harold, "The Value of Fidelity in Adaptation," 89–100.
14. KVN is a humorous TV show that broadcasts a team competition where participants improvise in exchanging funny questions and answers, singing, dancing, presenting tongue-in-cheek sketches, etc.
15. It also should be pointed out that the selection of Nikolay V. Maklakov's translation for this citation is atypical. We have not found this Russian version of "To be or not to be" in any other staging or production.
16. "Putz" is a slang word borrowed from Yiddish. In this case it is used in a figurative meaning "fool, simpleton." Cf., the name "Hamlet" is probably derived from *Amleth, Amlóði, Hamblett*—the name of the hero from the lost *Skjöldunga saga*. In nineteenth-century Iceland the word "Amlóði" was used to refer to a narrow-minded and silly person. In contemporary Icelandic it is used to denote a lazy and foolish idler. See more details, for example in: Gaydin, *Vechnye obrazy kak konstanty kul'tury*, 53.
17. Zhuchka is a common name for mongrels in Russia.
18. Zhorik is a colloquial variant of the name Georgy (Yuri, Yegor, Igor).
19. "Boren'ka" is a pet form of Boris.
20. Viktor I. Anpilov was a Russian Communist politician.
21. It is a hint at the fact that Kostikov was sent as an ambassador to the Holy See and the Order of Malta after his resignation.
22. The Russian Emperor Paul I is called "Russian Hamlet," because his father, Peter III, was allegedly assassinated, his mother, Catherine the Great, did not want to hand over the reins of power to him and, finally, he has murdered himself after less than five years of his reign.
23. Nowadays he is the sixth and current president of Ukraine.
24. Yulia V. Tymoshenko is a Ukrainian politician and businesswoman.
25. Petro O. Poroshenko is a well-known Ukrainian oligarch, the founder of Roshen Confectionery Corporation; he was the fifth President of Ukraine.
26. Viktor F. Yanukovych is a Ukrainian politician. He served as the fourth President of Ukraine.

27. For more details about these concepts mainly in the Russian context see, for example: Zakharov, *Shekspirizm russkoi klassicheskoi literatury*; Lukov and Zakharov, "Shekspirizatsiia i shekspirizm," 253–56; Zakharov and Lukov, *Shekspir, shekspirizatsiia*; Zakharov and Lukov, *Genii na veka*.
28. See: Gaydin, "Neoshekspirizatsiia," 345–54; Gaydin, *Neoshekspirizatsiia v sovremennoi khudozhestvennoi kul'ture*; Gaydin, *Shekspir v sovremennoi russkoi kul'ture: natsional'noe i global'noe*; Lisovich et al. *Shekspirosfera: Virtual'nye miry Shekspira i ego sovremennikov*.
29. Bartoshevich, "Gamlety nashikh dnei," 211.

Works Cited

Alekseev, Mikhail, ed. *Shekspir i russkaia kul'tura* [Shakespeare and Russian culture]. Moscow: Nauka Publ., 1965. (In Russ.).

Bardovsky, Alexander. "Russkii Gamlet" [Russian Hamlet]. In *Russkoe proshloe. Istoricheskie sborniki* [Russian Past. Historical Collections], book 4, edited by Sergey Platonov, Alexander Presniakov, and Julius Gessen, 135–45. Petrograd and Moscow: Petrograd Publ., 1923. (In Russ.).

Bartoshevich, Alexey. "Gamlety nashikh dnei" [Hamlets of Our Time]. In *Shekspirovskie chteniia* [Shakespeare Readings], edited by Alexey Bartoshevich, 209–16. Moscow: Moscow University for the Humanities Publ., 2010. (In Russ.).

Gaydin, Boris. "Neoshekspirizatsiia" [Neo-Shakespearization]. *Znanie. Ponimanie. Umenie*, no. 4 (2014): 345–54. (In Russ.).

Gaydin, Boris. *Neoshekspirizatsiia v sovremennoi khudozhestvennoi kul'ture* [Neo-Shakespearization in Contemporary Artistic Culture]. Moscow: Moscow University for the Humanities Publ., 2014. (In Russ.).

Gaydin, Boris. *Shekspir v sovremennoi russkoi kul'ture: natsional'noe i global'noe* [Shakespeare in Contemporary Russian Culture: The National and Global]. Moscow, forthcoming. (In Russ.).

Gaydin, Boris. *Vechnye obrazy kak konstanty kul'tury: tezaurusnyi analiz "gamletovskogo voprosa"* [Eternal Images as Constants of Culture: Thesaurus Analysis of the "Hamlet's Question"]. Saarbrücken: Lambert Academic Publishing, 2011. (In Russ.).

Gibian, George. "Russia." In *A Shakespeare encyclopaedia*, edited by Oscar James Campbell and Edward G. Quinn, 728. London and New York: Methuen & Co LTD, 1966.

Gibian, George. "Shakespeare in Russia." PhD diss., Harvard University, 1951.

Gorbunov, Andrey. "K istorii russkogo «Gamleta»" [On the History of Russian "Hamlet"]. In Shakespeare, William. *Gamlet* [Hamlet], selected translations, 7–26. Moscow: Raduga Publ., 1985. (In Russ.).

Harold, James. "The Value of Fidelity in Adaptation." *British Journal of Aesthetics* 58, no. 1 (2018): 89–100. https://doi.org/10.1093/aesthj/ayx041.

Levin, Yuri. *Shekspir i russkaia literatura XIX veka* [Shakespeare and 19th Century Russian Literature]. Leningrad: Nauka Publ., 1988. (In Russ.).

Lisovich, Inna, and Vladimir Makarov. "Nauchno-issledovatel'skii proekt «Virtual'naia shekspirosfera: transformatsii shekspirovskogo mifa v sovremennoi kul'ture»" [Research Project "Virtual Shakespearean Sphere: Transformations of Shakespearean Myth in Modern Culture"]. *Znanie. Ponimanie. Umenie*, no. 2 (2014): 264–82. (In Russ.).

Lisovich, Inna, Nikolay Zakharov, Vladimir Makarov, Boris Gaydin, Valery Lukov, and Vladimir Lukov. *Shekspirosfera: Virtual'nye miry Shekspira i ego sovremennikov* [The Shakespearean Sphere: Virtual Worlds of Shakespeare and His Contemporaries]. Moscow: Moscow University for the Humanities Publ., 2016. (In Russ.).

Lukov, Vladimir. "Pushkin: russkaia 'vsemirnost''" [Pushkin: Russian 'Universalness']. *Znanie. Ponimanie. Umenie*, no. 2 (2007): 58–73. (In Russ.).

Lukov, Vladimir, and Nikolay Zakharov. "Shekspirizatsiia i shekspirizm" [Shakespearization and Shakespeareanism]. *Znanie. Ponimanie. Umenie*, no. 3 (2008): 253–56. (In Russ.).

Lukov, Valery, and Vladimir Lukov. "Shekspirosfera i kul'turnye konstanty" [The Shakespearean Sphere and Cultural Constants]. *Znanie. Ponimanie. Umenie*, no. 2 (2014): 200–8. (In Russ.).

Lukov, Valery, Nikolay Zakharov, Vladimir Lukov, and Boris Gaydin. "Shekspirosfera (Shekspir, ego sovremenniki, ego epokha v kul'ture povsednevnosti)" [The Shakespearean Sphere (Shakespeare, His Contemporaries, His Age in the Culture of Everyday Life)]. *Informatsionnyi gumanitarnyi portal "Znanie. Ponimanie. Umenie"*, no. 3 (2012). Accessed March 31, 2020. http://zpujournal.ru/e-zpu/2012/3/Lukov~Zakharov~Lukov~Gaydin~Shakespeare-sphere/. (In Russ.).

Mokulsky, Stefan. "Komediia" [Comedy]. In *Literaturnaia entsiklopediia* [Literary Encyclopedia], 11 vols. [Moscow], 1929–1939, edited by Vladimir Fritzsche and Anatoly Lunacharsky, clmns. 407–32. Moscow: The Communist Academy Publ., 1931. Vol. 5. (In Russ.).

Parfenov, Alexandr, and Joseph G. Price, ed. *Russian Essays on Shakespeare and His Contemporaries*. Newark, NJ: University of Delaware Press; London: Associated University Presses, 1998.

Pushkin, Alexander. "Table-talk." In Pushkin, Alexander. *Polnoe sobranie sochinenii* [Complete Works] : in 10 vols., 64–83. Leningrad: Nauka Publ., Leningrad Branch, 1978. Vol. 8: *Avtobiograficheskaia i istoricheskaia proza. Istoriia Pugacheva. Zapiski Moro de Braze* [Autobiographical and Historical Prose. Pugachev's Story. The Notes of Moro de Braze]. (In Russ.).

Rowe, Eleanor. *Hamlet: A Window on Russia*. New York: New York University Press, 1976.

Ryazanov, Eldar. *Grustnoe litso komedii, ili Nakonets podvedennye itogi* [The Unhappy Face of Comedy, or Ultimately Final Results]. Moscow: ProzaiK Publ., 2010. (In Russ.).

Stříbrný, Zdeněk. *Shakespeare and Eastern Europe*. Oxford and New York: Oxford University Press, 2000.

Vinogradov, Leonid, and Karen Stepanyan. "Karen Stepanyan o Dostoevskom, chitavshem Servantesa, i poiskakh Boga v literature" [Karen Stepanyan on Dostoevsky Who Read Cervantes and the Search for God in Literature]. *Pravoslavie i Mir*. Accessed March 31, 2020. http://pravmir.ru/karen-stepanyan-o-dostoevskom-servantese-i-poiskax-boga-v-literature/. (In Russ.).

Zakharov, Nikolay. "Shekspirizm Pushkina" [Pushkin's Shakespeareanism]. *Znanie. Ponimanie. Umenie*, no. 3 (2006): 148–55. (In Russ.).

Zakharov, Nikolay. "Shekspirovskii tezaurus v tvorchestve Pushkina" [Shakespeare's Thesaurus in Pushkin's Oeuvre]. *Vestnik Mezhdunarodnoi akademii nauk (Russkaia sektsiia)*, no. 1 (2006): 75–77. (In Russ.).

Zakharov, Nikolay. *Shekspirizm russkoi klassicheskoi literatury: tezaurusnyi analiz* [Shakespeareanism of Russian Classical Literature: The Thesaurus Analysis], edited by Vladimir Lukov. Moscow: Moscow University for the Humanities Publ., 2008. (In Russ.).

Zakharov, Nikolay. "Productions of Hamlet on the Post-Soviet Stage in Russia." *Znanie. Ponimanie. Umenie*, no. 4 (2015): 246–56. https://doi.org/10.17805/zpu.2015.4.23.

Zakharov, Nikolay. "Iconic Characters: Hamlet as Iconic Image in Russian Culture." In *The Cambridge Guide to the Worlds of Shakespeare*, 2 vols, edited by Bruce R. Smith et al., 1336–38. New York: Cambridge University Press, 2016. Vol. 2: The World's Shakespeare 1660–Present. https://doi.org/10.1017/9781316137062.184.

Zakharov, Nikolay, and Vladimir Lukov. *Shekspir, shekspirizatsiia* [Shakespeare, Shakespearization]. Moscow: Moscow University for the Humanities Publ., 2011. (Shakespeare Studies XVII). (In Russ.).

Zakharov, Nikolay, and Vladimir Lukov. *Genii na veka: Shekspir v evropeiskoi kul'ture* [A Genius for Centuries: Shakespeare in European Culture]. Moscow: Humanities Institute of TV & Radio Broadcasting Publ., 2012. (In Russ.).

Zakharov, Nikolay, Valery Lukov, and Vladimir Lukov. "Shekspirosfera" [The Shakespearean Sphere]. *Elektronnoe periodicheskoe nauchnoe izdanie "Vestnik Mezhdunarodnoi akademii nauk. Russkaia sektsiia"*, no. 2 (2012): 70–75. Accessed March 31, 2020. http://heraldrsias.ru/online/2012/2/238/. (In Russ.).

Afterword

It is only a fifteen-minute short film and, compared to Shakespeare's lengthier, voluminous *Hamlet* (the source of its inspiration, according to the credits), arguably no more than a fragment. Yet, set in the old city of Valletta, Malta, and having achieved global exposure thanks to festival take-up and awards, *Daqqet ix-Xita/Plangent Rain* (dir. Kenneth Scicluna, 2010) operates brilliantly as a meditation on Shakespeare's most celebrated play.[1] It does so through allusion. *Daqqet ix-Xita/Plangent Rain*'s plot, as might be anticipated, can be quickly summarised. A young man (Sean Decelis), the son of sailor, is damned to rowing his boat back and forth across Valletta's Grand Harbour, locked in conscience-stricken behaviour. The boat criss-crosses in a movement emblematic of cyclical rhythms and deferral/delay. Incapable of action, but ignited by suspicion, the young man is plagued by the indecent union of his mother and uncle. The source of his angst? The death of his father, a presence we never quite see but a figure referred to by the elderly boat passenger (Manuel Cauchi) who, bringing Horatio to mind, reflects: 'Of course I knew your father. If ever there was a gentleman, it was he'. As part of its retrospective *mise-en-scène*, *Daqqet ix-Xita/Plangent Rain* foregrounds the son's memorial romanticisation of—and attachment to—the father, splicing in shots of a sailor on leave and tantalising viewers with bedroom glimpses of the picture of a ship and the model of a boat. For the young man, there is no easy alleviation from suffering. Typically, the film limns him labouring up the old town's constricted Strait Street, bearing his oars like burdens. Martyr-like, he traverses a kind of Via Dolorosa, a road to

A. A. Joubin and V. Bladen (eds.), *Onscreen Allusions to Shakespeare*,
Global Shakespeares, https://doi.org/10.1007/978-3-030-93783-6

cavalry, that leads not to the cross but to an ancient tenement. Focusing repeatedly on baroque properties, *Daqqet ix-Xita/Plangent Rain* here declares the second of its inspirational debts, which the credits simultaneously acknowledge, the city of Valletta itself along with its intersecting cultures and histories.

The island of Malta is steeped in a rich maritime past. Situated at an oceanic crossroads, Malta was long an island nation, energised by mutually fertilising influences, and strategically critical to the early modern Mediterranean power-balance. Maltese, English, Sicilian, and Italian are among its historical languages, and, not surprisingly, the dominant image of Valletta in popular representation is still its docks, creeks, spur, wharfs, and forts, illustrative of commerce and trade. Malta is also the island long associated with the Knights of St John, bastions of faith and crusaders of Christendom, as enshrined in accounts of the 1565 Siege of Malta at which the one-time hospitallers famously defended their fortifications against the onslaught of the 'Ottoman'. In its discovery of Valletta, *Daqqet ix-Xita/Plangent Rain* admits of no such straightforward triumphalism. Instead, and aided by a black-and-white cinematography that approves melancholy and dreariness, the film underscores motifs of soddenness and rottenness. Wetness is omnipresent—the boat the young man rows is full of holes; the old city is engulfed by puddles; a gutter is overflowing, there being excess rain to accommodate. The familiar edifices of Strait Street appear decaying, while the basement of the tenement to which the young man returns is flooded, blurring the point at which the harbour ends, and the city begins. In fact, in periodically merging its black-and-white palette with a greenish tinge, *Daqqet ix-Xita/Plangent Rain* alludes to disease and to the 'leprous' (1.5.64) milieu of *Hamlet*.

Hamlet is most obviously apprehended in the film's vernacular transliteration of the play's dialogue. First, in Maltese, but with English subtitles, *Daqqet ix-Xita/Plangent Rain* approximates many of the play's aphorisms and injunctions. 'Sooner or later, everyone gets his turn', the uncle (Philip Mizzi) upbraids in the kitchen, recalling Claudius' line, 'you must know your father lost a father,/That father lost his' (1.2.89–90).[2] 'Go change', the mother (Polly March) instructs her son, this conjuring Gertrude's request that Hamlet 'cast[s] [his] nighted colour off' (1.2.68). Uncle and mother are signposted via dialogue, but so too is the Ghost, as when, in a night-time segment, a voice intones, 'Remember', in such a way as to suggest 'remember me' (1.5.91). Some of these transliterations are playful, parodic even. Hence, as the young man struggles with Strait Street, we hear the exclamation, 'Foul! An incredible foul!', a football commentator's remark that comically surrogates for the Ghost's accusation. Others are felicitously intriguing. Crucially, *Daqqet ix-Xita/Plangent Rain* prioritises voices that are off-stage, or obscene, and that cannot be pinned down to source. There is obvious—and affective—flouting of conventional diegesis here, as television noise bleeds into shards of sepulchral speeches that bleed in turn into charges of criminality from beyond the grave. (The soundscape is also confused in gendered terms, women's voices combining with men's in evocative conjunctions). Second, *Daqqet ix-Xita/Plangent Rain* supplements transliteration with verbal expressions that fill in for what *Hamlet* neglects to tell us or only ever intimates. In this sense, the film, despite its brevity, works in an additive capacity. 'Don't let impotence wreck your marriage' a disembodied self-help book warning sounds: the implication is that, in the father-wife/Old Hamlet-Gertrude relationship, there were sexually divisive bones of contention. 'The years rolled by, and no one caught on to anything' is a further fragment of narrative that swells the *mise-en-bande*, a third-person account of duplicity even more unsettling for never being quite clarified. Finally, the eavesdropping young man overhears his mother and uncle in a recriminatory exchange: 'Swear on my mother's soul … Look at us … leaving empty-handed'. (Not an arras at this point but muffling doors). Clearly, there are further scheming histories here, now nuanced as 'purposes mistook/Fallen on th'inventors' heads' (5.2.368–69), but the larger point is how the film furnishes us with a backstory. In its allusions to prior malpractice, *Daqqet ix-Xita/Plangent Rain* concerns itself not just with *Hamlet* but with Hamlet before *Hamlet*, coming to life as an adaptation that answers to some of the play's perennial questions.[3]

In several respects, *Daqqet ix-Xita/Plangent Rain* does not really need dialogue, so obviously supported is it by a reservoir of resonant visuals. The roving camera focuses in on Strait Street's grilles and narrow doorways, metaphors for Denmark as prison, and, in interior segments, equally concentrates via close-up on an ear, the orifice, of course, through which Old Hamlet meets his end. Dancing couples celebrating the wedding on the tenement's rooftop are an interpolation, but the image finds its logic in an accompanying shot of crumpled sheets, graphic reminders of the 'enseamed bed' (3.4.90) and the Shakespearean protagonist's soiled fantasies. Certainly, in the prominence given to a busy waiter bearing pastries on a plate in the grotesquely festive montage, an echo of Hamlet's joke, 'the funeral baked meats/Did coldly furnish forth the marriage tables' (1.2.179–80), is heard. And then there is the young—unspeaking—woman (Ilaria Falzon) clothed in cool white arranging flowers in a vase. As the young man takes refuge in the tenement after being drenched in the rain, she shows solicitude, drying him with a towel and, in the film's metaphorical order of things, endeavouring to rid him of rottenness. But this rare moment of tenderness soon evaporates. In addition, the flowers are fading and dried ('[my] violets ... withered all when my father died' [4.5.177–78], states Ophelia)—the young woman, it is established, has missed the *carpe diem* moment of their beauty, and she does not reappear. Tellingly, the flowers are individually laid out on a dusty trunk like so many corpses, suggesting a rollcall of the dead.

Although separated by time and place, this segment of *Daqqet ix-Xita/Plangent Rain* recalls the experimental Danish adaptation of *Hamlet*, *Ofelias Blomster/Ophelia's Flowers* (dir. Jørgen Leth, 1968), another short film that looks to image and association for its rationale. Indeed, a consistent tendency is for *Daqqet ix-Xita/Plangent Rain* to summon the spectres of earlier *Hamlet* adaptations, acting thereby as a palimpsest of the Shakespearean interpretive impetus. The film's sources of inspiration, then, are in fact multiple, from *Hamlet* (dir. Laurence Olivier, 1948), distinguished by its sharp-angled architectural envisioning of Elsinore, to *Gamlet* (dir. Grigori Kozintsev, 1964), marked by a mostly monochrome appearance congruent with a pessimistically political mindset. Both adaptations are part of *Daqqet ix-Xita/Plangent Rain*'s representational armoury, whether this be suggested in the opening shot of falling spear-like rain or in the lensing of Valletta's harbour, which is low lit to play up *chiaroscuro* and a darkened edge to the frame. Intertextual indebtedness is also at work in the film's score. At the start, a wailing flute intrudes on the soundscape, Ruben Zahra's alternately lyrical and shrieking minor chord patterns alluding to Akira Kurosawa's use of the *nohkan* in his Shakespeare film adaptations and confirming the music of *Daqqet ix-Xita/Plangent Rain* as 'lament'. Mesmerising and recurrent, the score is embellished by folksy percussion, xylophone, and a militaristic drumroll at the film's end, although not with any lessening of discordance. The clattering cacophony of the 'lament' draws heightened attention to the scene as the young man rows his mother and uncle out into the harbour, only to begin manically rocking the boat in an attempted suicidal sinking. Having been privy to their conspiratorial talk—the young man's play-within-the-play revelation—he is precipitated into action, while the appalled reaction shot of his mother conveys her recognition of his recognition of her culpability. Privileged at this point, then, is the revenge plot of *Hamlet*, the outcome of which, however, remains open-ended. Via an expressive dissolve that shifts us from the boat's unhappy occupants, the image with which we are left is of flowers and petals floating in the current. It is an abundantly allusive composition, one that brings into play scraps of relationships, pieces of a past, Valletta's contexts, and Shakespearean stories. Emboldened by the score, the conclusion gestures, but again without explicitly delivering on the cue, to a Fortinbras-like entrance even as it also underwrites the sense of a passing owned and journeys completed. And, as waves take over as the dominant sound, *Daqqet ix-Xita/Plangent Rain* reiterates notes of liquidity and fluidity and reverts to its maritime environs, closing with the flotsam and jetsam of romance and intrigue and alluding to the flows and eddies of the adaptive process.

The exciting chapters in this collection wrestle with the question of what constitutes a Shakespearean cinematic allusion. For some contributors, an allusion is an inset or a quotation. For others, it manifests itself in a citation or an image. For yet more, it can be grasped in the form of a scene-within-a-scene. Many of the chapters confess to the allusion as a fragment or tatter which borders on a spectral dimension. So it is that Maurizio Calbi in his chapter explores two Italian films and one Filipino Shakespeare film that test the boundaries of citation in a way that resurrects the Shakespeare-on-film boom of the 1990s. In inviting us to cogitate what a Shakespeare film was, is, and how it might be, his chapter serves as an eloquent preface to Victoria Bladen's stimulating essay on linguistic intertexts in some Australian cinematic examples. Bladen convincingly demonstrates the extent to which Shakespeare is a shaping force in confronting postcolonial relations, not least through a metaphorically suggestive film vocabulary that pushes at issues of cultural register and class. Her reflections pave the way for the similarly attuned chapter by Chris Thurman in which, introducing *Otello Burning* (dir. Sara Blecher, 2011), a South African film set outside Durban in the late 1980s, he problematises the use of *Othello* as a reference-point. Thurman's cautionary contribution is to encourage us to move away from better-known South African adaptive examples, such as television's 'Shakespeare in Mzansi' (2008), in order to investigate slippages and discontinuities in Shakespeare's authorising functions. Poonam Trivedi is also interested in authorising functions, and her chapter, capped by stylish concluding observations, maps a range of allusions to Shakespeare in Hindi-language cinema. Distinctive in Trivedi's exploration, and dovetailing with some aspects of *Daqqet ix-Xita/Plangent Rain*, is a difficult-to-ignore *extent* of reference (parodic, reverential, conscious, unconscious). Is a taxonomy of allusion possible, Trivedi asks? Her chapter compels us to consider the prospect in its incisive construction of Shakespeare as pop and postmodern icon.

The remaining chapters continue the exploration of allusion by flagging context, noting generic diversity, and arguing for the vitality of a spectrum of global film industries. Germane is Aimara da Cunha Resende's chapter on representations of *Romeo and Juliet*'s balcony scene in Brazilian cinema and television, her discussion expertly identifying the significances of the *novela* (soap opera) genre. Her application to her examples of theories of anthropophagy—eating, digesting, and incorporating are positives, she contends—trenchantly spotlights how Shakespeare is positioned within an allusive Latin American matrix. Often, an allusion is mediated via other allusions. Nathalie Vienne-Guerrin, in her chapter, addresses a French film, *Mon petit doigt m'a dit* (dir. Pascal Thomas, 2005), which is based on an Agatha Christie novel, which itself alludes to Shakespeare, and thereby offers a stellar reading of adaptation as a palimpsestuous operation. Guerrin's thesis is that allusions make up multiply remediated presences that either enlighten or obscure, and in this far-reaching extrapolation her chapter invites comparison with the self-consciousness of *Daqqet ix-Xita/Plangent Rain*. Allusions are illuminating, but they are not always easy to spot. Mariacristina Cavecchi in her chapter provides fascinating insights into what may or may not be an allusion to *Julius Caesar* in *Roma* (dir. Federico Fellini, 1972), prompting us thereby to ponder the relationship between Shakespeare, Italian cultures, and Fascist history. The chapter's speculation about an unmade Fellini film adaptation of *Othello* is particularly enriching in this respect. Also encompassing other ventures in adaptation, Márta Minier's chapter on Shakespeare and 'East-Central Europe' indisputably establishes the recuperative cultural work performed by a Polish television film and an international biopic. In them, she refreshingly demonstrates, we find both a ready familiarity with Shakespearean allusion and an interpretive terrain that can simultaneously engage the novels of Dickens and autobiographical experiment. Minier's focus on region/nation leads onto the collection's final chapter in which Boris N. Gaydin and Nikolay V.

Zakharov pursue the concept of 'Hamletisation' into Russian television shows and feature films. 'Why Hamlet?' they ask or, rather, 'Why parts of him?'. Considering an impressive array of instances, Gaydin and Zakharov make thrillingly visible a panoply of allusions to Shakespeare's prince and situate the fascination he exercises in Soviet and post-Soviet praxes, altering us in so doing to the adaptive *Hamlet*'s political utility.

On Shakespeare and allusions, the criticism of Mariangela Tempera, until her untimely death Professor of English Literature at the University of Ferrara, is quoted in this collection. But, even aside from her excellent scholarship, Mariangela's voice infuses these contents. Perhaps more allusively, I hear her in the chapters; I see her in many of their approaches. Bob-haired, and with an irrepressible intellect, she was passionate about Shakespeare in all his iterations and manifestations. She spearheaded the study of Shakespeare and media, founded a long-running conference and book series ('Dal testo alla scena') on the Shakespeare page-stage relationship; and made sterling contributions to developing civic connections between academia and schools. For me, it was her love of learning from Shakespeare and cinema—and world examples—that meant that we bonded. We would spend lunches and coffees together—in Stratford-upon-Avon and elsewhere—trading instances, concepts, angles. Mariangela was always savvy and acute on position and privilege. 'That Italian Shakespeare film has caused controversy because of its representation of the south!' would be a typical remark. At conferences, we would put on student competitions, with Mariangela generously supporting the spirit of the occasion while also being a stickler for propriety, ringing a bell with smiling exactitude when the time was up. She came to Belfast for an inspirational lecture and mentoring workshop: student development was close to her heart. 'Don't say "might" in your CVs, be confident and say "will"', she would recommend. Her manifold talents and abilities were fully on view at the symposium she organised in Ferrara in 2013. (Many of the contributors to this collection were there.) Her paper at that meeting was on Shakespeare and the Euro-Western, that well-known but understudied cinematic genre that mixes and matches so many influences, players, and languages. 'This character says he's quoting Shakespeare; let me tell you, he's not!' Mariangela insisted. She was invigorating in opinion, forthright in view and never anything less than outward-looking. For the symposium, we were accommodated in a hotel that had been a monastery. Without wi-fi, we were thrown into each other's company, but it was really Mariangela's social skills that encouraged conviviality. One evening, over dinner, we broke into song, each symposium participant performing his or her party-piece. Echoes of monastic chants were replaced by the fun and laughter of contemporary popular musical theatre.

This collection also refers to Mariangela's 'archive'. A word about that. As part of her work at the 'Centro Shakespeariano', Mariangela (with Vanni Borghi of the Council of Ferrara) was the compiler of a quite magnificent catalogue. This 'Catalogo e Inventario' *magnus opus* lists not only a huge number of Shakespeare films but also cartoons, opera, ballet, educational works, interviews, and documentaries—on a world-wide basis—that reference Shakespeare or take Shakespeare as their starting-point. The last version of the catalogue I have, the one in front of me as I write, runs to 247 (tiny print) pages. A forerunner of digital platforms and resources, the catalogue is extraordinarily comprehensive: coded and codified, it is so organised as to provide information about play, director, cast, genre, and length. And, incredibly helpfully for enthusiasts, it comes with detail about who said what, in which film, Shakespeare-wise. To keep the catalogue going, Mariangela relied on an army of volunteers who sent her references: I was one of them, part-time. We probably all were in one way or another. Wherever Mariangela went, she would be on the look-out as she was continually adding, rewriting, updating. On a train once, we had a conversation about how she could find a copy of an elusive Italian film adaptation of *Measure for Measure*. Where could one try? Who could one contact? When she came to my own university, she asked my students about a title, and they basked in the glow of her attention. Increasingly, I found it challenging to come up with examples Mariangela didn't know about—it was a shared joke between us that there really wasn't much that escaped her—but I did, and our conversations continued. And what of the wonderful short film that chimes with and gets us thinking hard about the subject of this collection, Kenneth Sciulana's *Daqqet ix-Xita/Plangent Rain*? It hardly needs saying the film is listed in Mariangela's catalogue. Just go to the section entitled—'*Hamlet*: Parodies, Citations, Fragments, Allusions'.[4]

Mark Thornton Burnett

Mark Thornton Burnett fellow of the English Association and Member of the Royal Irish Academy, is Professor of Renaissance Studies at Queen's University, Belfast. He is the author of *Masters and Servants in English Renaissance Drama and Culture: Authority and Obedience* (Basingstoke:

Macmillan, 1997), *Constructing 'Monsters' in Shakespearean Drama and Early Modern Culture* (Basingstoke: Palgrave, 2002), *Filming Shakespeare in the Global Marketplace* (Basingstoke: Palgrave, 2007; 2nd ed. 2012), *Shakespeare and World Cinema* (Cambridge: Cambridge University Press, 2013) and *'Hamlet' and World Cinema* (Cambridge: Cambridge University Press, 2019). He is editor of the 'Shakespeare and Adaptation' series published by Bloomsbury Academic.

Notes

1. The film won two awards at the Malta International TV Short Film Festival (direction and cinematography) and has been screened at the Cannes Film Festival, the Cyprus International Film Festival, the New York International Film Festival, and the Oaxaca International Film Festival. For a full listing of screenings, see 'Plangent Rain: A Story of Strait Street', http://www.stradastretta.com/fs_screenings_eng.html (accessed 7 March 2013).
2. William Shakespeare, *Hamlet*, edited by Ann Thompson and Neil Taylor, revised edition (London and New York: Bloomsbury Arden Shakespeare, 2016). All further references appear in the text.
3. *Hamlet* invites prequels, Ann Thompson argues, because the play 'raises important questions it does not answer' and only intermittently deigns to 'explain [its] events' ('*Hamlet*: Looking Before and After: Why So Many Prequels and Sequels?', in Sarah Annes Brown, Robert I. Lublin and Lynsey McCulloch, eds, *Reinventing the Renaissance: Shakespeare and his Contemporaries in Adaptation and Performance* [Basingstoke: Palgrave, 2013], pp. 17–31, esp. p. 18). asmlet.
4. My thanks to Alexa Alice Joubin and Victoria Bladen for the invitation to write this afterword and to Kenneth Scicluna for courtesies and stimulating conversations.

Works Cited

8audreyrose, "Mon petit doigt m'a dit 2005 Trailer.flv," 8 October 2011. Accessed 15 September 2020. https://www.youtube.com/watch?v=X3SSVBlCkRE.

Alekseev, Mikhail, ed. *Shekspir i russkaia kul'tura* [Shakespeare and Russian culture]. Moscow: Nauka Publ., 1965. (In Russ.).

Andrade, Oswald. "Manifesto Antropófago." In Gilberto Mendonça Teles, *Vanguarda Europeia e Modernismo Brasileiro*, 226–32. Petrópolis: Vozes, 1973.

Andrew, Dudley. *Concepts in Film Theory*. New York: Oxford University Press, 1984.

Aristotle. *Poetics*. London: Penguin, 1996.

Ashcroft, Bill. "Madness and Power: *Lilian's Story* and the Decolonised Body." In *Lighting Dark Places: Essays on Kate Grenville*, edited by Sue Kossew, 55–72. Netherlands: Rodopi, 2010.

Augusto, Sérgio. *Este Mundo É Um Pandeiro: a chanchada de Getúlio a JK*, São Paulo: Companhia das Letras, 2001.

Bakhtin, Mikhail. *Rabelais and His World*, translated by Helene Iswolsky. Bloomington: Indiana University Press, 1984.

Bakhtin, Mikhail. *Problems of Dostoevsky's Poetics*, edited and translated by Caryl Emerson. Minneapolis: University of Minnesota Press, 1985.

Bakhtin, Mikhail. *The Dialogic Imagination: Four Essays by Mikhail Bakhtin*, edited by Michael Holquist, translated by Caryl Emerson. Austin: University of Texas Press, 1985.

A. A. Joubin and V. Bladen (eds.), *Onscreen Allusions to Shakespeare*, Global Shakespeares, https://doi.org/10.1007/978-3-030-93783-6

Barcan, Ruth. "'Mobility Is the Key': Bodies, Boundaries and Movement in Kate Grenville's *Lilian's Story*." *Ariel: A Review of International English Literature* 29, no. 2 (1998): 31–55.
Bardovsky, Alexander. "Russkii Gamlet" [Russian Hamlet]. In *Russkoe proshloe. Istoricheskie sborniki* [Russian Past. Historical Collections], book 4, edited by Sergey Platonov, Alexander Presniakov, and Julius Gessen, 135–45. Petrograd and Moscow: Petrograd Publ., 1923. (In Russ.).
Bartoshevich, Alexey. "Gamlety nashikh dnei" [Hamlets of Our Time]. In *Shekspirovskie chteniia* [Shakespeare Readings], edited by Alexey Bartoshevich, 209–16. Moscow: Moscow University for the Humanities Publ., 2010. (In Russ.).
Bassi, Shaul. *Shakespeare's Italy and Italy's Shakespeare. Place, "Race," Politics*. London: Palgrave Macmillan US, 2016.
Bassnett, Susan. "Influence and Intertextuality: A Reappraisal." *Forum for Modern Language Studies* 43, no 2 (2007): 134–46.
Bellanta, Melissa. "A Masculine Romance: *The Sentimental Bloke* and Australian Culture in the War and Early Interwar Years." *Journal of Popular Romance Studies* 4, no. 2 (2014): 0–20. Accessed 12 May 2020. www.jprstudies.org/2014/10/a-masculine-romance-the-sentimental-bloke-and-australian-culture-in-the-war-and-early-interwar-yearsby-melissa-bellanta/.
Bigliazzi, Silvia. "Julius Caesar 1935. Shakespeare and Censorship in Fascist Italy." Verona: Skenè Texts, Supplement to *Skenè. Journal of Theatre and Drama Studies*, 3 (2019).
Bladen, Victoria. "The Rock and the Void: Pastoral and Loss in Joan Lindsay's *Picnic at Hanging Rock* and Peter Weir's Film Adaptation." *Colloquy: text theory critique* 23 (2012): 0–26. Accessed 12 May 2020. https://www.monash.edu/__data/assets/pdf_file/0003/1764300/bladen.pdf.
Bladen, Victoria. "*Othello* on Screen: Monsters, Marvellous Space and the Power of the Tale." In *Shakespeare on Screen: Othello*, edited by Sarah Hatchuel and Nathalie Vienne-Guerrin, 24–42. Cambridge: Cambridge University Press, 2015.
Bladen, Victoria. "Looking for Lear in *The Eye of the Storm*." In *Shakespeare on Screen:* King Lear, edited by Victoria Bladen, Sarah Hatchuel, and Nathalie Vienne-Guerrin, 185–201. Cambridge: Cambridge University Press, 2019.
Blecher, Sara, dir. *Otelo Burning*. 2011; Johannesburg: Cinga Productions. Film [DVD].
Blecher, Sara. Interview with the author, 11 October 2013.
Bosman, Anston. "Shakespeare and Globalization." In *The New Cambridge Companion to Shakespeare*, 2nd ed., edited by Margreta de Grazia and Stanley Wells, 285–301. Cambridge: Cambridge UP, 2010.
Bosworth, Richard J.B. *Whispering City: Rome and Its Histories*. New Haven and London: Yale University Press, 2011.

Boyd, David. "The Public and Private Lives of a Sentimental Bloke." *Cinema Journal* 37, no. 4 (1998): 3–18.

Brand, John. *Observations of the Popular Antiquities of Great Britain*, vol. 3. London: Bell & Daldy, 1872.

Brunetta, Gian Piero. "Cinema." In *Dizionario del fascismo*. Torino: Einaudi, 2002.

Burnett, Mark Thornton. *Shakespeare and World Cinema*. Cambridge: Cambridge University Press, 2013.

Burt, Richard. "To E—Or Not to E -?: Disposing of Schlockspeare in the Age of Digital Media." Introduction to *Shakespeare After Mass Media*, edited by Richard Burt. New York: Palgrave, 2002.

Burt, Richard, ed. *Shakespeares After Shakespeare. An Encyclopedia of the Bard in Mass Media and Popular Culture*. Westport, Connecticut and London: Greenwood Press, 2007.

Burt, Richard. "Introduction: Shakespeare, More or Less? From Shakespearec-centricity to Shakespearecentricity and Back." Burt, *Shakespeares* 1–9.

Burt, Richard and Lynda Boose, eds. "Shakespeare and Asia in Postdiasporic Cinemas: Spinoffs and Citations." In *Shakespeare, the Movie II: Popularizing the Plays on Film, TV, Video and DVD*. New York: Routledge, 2003.

Calbi, Maurizio. *Spectral Shakespeares. Media Adaptations in the Twenty-First Century*. New York and London: Palgrave Macmillan, 2013.

Calbi, Maurizio. "'In States Unborn and Accents Yet Unknown': Spectral Shakespeare in Paolo and Vittorio Taviani's *Cesare deve morire* (*Caesar Must Die*)." *Shakespeare Bulletin* 32, no. 2 (2014): 235–53.

Caponi, Paolo. *Otello in camicia nera. Shakespeare, la censura e la regia nel ventennio fascista*. Roma: Bulzoni, 2018.

Carrera, Alessandro. *Fellini's Eternal Rome: Paganism and Christianity in Federico Fellini's Films*. London: Bloomsbury 2019.

Cartelli, Thomas. Rev. of *Shakespeare and the Problem of Adaptation*, by Margaret Jane Kidnie. Semenza, 218–24.

Catania, Saviour. "The Hanging Rock Piper: Weir, Lindsay, and the Spectral Fluidity of Nothing." *Literature/Film Quarterly* 40, no. 2 (2012): 84–95.

Chillington Rutter, Carol. "Remind Me: How Many Children Had Lady Macbeth?" *Shakespeare Survey* 57 (2004): 38–53. Rpt. in revised, expanded form as "Precious Motives, Seeds of Time: Killing Futures in *Macbeth*." In *Shakespeare and Child's Play: Performing Lost Boys on Stage and Screen*, 154–204. London and New York: Routledge, 2007.

Christie, Agatha. *By The Pricking of My Thumbs* [1968]. London: Harper Collins Publishers, 2001. *Agatha Christie Official Website*. Accessed 15 September 2020.

Clemen, Wolfgang. *Shakespeare's Soliloquies*, translated by Charity Scott Stokes. London and New York: Routledge, 2010 [1987].

Collins, Felicity, Jane Landman, and Susan Bye. *A Companion to Australian Cinema*. Hoboken, NJ: Wiley-Blackwell, 2019.
Compagnon, Antoine. *La Seconde main ou le travail de la citation*. Paris: Seuil, 1979.
Corradini, Enrico. *Giulio Cesare: dramma in 5 atti*. Milano: Mondadori, 1926.
Croce Benedetto. *Shakespeare*, edited by Gian N. Orsini. Bari: Laterza, 1960.
Cuarón, Alfonso, dir. *Harry Potter and the Prisoner of Azkaban*. 2004; Warner Bros.
Curran, John. *Agatha Christie's Murder in the Making. Stories and Secrets from her Archive*. London: HarperCollins Publishers, 2011.
D'Angelo, Frank J. "The Rhetoric of Intertextuality." *Rhetoric Review* 29, no 1 (2009): 31–47.
Deane, Laura. "Cannibalism and Colonialism: *Lilian's Story* and (White) Women's Belonging." *Journal of the Association for the Study of Australian Literature* 14, no. 3 (2014): 1–13.
Demasi, Domingos. *Chanchadas e Dramalhões*. Rio de Janeiro: Funarte, 2001.
Demby, Gene and Meraji, Shereen Marisol. "All That Glisters Is Not Gold." *Code Switch* (NPR), 21 August 2019. Online (transcript). https://www.npr.org/transcripts/752850055.
Dennis, C.J. *The Songs of a Sentimental Bloke*. Melbourne, Australia: Text Publishing, 2012.
Derrida, Jacques. *Archive Fever*, translated by Eric Prenowitz. Chicago and London: University of Chicago Press, 1995.
Derrida, Jacques. *Specters of Marx. The State of the Debt, the Work of Mourning and the New International*, translated by Peggy Kamuf. London and New York: Routledge, 1994.
Desai, Ashwin. *Reading Revolution: Shakespeare on Robben Island*. Pretoria: Unisa Press, 2012.
Desmet, Christy. "Dramas of recognition: *Pan's Labyrinth* and *Warm Bodies* as Accidental Shakespeare." In *Shakespeare/Not Shakespeare*, edited by Christie Desmet, Natalie Loper, and Jim Casey, 275–91. New York: Palgrave Macmillan, 2017.
Desmet, Christy and Robert Sawyer, eds. *Shakespeare and Appropriation*. London: Routledge, 1999.
Desmet, Christy, Natalie Loper, and Jim Casey, eds. *Shakespeare Not Shakespeare*. London: Palgrave Macmillan, 2017.
Distiller, Natasha. *Shakespeare, South Africa, and Post-Colonial Culture*. Lampeter: Edwin Mellen, 2005.
Distiller, Natasha. *Shakespeare and the Coconuts: On Post-apartheid South African Culture*. Johannesburg: Wits University Press, 2012.
Domaradzki, Jerzy, dir. *Lilian's Story*. 1996; Australia: Movieco Australia. DVD.

Dorval, Patricia and Nathalie Vienne-Guerrin, eds. "Shakespeare on Screen in francophonia Database." Accessed 5 July 2021. http://shakscreen.org/.

Dunnett, Jane. "The Rhetoric of Romanità: Representations of Caesar in Fascist Theatre." In *Julius Caesar in Western Culture*, edited by Maria Wyke, 244–65. Oxford: Blackwell, 2006.

Eco, Umberto. *Quase A Mesma Coisa*, translated by Eliana Aguiar. Rio de Janeiro-São Paulo: Editora Record, 2007.

Edwards, Catharine. *Roman Presences: Receptions of Rome in European Culture, 1789–1945*. Cambridge: Cambridge University Press, 1999.

Elsom, John. *Is Shakespeare Still Our Contemporary?* New York: Routledge, 1989.

Falkowska, Janina. "New Cinema of Nostalgia in Poland." In *Small Cinemas in Global Markets: Genres, Identities, Narratives*, edited by Lenuta Giukin, Janina Falkowska, and David Desser, 17–30. Lanham and London: Lexington Books (Rowman and Littlefield), 2014.

Fellini, Federico. *Roma di Federico Fellini*, edited by Bernardino Zapponi. Bologna: Cappelli, 1972.

Fiennes, Ralph. *Coriolanus*. 2011; Valley Village: Hermetof Pictures / Magna Films. Film.

Flaherty, Kate. *Ours as We Play It: Australia Plays Shakespeare*. Crawley, WA: UWA Publishing, 2011.

Galfré, Monica. *Una riforma alla prova. La scuola media di Gentile e il fascismo*. Milano: Franco Angeli, 2000.

Garber, Marjorie. "(Quotation Marks)." *Critical Inquiry* 25, no. 4 (1999): 653–79.

Garber, Marjorie. *Shakespeare's Ghost writers: Literature as Uncanny Causality*. First published in 1987 by Methuen. New York: Routledge, 2010.

Gaydin, Boris. *Vechnye obrazy kak konstanty kul'tury: tezaurusnyi analiz "gamletovskogo voprosa"* [Eternal Images as Constants of Culture: Thesaurus Analysis of the "Hamlet's Question"]. Saarbrücken: Lambert Academic Publishing, 2011. (In Russ.).

Gaydin, Boris. "Neoshekspirizatsiia" [Neo-Shakespearization]. *Znanie. Ponimanie. Umenie*, no. 4 (2014): 345–54. (In Russ.).

Gaydin, Boris. *Neoshekspirizatsiia v sovremennoi khudozhestvennoi kul'ture* [Neo-Shakespearization in Contemporary Artistic Culture]. Moscow: Moscow University for the Humanities Publ., 2014. (In Russ.).

Gaydin, Boris. *Shekspir v sovremennoi russkoi kul'ture: natsional'noe i global'noe* [Shakespeare in Contemporary Russian Culture: The National and Global]. Moscow, forthcoming. (In Russ.).

Genette, Gérard. *Paratexts: Thresholds of interpretation*. Cambridge: Cambridge University Press, 1997. Originally published in French as *Seuils*. Paris: Éditions du Seuil, 1987.

Gevisser, Mark. *Thabo Mbeki: The Dream Deferred*. Johannesburg: Jonathan Ball, 2007.

Gibian, George. "Russia." In *A Shakespeare encyclopaedia*, edited by Oscar James Campbell and Edward G. Quinn, 728. London and New York: Methuen & Co LTD, 1966.

Gibian, George. "Shakespeare in Russia." PhD diss., Harvard University, 1951.

Gibińska, Marta and Jerzy Limon, eds. *Hamlet East-West*. Gdańsk: Theatrum Gedanense Foundation, 1998.

Gilbert, Helen and Joanne Tompkins. *Post-Colonial Drama: Theory, Practice, Politics*. London: Routledge, 1996.

Gillis, Jackson, Richard Levinson, William Link, writers. *Columbo*. Season 2 Episode 4, "Dagger of the Mind." Directed by Richard Quine. Aired 26 November 1972, in broadcast syndication. NBC.

Giukin, Lenuta, Janina Falkowska, and David Desser, eds. *Small Cinemas in Global Markets: Genres, Identities, Narratives*. Lanham and London: Lexington Books (Rowman and Littlefield), 2014.

Golder, John and Richard Madelaine. *O Brave New World: Two Centuries of Shakespeare on the Australian Stage*. Sydney: Currency Press, 2001.

Gorbunov, Andrey. "K istorii russkogo «Gamleta»" [On the History of Russian "Hamlet"]. In Shakespeare, William. *Gamlet* [Hamlet], selected translations, 7–26. Moscow: Raduga Publ., 1985. (In Russ.).

Gordon, Robert. "Iago and the *swaart gevaar*: The Problems and Pleasures of a (Post)colonial *Othello*." In *Shakespearean International Year Book* 9, edited by Graham Bradshaw, Tom Bishop, and Laurence Wright. Abingdon: Ashgate, 2009.

Gori, Gianfranco Miro "Il dialetto di Federico." In *Federico Fellini: La mia Rimini*, edited by Mario Guaraldi and Loris Pellegrini. Rimini: Guaraldi, 2007.

Grenville, Kate. *Lilian's Story*. St. Leonard's, NSW: Allen & Unwin, 1997 rev. ed. [1985].

Gross, John. *After Shakespeare: Writing Inspired by the World's Greatest Author*. Oxford: Oxford University Press, 2002.

Guagnelini Giovanni and Re, Valentina. *Visioni di altre visioni: intertestualità e cinema*. Firenze: Archetipolibri - Gedit Edizioni, 2007.

Guglielmi, Nino. *Giulio Cesare: quattro momenti e sei quadri*. Roma: Edizioni Fascismo, 1939.

Harold, James. "The Value of Fidelity in Adaptation." *British Journal of Aesthetics* 58, no. 1 (2018): 89–100. https://doi.org/10.1093/aesthj/ayx041.

Harries, Martin. *Scare Quotes from Shakespeare. Marx, Keynes, and the Language of Reenchantment*. Stanford, CA: Stanford University Press, 2000.

Harwood, Ronald. *The Pianist*. In *The Pianist & Taking Sides*, 1–115. London: Faber and Faber, 2002.

Hatchuel, Sarah and Vienne-Guerrin, Nathalie, eds. *Shakespeare on Screen: The Roman Plays*. Mont-Saint-Aignan Cedex: Publications des universités de Rouen et du Havre, 2009.

Hatchuel, Sarah and Vienne-Guerrin, Nathalie. "'Is This an Umbrella Which I See Before Me?': *Columbo* goes to Scotland Yard." In *Shakespeare on Screen*: Macbeth, edited by Sarah Hatchuel and Nathalie Vienne-Guerrin, 397–410. Rouen: Presses Universitaires de Rouen et du Havre, 2013.

Healy, Alice. "'Impossible Speech' and the Burden of Translation: *Lilian's Story* from Page to Screen." *Journal of the Association for the Study of Australian Literature* 5 (2006): 162–77.

Hofmeyr, Isabel. "Reading Debating / Debating Reading: The case of the Lovedale Debating Society, or Why Mandela quotes Shakespeare." In *Africa's Hidden Histories: Everyday literacy and making the self*, edited by Karin Barber, 258–77. Bloomington: Indiana University Press, 2006.

Holmes, Jonathan. "'A World Elsewhere': Shakespeare in South Africa." *Shakespeare Survey* 55 (2002): 271–84.

Homqvist, Jytte. "Contrasting Cultural Landscapes and Spaces in Peter Weir's film *Picnic at Hanging Rock* (1975), Based on Joan Lindsay's 1967 Novel with the Same Title." *Coolabah* 11 (2013): 25–35.

Hopkins, Lisa. *Shakespearean Allusion in Crime Fiction. DCI Shakespeare*. London: Palgrave, 2016.

Houseman, John. *Unfinished Business—Memoirs: 1902–1988*. New York: Applause Theatre Books, 1989.

Huang, Alexa and Elizabeth Rivlin, eds. *Shakespeare and the Ethics of Appropriation*. New York: Palgrave Macmillan, 2014.

Hutcheon, Lynda and Syobhan O'Flynn. *A Theory of Adaptation*. 2nd ed., 121–22. London and New York: Routledge, 2013.

Ick, Judy Celine. "The Undiscovered Country: Shakespeare in Philippine Literatures." *Kritika Kultura* 21/22 (2013/2014): 185–209.

Iordanova, Dina. "Unseen Cinema, Notes on Small Cinemas and the Transnational." In *Small Cinemas in Global Markets: Genres, Identities, Narratives*, edited by Lenuta Giukin, Janina Falkowska, and David Desser, 213–220. Lanham and London: Lexington Books (Rowman and Littlefield), 2014.

Isenberg, Nancy. "'Caesar's Word Against the World': Caesarism and the Discourses of Empire." In *Shakespeare and the Second World War: Memory, Culture, Identity*, edited by Irena R. Makaryk and Marissa McHugh, 83–105. Toronto: University of Toronto Press, 2012.

Johnson, David. *Shakespeare and South Africa*. Oxford: Oxford University Press, 1996.

Johnson, David. "Beyond Tragedy: *Otelo Burning* and the Limits of Post-apartheid Nationalism." *Journal of African Cultural Studies* 26, no. 3 (2014): 348–51.

Johnson, David. "Coriolanus in South Africa." In *The Cambridge Guide to the Worlds of Shakespeare* (XVII: Shakespeare as Cultural Icon), edited by Bruce R. Smith et al, 1235–41. Cambridge: Cambridge University Press, 2016.

Joubin, Alexa Alice and Rivlin Elizabeth, eds. *Shakespeare and the Ethics of Appropriation*. Palgrave Macmillan, 2014.

Kani, John. *Apartheid and Othello*. "Living Shakespeare" series, edited by Virginia Compton. London: British Council, 2016. Online: https://literature.britishcouncil.org/assets/Uploads/06.-shakespeare-lives-south-africa-john-kani-digital-download.pdf.

Kashner Sam and Schoenberger, Nancy. *Furious love. Liz Taylor, Richard Burton: la storia d'amore del secolo*. Milano: Il Saggiatore (2010), 2011.

Kennedy, Dennis, Young Li Lan. "All that Remains of Shakespeare in Indian Film." In *Shakespeare in Asia: Contemporary Performance*. Cambridge: Cambridge University Press, 2010.

Kerner, Aaron. *Film and the Holocaust: New Perspectives on Dramas, Documentaries, and Experimental Film*. New York and London: Continuum, 2011.

Kezich, Tullio. *Federico Fellini. Il libro dei film*. Milano: Rizzoli, 2009.

Kidnie, Margaret J. *Shakespeare and the Problem of Adaptation*. London and New York: Routledge 2009.

Klapish, Cédric, dir. *Un air de famille*. 1996; Téléma.

Knights, L. C. "How Many Children Had Lady Macbeth? An Essay in the Theory and Practice of Shakespeare Criticism." In *Explorations*, 15–54. New York: New York University Press, 1964.

Kott, Jan. *Shakespeare Our Contemporary*, translated by Boleslaw Taborski. New York and London: W.W. Norton & Company, 1964.

Kristeva, Julia. *Revolution in Poetic Language*, translated by Margaret Waller. New York: Columbia University Press, 1984.

Kujawińska, Courtney Krystyna. "Celebrating Shakespeare under the Communist Regime in Poland." In *Shakespeare in Cold War Europe: Conflict, Commemoration, Celebration*, edited by Erica Sheen and Isabel Karreman, 23–35. London: Palgrave Macmillan, 2016.

Kullmann, Thomas. "Shakespeare on the Internet: Global and South Asian Appropriations." In *Asian Interventions in Global Shakespeare: 'All the World's his Stage'*, edited by Poonam Trivedi, Paromita Chakravarti, and Ted Motohashi. New York: Routledge, 2020.

Kürti, László and Peter Skalník. *Postsocialist Europe: Anthropological Perspectives from Home*. New York and Oxford: Berghahn Books, 2009.

Landy, Marcia. *Italian Film*. Cambridge: Cambridge University Press, 2000.

Lanier, Douglas. "Introduction. On the Virtues of Illegitimacy: Free Shakespeare on Film." Burt, *Shakespeares*, 132–37.

Lanier, Douglas. "Recent Shakespeare Adaptation and the Mutations of Cultural Capital." Semenza 104–13.

Lanier, Douglas. *Shakespeare and Modern Popular Culture*. Oxford: Oxford University Press, 2002.

Lanier, Douglas. "Will of the People: Recent Shakespeare Film Parody and the Politics of Popularization." In *A Concise Companion to Shakespeare on Screen*, edited by Diana E. Henderson. Malden, MA: Blackwell Publishing, 2006.

Lanier, Douglas. "On the Virtues of Illegitimacy: Free Shakespeare on Film." In *Shakespeares After Shakespeare. An Encyclopedia of the Bard in Mass Media and Popular Culture*, edited by Richard Burt, vol. 1, 132–37. Westport, Connecticut and London: Greenwood Press, 2007.

Lanier, Douglas. "Post-Racial Othello." 2010 Lindberg Lecture, University of New Hampshire. 29 June 2012. Online: http://www.youtube.com/watch?v=ScroEtGwmOQ.

Lanier, Douglas. *Larrikins: A History*. Brisbane: University of Queensland Press, 2012.

"La Roma di Fellini: città eterna, città interna." *Doppiozero*, January 20, 2020. Accessed 20 July 2021. https://www.doppiozero.com/materiali/la-roma-di-fellini-citta-eterna-citta-interna.

Levin, Yuri. *Shekspir i russkaia literatura XIX veka* [Shakespeare and 19th Century Russian Literature]. Leningrad: Nauka Publ., 1988. (In Russ.).

Levine, Lawrence W. *Highbrow/Lowbrow: The Emergence of Cultural Hierarchy in America*. Cambridge, MA: Harvard University Press, 1988.

Lévi-Strauss, Claude. *Raça e História*, translated by Inácio Canelas. Lisboa: Editorial Presença, 1996.

Lindsay, Joan. *Picnic at Hanging Rock*. Harmondsworth: Penguin, 1970 [1967].

Lindsay, Joan, Beatrix Christian, and Alice Addison, Writers. *Picnic at Hanging Rock*. Directed by Larysa Kondracki, Michael Rymer and Amanda Brotchie, featuring Natalie Dormer and Lily Sullivan. Aired 2018. Amazon Studios, FremantleMedia Australia and Screen Australia. Blu-Ray.

Lisovich, Inna, and Vladimir Makarov. "Nauchno-issledovatel'skii proekt «Virtual'naia shekspirosfera: transformatsii shekspirovskogo mifa v sovremennoi kul'ture»" [Research Project "Virtual Shakespearean Sphere: Transformations of Shakespearean Myth in Modern Culture"]. *Znanie. Ponimanie. Umenie*, no. 2 (2014): 264–82. (In Russ.).

Lisovich, Inna, Nikolay Zakharov, Vladimir Makarov, Boris Gaydin, Valery Lukov, and Vladimir Lukov. *Shekspirosfera: Virtual'nye miry Shekspira i ego sovremennikov* [The Shakespearean Sphere: Virtual Worlds of Shakespeare and His Contemporaries]. Moscow: Moscow University for the Humanities Publ., 2016. (In Russ.).

Livett, Kate. "Homeless and Foreign: the Heroines of *Lilian's Story* and *Dreamhouse*." In *Lighting Dark Places: Essays on Kate Grenville*, edited by Sue Kossew, 119–34. Netherlands: Rodopi, 2010.

Longford, Raymond, dir. *The Sentimental Bloke*. 1919; Australia, Madman Entertainment Pty Ltd. DVD.

Lukov, Vladimir. "Pushkin: russkaia 'vsemirnost''" [Pushkin: Russian 'Universalness']. *Znanie. Ponimanie. Umenie*, no. 2 (2007): 58–73. (In Russ.).

Lukov, Vladimir, and Nikolay Zakharov. "Shekspirizatsiia i shekspirizm" [Shakespearization and Shakespeareanism]. *Znanie. Ponimanie. Umenie*, no. 3 (2008): 253–56. (In Russ.).

Lukov, Valery, and Vladimir Lukov. "Shekspirosfera i kul'turnye konstanty" [The Shakespearean Sphere and Cultural Constants]. *Znanie. Ponimanie. Umenie*, no. 2 (2014): 200–8. (In Russ.).

Lukov, Valery, Nikolay Zakharov, Vladimir Lukov, and Boris Gaydin. "Shekspirosfera (Shekspir, ego sovremenniki, ego epokha v kul'ture povsednevnosti)" [The Shakespearean Sphere (Shakespeare, His Contemporaries, His Age in the Culture of Everyday Life)]. *Informatsionnyi gumanitarnyi portal "Znanie. Ponimanie. Umenie"*, no. 3 (2012). Accessed 31 March 2020. http://zpu-journal.ru/e-zpu/2012/3/Lukov~Zakharov~Lukov~Gaydin~Shakespeare-sphere/. (In Russ.).

Malpiero, Gian Francesco. *Giulio Cesare* in *L'Armonioso Labirinto: Teatro da musica 1913–1970*, edited by Marzio Pieri, 225–69. Venezia: Marsilio, 1992.

Manetti, Daniela. *"Un'arma poderosissima." Industria cinematografica e Stato durante il fascismo. 1922–1943*. Milano: Franco Angeli, 2012.

Márkus, Zoltán. "Shakespeare in Quotation Marks." Ed. Bruce Smith and Katherine Rowe, *Cambridge World Shakespeare Encyclopedia* (forthcoming).

Marsden, Jean I., ed. *The Appropriation of Shakespeare*. Hemel Hempstead: Harvester Wheatsheaf, 1991.

Mazierska, Ewa. "In the Name of Absent Fathers and Other Men: Representation of Motherhood in the Polish Post Communist Cinema." *Feminist Media Studies* 1 (2006): 67–83.

Mazierska, Ewa. *Roman Polanski: The Cinema of a Cultural Traveller*. London and New York: I.B. Tauris, 2007.

Mazierska, Ewa. *Masculinities in Polish, Czech and Slovak Cinema: Black Peters and Men of Marble*. New York and Oxford: Berghahn Books, 2008.

Moana. Dir. Alfredo Peyretti. Sky Cinema and Polivideo. 2009. Film.

Mokulsky, Stefan. "Komediia" [Comedy]. In *Literaturnaia entsiklopediia* [Literary Encyclopedia]: in 11 vols. [Moscow], 1929–1939, edited by Vladimir Fritzsche and Anatoly Lunacharsky, clmns., 407–32. Moscow: The Communist Academy Publ., 1931. Vol. 5. (In Russ.).

Mônica e Cebolinha no mundo de Romeu e Julieta. Accessed 30 March 2020. https://www.youtube.com/watch?v=lAEOiotIa7s.

Mushakavanhu, Tinashe. "Shakespeare in Mzansi: A South African Perspective." *Sentinel Literary Quarterly* 4, no. 1 (2010). Online: http://www.sentinelpoetry.org.uk/slq/4-1-oct2010/interviews/tinashe-mushakavanhu.html.

Mushakavanhu, Tinashe. "Shakespeare in Mzansi: A South African Perspective." *Sentinel National Film and Sound Archive*. http://www.nfsa.gov.au/.

O'Loughlin, Thomas. *The Eucharist: Origins and Contemporary Understandings*. London: Bloomsbury, 2015.

O'Regan, Tom. *Australian National Cinema*. London: Routledge, 1996.

Orkin, Martin. *Shakespeare against Apartheid*. Johannesburg: Ad Donker, 1987.

Orkin, Martin. *Drama and the South African State*. Manchester: Manchester University Press, 1991.

Parfenov, Alexandr, and Joseph G. Price, ed. *Russian Essays on Shakespeare and His Contemporaries*. Newark, NJ: University of Delaware Press; London: Associated University Presses, 1998.

Parsons, Keith and Mason, Pamela, eds. *Shakespeare in Performance*. London: Salamander Books, 1995.

Paul, Joanna. "Rome Ruined and Fragmented: The Cinematic city in Fellini's Satyricon and Roma." In *Cinematic Rome*, edited by Richard Wrighley, 109–20. Leicester: Troubador Publishing, 2008.

Pavis, Patrice. *Theatre at the Crossroads of Culture*, translated by Loren Kruger. London: Routledge, 1992.

Pearce, Brian. "Review: *Coriolanus* (dir. Debbie Lutge)." *Shakespeare in Southern Africa* 21 (2009): 83–84.

Pearce, Brian. "British Directors in Post-Colonial South Africa." In *Shakespeare in Stages: New Theatre Histories*, edited by Christine Dymkowski and Christie Carson, 264–76. Cambridge: Cambridge University Press, 2010.

Pennacchia Punzi, Maddalena. *Shakespeare intermediale. I drammi romani*. Spoleto: Editoria & Spettacolo, 2021.

Pettigrew, Damian. *I'm born a Liar. A Fellini Lexicon*. New York: Harry N. Abrams Inc., 2003.

Pilch, Jerzy. *The Mighty Angel*, translated by Bill Johnston. University of Rochester: Open Letter, 2009 [2000].

Pushkin, Alexander. "Table-talk." In Pushkin, Alexander. *Polnoe sobranie sochinenii* [Complete Works]: in 10 vols., 64–83. Leningrad: Nauka Publ., Leningrad Branch, 1978. Vol. 8: *Avtobiograficheskaia i istoricheskaia proza. Istoriia Pugacheva. Zapiski Moro de Braze* [Autobiographical and Historical Prose. Pugachev's Story. The Notes of Moro de Braze]. (In Russ.).

Putuma, Koleka. *Collective Amnesia*. Cape Town: uHlanga Press, 2017.

Ravara Montebelli, Cristina. *Guida alla mostra documentaria Alea Iacta Est. Giulio Cesare a Savignano sul Rubicone*. Cesena: Società Editrice Il Ponte Vecchio, 2010.

Rivière, François. *Agatha Christie, La Romance du Crime*. Paris: Éditions de La Martinière, 2012.

Rome and Juliet. Dir. Connie Macatuno. Regal Capital & Regal Entertainment. 2006. Film.

Romeu e Julieta, by Fábio Jr e Lucélia Santos. Youtube, 1980. Accessed 28 March 2020. https://www.youtube.com/watch?v=iwN2yrMd7Kg.

"Romeu e Julieta (1968)—Hebe Camargo e Ronald Golias." YouTube, September 22, 2007. Accessed 27 March 2020. https://www.youtube.com/watch?v=HTr97lTecg4.

Rossi, Ernesto. *Studi drammatici e lettere autobiografiche*. Firenze: Le Monnier, 1885.

Roux, Daniel. "Shakespeare and Tragedy in South Africa: From *Black Hamlet* to *A Dream Deferred*." *Shakespeare in Southern Africa* 27 (2015): 1–14.

Rowe, Eleanor. *Hamlet: A Window on Russia*. New York: New York University Press, 1976.

Ryazanov, Eldar. *Grustnoe litso komedii, ili Nakonets podvedennye itogi* [The Unhappy Face of Comedy, or Ultimately Final Results]. Moscow: ProzaiK Publ., 2010. (In Russ.).

Sanders, Julie. *Adaptation and Appropriation*. London and New York: Routledge, 2006.

Sanesi, Ireneo. "Enrico Corradini - *Giulio Cesare*, dramma in cinque atti" - Roma, Rassegna Internazionale, 1902, in *La critica. Rivista di Letteratura, Storia e Filosofia diretta da Benedetto Croce* 1 (1903): 104–18.

SBT 2003. Accessed 30 March 2020. www.youtube.com/watch?v=dRYzsabiL8c.

SBT, 1990. Accessed March. www.youtube.com/watch?v=hecm9syK3BM.

Schalkwyk, David. *Hamlet's Dreams: The Robben Island Shakespeare*. London: Bloomsbury, 2013.

Schandl, Veronika. *Socialist Shakespeare Productions in Kadar-regime Hungary: Shakespeare Behind the Iron Curtain*. Lewiston, New York: Edwin Mellen Press, 2008.

Schepisi, Fred. dir. *The Eye of the Storm*. 2011; Australia: Paper Bark Films Pty. Ltd. DVD.

Scott-Douglass, Amy. *Shakespeare Inside. The Bard Behind Bars*. London: Continuum, 2007.

Sedgwick, Eve Kosofsky. *Tendencies*. London and New York: Routledge, 1998 [1993].

Seeff, Adele. *South Africa's Shakespeare and the Drama of Language and Identity*. London: Palgrave Macmillan, 2018.

Segel, Harold B., ed. *The Columbia Guide to the Literatures of Eastern Europe Since 1945*. New York: Columbia University Press, 2003.

Semenza, Greg, ed. *After Shakespeare on Film*. Spec. issue of *Shakespeare Studies* 38 (2010): 1–285.

Sennett, Richard. *The Fall of Public Man: On the Social Psychology of Capitalism.* New York: Vintage, 1974.
Sestito, Marisa. *Julius Caesar in Italia.* Bari: Adriatica, 1978.
Shakespeare, William. *Gamlet* [Hamlet], selected translations, 7–26. Moscow: Raduga Publ., 1985. (In Russ.).
"Shakespeare / Not Shakespeare: Afterword" in *Shakespeare / Not Shakespeare,* edited by Christy Desmet, Natalie Loper, and Jim Casey, 293–303. Palgrave Macmillan, 2017.
"Shakespearean Rhizomatics: Adaptation, Ethics, Value." In *Shakespeare and the Ethics of Appropriation*, edited by E. Rivlin and A. Huang, 21–40. New York: Palgrave Macmillan, 2014.
Shakespeare, William. *Macbeth*, edited by Kenneth Muir. Arden 2, Methuen, 1951.
Shakespeare, William. *Romeo and Juliet*, edited by Jill L. Levenson. Oxford: Oxford University Press, 2000.
Shakespeare, William. *William Shakespeare: The Complete Works*, edited by Stanley Wells and Gary Taylor, 2nd ed. Oxford: Clarendon Press, 2005.
Shakespeare, William. *The Norton Shakespeare*, 3rd ed., edited by Stephen Greenblatt, Walter Cohen, Suzanne Gossett, Jean E. Howard, Katherine Eisaman Maus, and Gordon McMullan. New York: Norton, 2016.
Shurbanov, Alexander and Boika Sokolova. *Painting Shakespeare Red: An East-European Appropriation.* Newark-London: University of Delaware Press. Associated University Presses, 2001.
Sierra, Horacio. *New Readings of The Merchant of Venice.* Newcastle-upon-Tyne: Cambridge Scholars Press. 2013.
Smith, Bruce R. "Shakespeare's Residuals: The Circulation of Ballads in Cultural Memory." In *Shakespeare and Elizabethan Popular Culture,* The Arden Critical Companions, edited by Stuart Gillespie and Neil Rhodes. London: Thomson Learning, 2006, 193–217.
Spiró, György. "Színészek dicsérete: Új lengyel filmek." *Filmvilág*, 8 August 2002.
"Staged by Quick Comedians: References to Shakespeare's Roman Plays on Screen." In *Shakespeare on Screen: The Roman Plays*, edited by Sarah Hatchuel and Nathalie Vienne-Guerrin, 305–28. Mont-Saint-Aignan Cedex: Publications des universités de Rouen et du Havre, 2009.
Staiger, Janet. *Perverse Spectators: The Practices of Film Reception.* New York and London: New York University Press, 2000.
Stříbrný, Zdeněk. *Shakespeare and Eastern Europe.* Oxford: Oxford University Press, 2000.
Sułkowski, Bogusław. "A Polish Reinterpretation of *Hamlet*." In *Hamlet East-West*, edited by Marta Gibińska and Jerzy Limon, 171–76. Gdańsk: Theatrum Gedanense Foundation, 1998.

Swan, Oscar E. *Kaleidoscope of Poland: A Cultural Encyclopedia*. Pittsburgh, PA: University of Pittsburgh Press, 2015.

Szpilman, Wladyslaw. *The Pianist: The Extraordinary Story of One Man's Survival in Warsaw, 1939–45*, translated by Anthea Bell. London: Phoenix, 2000.

Tassone, Aldo. "From Romagna to Rome: The Voyage of a Visionary Chronicler (*Roma* and *Amarcord*)." In *Federico Fellini Essays in Criticism*, edited by Peter Bondanella, 261–88. Oxford: Oxford University Press, 1978.

Taylor, Gary. *Reinventing Shakespeare*. Oxford: Oxford University Press, 1989.

Taylor, Jerome. "The Big Question: How Big Is the Agatha Christie Industry, and What Explains Her Enduring Appeal?" *The Independent*, Wednesday February 25, 2009. Accessed 15 September 2020. http://www.independent.co.uk/arts-entertainment/books/features/the-big-question-how-big-is-the-agatha-christie-industry-and-what-explains-her-enduring-appeal-1631296.html.

Teague, Fran. "Shakespeare, Beard of Avon." In *Shakespeare After Mass Media*, edited by Richard Burt, 221–41. New York: Palgrave, 2002.

Tempera, Mariangela. "Political Caesar. Julius Caesar on the Italian Stage." In *Julius Caesar: New Critical Essays*, edited by Horst Zander, 333–43. New York, London: Routledge, 2005.

Tempest and its implications for critical practice." *Social Dynamics* 36.2 (June 2010): 315–27.

The Norton Shakespeare, edited by Stephen Greenblatt, Walter Cohen, Jean E. Howard and Katherine Eisaman Maus. New York: Norton, 1997.

Theodorakopoulos, Elena. "The Sites and Sights of Rome in Fellini's Films: 'Not a Human Habitation but a Psychical Entity'." In *The Sites of Rome*, edited by Larmour, David H. James, and D. Spencer, Diana, 353–84. Oxford: Oxford University Press, 2007.

Thomas, Pascal, dir. *La Dilettante*. 1999; Ah! Victoria! Films.

Thomas, Pascal, dir. *Mon Petit Doigt m'a dit*. 2005; Ah! Victoria! Films.

Thomas, Pascal, dir. *Le Crime est notre Affaire*. 2008; Les Films Français.

Thomas, Pascal, dir. *Associés Contre le Crime*. 2012; Les Films Français.

Thompson, John B. *A Mídia e a Modernidad*e, translated by Wagner de Oliveira Brandão. Petrópolis: Vozes, 2002.

Thompson, Karenlee. "The Australian Larrikin: C.J. Dennis's [Un]Sentimental Bloke." *Antipodes* 21, no. 2 (2007): 177–83.

Thornton Burnett, Mark, *Shakespeare and World Cinema*. Cambridge: Cambridge University Press, 2013.

Thurman, Chris. *Guy Butler: Reassessing a South African Literary Life*. Scottsville: University of KwaZulu-Natal Press, 2010.

Thurman, Chris. "Editorial." *Shakespeare in Southern Africa* 24 (2012): iii–v.

Thurman, Chris, ed. *South African Essays on 'Universal' Shakespeare*. Burlington: Ashgate, 2014.

Thurman, Chris. "After *Titus*: Towards a Survey of Shakespeare on the Post-apartheid Stage." In *New Territories: Reconfiguring Theatre and Drama in Post-apartheid South Africa*, edited by Greg Homann and Marc Maufort, 75–104. Brussels: Peter Lang, 2015.

Thurman, Christopher. "Sher and Doran's *Titus Andronicus* (1995): Importing Shakespeare, Exporting South Africa." *Shakespeare in Southern Africa* 18 (2006): 29–36.

Timothy, Eubulus. *Othello: A South African Tale*. 2011; Johannesburg: The Other Theatre Company. Film [videotape].

Trivedi, Poonam and Paromita Chakravarti, eds. *Shakespeare and Indian Cinemas: 'Local Habitations.'* New York: Routledge, 2018.

Trivedi Poonam, Paromita Chakravarti, and Ted Motohashi, eds. *Asian Interventions in Global Shakespeare: 'All the World's His Stage.'* New York: Routledge, 2020.

Turcotte, Gerry, "'The Ultimate Oppression': Discourse Politics in Kate Grenville's Fiction." *World Literature Written in English* 29, no. 1 (Spring 1989): 64–85.

Tutta colpa di Giuda. Dir. Ferrario, Davide. Warner Bros and Rossofuoco. 2008. Film.

Uys, Pieter-Dirk. *MacBeki—A Farce to Be Reckoned With*. Darling: Peninsula/Junkets, 2009.

Van Watson, William. "Fellini and Lacan: The Hollow Phallus, the Male Womb, and the Retying of the Umbilical." In *Federico Fellini: Contemporary Perspectives*, edited by Francis Burke and Marguerite R. Waller, 65–91. Toronto, Buffalo, London: University of Toronto Press, 2002.

Vauchez, André and Giardina, Andrea, eds. *Il mito di Roma da Carlo Magno a Mussolini*. Bari: Laterza, 2008.

Vico Lodovici, Cesare. "*Cesare* di Forzano. Rev. of Cesare Written by Giovacchino Forzano (and Benito Mussolini), *Scenario* 8, no. 5 (May 1939).

Viera, Else Ribeiro Pires. "Liberating Calibans: Readings of Antropofagia and Harold de Campos' Poetics of Transcreation." In *Post-Colonial Translation: Theory and Practice*, edited by Susan Bassnett and Harish Trivedi. London: Routledge, 1999.

Vinogradov, Leonid, and Karen Stepanyan. "Karen Stepanyan o Dostoevskom, chitavshem Servantesa, i poiskakh Boga v literature" [Karen Stepanyan on Dostoevsky Who Read Cervantes and the Search for God in Literature]. *Pravoslavie i Mir*. Accessed 31 March 2020. http://pravmir.ru/karen-stepanyan-o-dostoevskom-servantese-i-poiskax-boga-v-literature/. (In Russ.).

Vladimir Lukov. *Shekspirosfera: Virtual'nye miry Shekspira i ego sovremennikov* [The Shakespearean Sphere: Virtual Worlds of Shakespeare and His Contemporaries]. Moscow: Moscow University for the Humanities Publ., 2016. (In Russ.).

Wagner, Geoffrey. *The Novel and the Cinema*. Rutherford, NJ and London: Fairleigh Dickinson University Press; Tantivy Press, 1975.
Weir, Peter, dir. *Picnic at Hanging Rock*. 1975; Australia: The Australian Film Commission; McElroy & McElroy. DVD.
White, Robert S. "*Eklavya*: Shakespeare meets the *Mahabharata*." In *Shakespeare and Indian Cinemas*, edited by Poonam Trivedi and Paromita Chakravarti. New York: Routledge, 2018.
Whyle, James. Interview with the Author, 30 September 2013.
Wilkinson, David Nicholas and Emlyn Price. *Ronald Harwood's Adaptations: From Other Works into Films*. Guerilla Books, 2007.
Willan, Brian. *Sol Plaatje: A Biography*. Johannesburg: Ravan Press, 1984.
Willan, Brian. "Whose Shakespeare? Early Black South African engagement with Shakespeare." *Shakespeare in Southern Africa* 24 (2012): 3–24.
Willan, Brian. "'A South African's Homage' at One Hundred: Revisiting Sol Plaatje's Contribution to the *Book of Homage to Shakespeare* (1916)." *Shakespeare in Southern Africa* 28 (2016): 1–19.
Williams, Raymond. *Culture*. Fontana New Sociology Series. Glasgow: Collins, 1981.
Williams, Raymond. *Culture*. Fontana New Sociology Series. Glasgow: Collins, 1981. US edition: *The Sociology of Culture*. New York: Schocken, 1982.
Wray, Ramona. "The Morals of *Macbeth* and Peace as Process: Adapting Shakespeare in Northern Ireland's Maximum Security Prison." *Shakespeare Quarterly* 62, no. 3 (2011): 340–63.
Wrighley, Richard, ed. *Cinematic Rome*. Leicester: Troubador Publishing, 2008.
Wright, Laurence. "Introduction: South African Shakespeare in the Twentieth Century." In *Shakespearean International Year Book* 9, edited by Graham Bradshaw, Tom Bishop, and Laurence Wright. Abingdon: Ashgate, 2009.
Wyke, Maria, ed. "Film Style and Fascism: Julius Caesar." *Film Studies* 4 (Summer 2004): 58–74.
Wyke, Maria, ed. *Julius Caesar in Western Culture*. Oxford: Blackwell, 2006.
Young, Sandra. "'Let Your Indulgence Set Me Free': Reflections on an 'Africanised' *Tempest* and Its Implications for Critical Practice." *Social Dynamics* 36, no. 2 (June 2010): 315–327.
Zakharov, Nikolay, and Vladimir Lukov. *Genii na veka: Shekspir v evropeiskoi kul'ture* [A Genius for Centuries: Shakespeare in European Culture]. Moscow: Humanities Institute of TV & Radio Broadcasting Publ., 2012. (In Russ.).
Zakharov, Nikolay. "Iconic Characters: Hamlet as Iconic Image in Russian Culture." In *The Cambridge Guide to the Worlds of Shakespeare*, 2 vols, edited by Bruce R. Smith et al., 1336–38. New York: Cambridge University Press, 2016. Vol. 2: The World's Shakespeare 1660—Present. https://doi.org/10.1017/9781316137062.184.

Zakharov, Nikolay. "Shekspirizm Pushkina" [Pushkin's Shakespeareanism]. *Znanie. Ponimanie. Umenie*, no. 3 (2006): 148–55. (In Russ.).

Zakharov, Nikolay. "Shekspirovskii tezaurus v tvorchestve Pushkina" [Shakespeare's Thesaurus in Pushkin's Oeuvre]. *Vestnik Mezhdunarodnoi akademii nauk (Russkaia sektsiia)*, no. 1 (2006): 75–77. (In Russ.).

Zakharov, Nikolay. *Shekspirizm russkoi klassicheskoi literatury: tezaurusnyi analiz* [Shakespeareanism of Russian Classical Literature: The Thesaurus Analysis], edited by Vladimir Lukov. Moscow: Moscow University for the Humanities Publ., 2008. (In Russ.).

Zakharov, Nikolay. "Productions of Hamlet on the Post-Soviet Stage in Russia." *Znanie. Ponimanie. Umenie*, no. 4 (2015): 246–56. https://doi.org/10.17805/zpu.2015.4.23.

Zakharov, Nikolay, and Vladimir Lukov. *Shekspir, shekspirizatsiia* [Shakespeare, Shakespearization]. Moscow: Moscow University for the Humanities Publ., 2011. (Shakespeare Studies XVII). (In Russ.).

Zakharov, Nikolay, Valery Lukov, and Vladimir Lukov. "Shekspirosfera" [The Shakespearean Sphere]. *Elektronnoe periodicheskoe nauchnoe izdanie "Vestnik Mezhdunarodnoi akademii nauk. Russkaia sektsiia"*, no. 2 (2012): 70–75. Accessed 31 March 2020. http://heraldrsias.ru/online/2012/2/238/. (In Russ.).

Index

A. A. Joubin and V. Bladen (eds.), *Onscreen Allusions to Shakespeare*, Global Shakespeares, https://doi.org/10.1007/978-3-030-93783-6

Milton Keynes UK
Ingram Content Group UK Ltd.
UKHW020705210924
1771UKWH00049B/269